The Folklore of the British Isles
General Editor: Venetia J. Newall

The Folklore
of Cornwall

The Folklore of Cornwall

Tony Deane
Tony Shaw

Introduction by Venetia J. Newall

Drawings by Gay John Galsworthy

ROWMAN AND LITTLEFIELD
Totowa, New Jersey

First published in the United States 1975
by Rowman and Littlefield, Totowa, N.J.

For Robert Husband of Penare

Library of Congress Cataloging in Publication Data

Deane, Tony.
The Folklore of Cornwall.

(The folklore of the British Isles)
Bibliography : p.
Includes indexes.
1. Folk-lore—England—Cornwall.
I. Shaw, Tony, joint author. II. Title.
GR142.C7D42 1975 398'.042'094237 75-5780
ISBN 0-87471—695—0

Printed in Great Britain

Contents

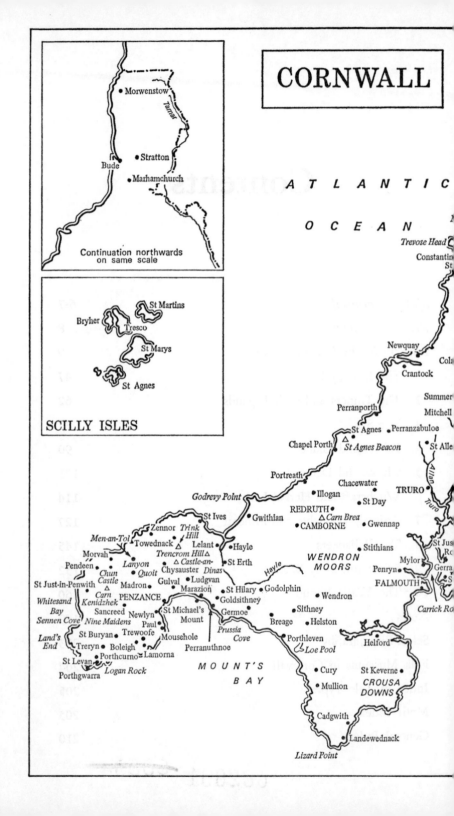

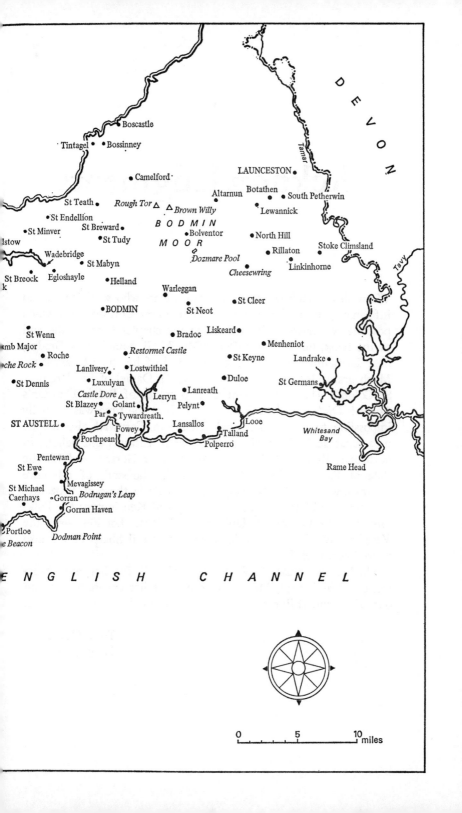

Acknowledgments

We wish to thank the many correspondents who willingly passed information to us, following our letters in the Cornish press; when possible, we have credited them in the chapter notes at the end of the book, but must single out Mrs M. E. Saunders of Bradoc, near Lostwithiel, who gave a great deal of her time to assist us. Much gratitude, too, is due to Mrs M. G. Daniel of Landare near St Columb Major, who sent us two copies of Ralph Dunstan's *Cornish Dialect and Folk Songs*, which at the time was virtually impossible to obtain. Personal friends in Cornwall also helped us a great deal with their recollections of customs and beliefs; in particular, Robert Husband of Penare, near Gorran, and Charlie Bate of Padstow should be mentioned. The staffs of reference libraries were constantly helpful, particularly those at Penzance, Falmouth and Truro, and, at Bromley and Kensington; the Folklore Society library in University College, London, and the Vaughan Williams Memorial Library in Cecil Sharp House also proved very useful.

Finally, we must thank Venetia Newall for her encouragement and assistance, Mrs G. Jennings for her expert typing and our wives and children for suffering 14 months of angry silence.

Tony Deane
Tony Shaw

Introduction

WITH THE PUBLICATION OF THIS BOOK, *The Folklore of the British Isles* reaches its sixth volume, and I want to take the opportunity to discuss briefly the problems of editing, or, for that matter, of contributing to, a series of this nature. Cornwall well illustrates some of the important issues, but first I must make a few general observations.

All our contributors either live in, or are closely familiar with, the areas about which they have written. Naturally authors in this position should be able to provide an objective survey of local tradition and lore. But they can also give us an insight into the way in which the folklore of their district is viewed by the inhabitants, and into what local people actually imagine their specific heritage to be.

In this context, I remember visiting a farmhouse built on the site of an Arthurian legend, though not in Cornwall. The farmer's wife, who was a local woman, knew the tradition and the tales connected with it, but refused to recount them because a certain book – the work of a well-loved local author – ' tells all that sort of thing better than I could '. Before directing me to the local library, she bemoaned the absence of her daughter, a schoolgirl, who had recently read that part of the book in class. It so happened that I knew the book to which she referred and its author, an attractive personality and good writer, but neither a shrewd nor particularly accurate reporter of local custom.

Here I was particularly familiar with the area and with the reasons for the influence which the author concerned exerts. Without this information, the bare bones of the account, as presented here, may be quite interesting, but they lack the perspective provided by a real knowledge of the social milieu, the local class structure and so on. Once or twice since the present series was launched, I have been asked whether I had considered organizing it on other than a geographical basis. The above anecdote illustrates only one way in which the local environment is, and always must be, relevant to folklore studies. Many additional factors – the persistence of loyalty to a formal geographical unit is one obvious example – embrace and influence various aspects of tradition, underscoring the value of this approach. My answer, therefore, is that, while it would be perfectly feasible to categorize British folklore into other analytical units, of which the occupational is perhaps the most obvious, a geographical treatment provides, in the current phase of folklore studies here, a schematic cast which is particularly useful.

In reality, the principles governing study of folklore within any group, whether we are concerned with geographical or other categories, do not greatly vary. Shared notions of exclusiveness, real or residual and whether conscious or not, provide a valid field for folkloric consideration, as indeed does any common background of experience. Tin mining, now only a memory in much of Cornwall, has a specially notable folklore containing some very puzzling elements, and also showing a marked persistence beyond the sphere of direct mining experience. This, as it were, temporal extension is paralleled by a spatial spread, so that local mining lore cannot at present be viewed outside the general scope of Cornish tradition. Even Gweal, an uninhabited islet off the west coast of Bryher in the Scillies, is claimed as a one-time mining area.

Devonshire miners had numerous traditions in common with their counterparts in Cornwall, and once the two communities were linked. Research elsewhere could show us to what extent the tin miners' beliefs and customs are duplicated in other areas and whether Cornish miners, now widely scattered in overseas countries, have carried their traditions with them. It is a local boast that ' where there are mines you will find Cornishmen ', and this same idea is echoed in song:

> *Yn tewlder an bal ha war donnow an mor,*
> *Pan eson ow quandra dre dyryow tramor,*
> *Yn pup le pynak, hag yn kenyver bro,*
> *Re dreleyen colonnow dhyso.*

Deep down underground, tossed on waves high and low,
To far distant climes though we wandering go,
Whatever the land or wherever the sea,
Our hearts may we turn back to thee.

This is part of a modern Cornish song, often performed at Old
Cornwall gatherings and other events where Cornish is used.
'The old Cornwall March' is also frequently heard on such
occasions, and here again tin – with fish and copper – makes up
part of the refrain: *Pysk, Sten ha Cober!* The song continues *Tre,
Pol ha Pen a dhe* [Here come Tre, Pol and Pen], taking up the
popular couplet:

By tre, pol and pen
You shall know the Cornishmen.

It really is true that these three words, Cornish for a homestead,
a lake or inlet and a headland, prefix dozens of local names. It
is in placenames that the old language survives most widely.

The first Old Cornwall Society was set up at St Ives in 1920,
followed quickly by others. Out of this grew the Federation of
Old Cornwall Societies, under the aegis of Henry Jenner and
R. Morton Nance. Jenner was the real pioneer of Cornish linguistic revival. He died in 1934, 86 years old and 30 years after
publication of his *Handbook of the Cornish Language* – this is
in the same year as he persuaded the Celtic Congress, meeting at
Caernarvon, to accept Cornwall as a member. Already, the year
before that, his speech in Cornish at the Lesneven (Finistère)
Congress of the *Union Régionaliste Breton* had been well received,
and 30 years earlier, in 1873, he had read a paper on the Cornish
language to the Philological Society.

Formal links between Cornwall and Brittany were always
ecclesiastical and linguistic rather than political, though Count
Alan of Brittany became Earl of Cornwall in 1140 – but not for
long. Bretons do, however, seem to have been frequent visitors to
the Earldom (later Duchy) until the Reformation, and a good number were actually resident. It is possible that intercourse between
the two countries helped to keep the language, very similar to
Breton, alive, though as early as 1328–9 the Bishop of Exeter
spoke of it as being 'in the uttermost parts of Cornwall'. By this
he may have meant beyond Truro. In 1362, 25 years after the
earldom became the Duchy, Latin and Norman French ceased to

be the official languages, and English was substituted. Middle English, the speech of the period, has been handed down to us – most notably by Chaucer. By the end of the seventeenth century, so Nicholas Boson reported, Cornish was still spoken, though not by the majority, from Land's End to St Michael's Mount, and towards St Ives and Redruth, as well as from the Lizard towards Helston and Falmouth.

In 1776 a Mousehole man, William Bodener, living in a district where Cornish persisted late, knew of only four or five folk in the village, evidently including himself, who could speak it. Traditionally the old language perished with Dolly Pentreath, aged 102, though the claim, like her age, probably owes more to legend than to fact. She died at Paul, a couple of miles from Mousehole, in 1777, and a memorial to her, partly in English and partly in Cornish, stands in the churchyard there. This was erected only 114 years ago, but Paul church contains a stone claimed as the only extant old example inscribed in Cornish. Dated 1709, this honours Captain Stephen Hutchens:

> *Bounas heb dueth, Eu poes karens wei*
> *Tha Pobl Bohodzhak Paull Han Egles nei.*

> Eternal life be his whose loving care
> Gave Paul an almshouse and the Church repair

As to the claim made for Dolly Pentreath, it is certainly untrue, a legend perhaps fostered by the picturesque detail that her memorial had as one of its sponsors the antiquarian linguist, Prince Louis Napoleon Bonaparte, a fact noted in the inscription. One or two at least of William Bodener's Cornish-speaking acquaintances must almost certainly have outlived her, and he himself survived until 1789. A different, and also rather obscure, claimant was given support by the St Ives Old Cornwall Society, when they erected a memorial in 1930. This is John Davey of St Just who died in 1844, having been born, at Boswednack, in 1770. St Just, it is true, lies four miles from Land's End, within the area of survival defined by Boson in about 1700, but the date seems too late for any but a sketchy knowledge. John Davey, Junior, (1812–91), who lived at Boswednack, just south of Zennor where both men are buried, is supposed to have shared his father's knowledge of Cornish, and outlived the old man by many years. Some authorities consider that the collapse of the tin-mining industry during the last four decades of the nineteenth century, which resulted in mass emigration from the county, finally put paid to the language more effectively than the absence of a vernacular literature. It is true that the mining industry did contribute to the spread of English, but that was at a much earlier date, when English-speaking tin miners from east Cornwall migrated in their hundreds to the new tin mines in the west. This was in the sixteenth century, when the Elizabethan era saw German experts imported to help set up the new mines, and ecclesiastical life was disrupted by the Reformation, with English established as the language of the Church.

Writing in *Cornish Review* some years ago, P. A. S. Pool said ' Cornish is not dead, and is not a foreign language but our own . . .' One can only concur, and it is worth remembering that, even during the black years of the mid-nineteenth century, when a passion for governmental and national uniformity only equalled since the war was affecting British life, there was some desultory publishing of Cornish texts.

Just before he died in 1959, Nance claimed that ' one generation has set Cornish on its feet. It is for another to make it walk.' It is worth adding that, as Pool pointed out, ' the younger generation of language bards have passed an examination of considerable severity.'

Like the early intellectual leadership of Irish nationalism, Nance recognised the importance of both language and folk tradition in upholding national – or regional – identity. As editor of *Old Cornwall* and, for many years, president of the Federation of Old Cornwall Societies, he devoted his energies to both subjects, and his monographs include: *The Plen an Gwary or Cornish Playing Place*; *Taboo-Names in Cornwall*; *Four Cornish Folk Tales*; and *Folk-Lore Recorded in the Cornish Language*. His *Lyver an Pymp Marthus Seleven* [Book of the Five Miracles of Seleven], which appeared just before the war, is also in the folk idiom. But probably his most influential work was *Cornish For All*, first published in 1929, and reissued with his new introduction in the year before his death. In it he included, with parallel Cornish and English texts, Nicholas Boson's version of the traditional tale *Jowan Chy an Horth, py An Try Foynt a Skyans* [John of Chyanhor, or the Three Points of Wisdom], dating from about 1667. Written out by Boson's son, John, the original manuscript is now in the British Museum.

Nance was very fond of an old Cornish triplet, originally taken

B

down from the Clerk of St Just in 1700, which reads in translation :

> Still true the ancient saw will stand –
> Too long a tongue, too short a hand,
> A tongueless man, though, lost his land.

This might be the watchword of those Celtic nationalists who
insist that without a language there is no people. Henry Jenner
put it slightly differently, saying that ' language is the audible and
visual sign of nationality.' In the Celtic situation, adjoining, as the
Celtic peoples do, nations who are more numerous, wealthy and
culturally vociferous than themselves, the argument holds much
force. Yet, whatever aspirations may be expressed, it remains true
that Celtic is the minority speech in each of the Celtic nations.
Despite this, national or regional consciousness remains strong
and, in the absence of a separate *Umgehungsprache*, it seems that
a vital linguistic awareness, probably coupled with an understanding of the value and unique status of the whole folk heritage, is sufficient to sustain a separate identity.

   Nonetheless, Cornwall does have special problems. Despite its
interesting and often unique traditions, it is not organized nor
run as a separate country, generally being simply regarded as one
of England's counties, with the same status as Somerset or
Devonshire. On 8 May, Helston Post Office provides a postmark
in Cornish, but that is about the summit of official recognition. Each
year the county suffers – or enjoys, perhaps – a major invasion by
English holiday-makers, and it is also an area of considerable
permanent immigration. In this, of course, one place nowadays
differs from another chiefly in matter of degree, and the question
to be asked is whether a local culture is sufficiently strong and
healthy to assimilate outsiders. In Cornwall's case, a positive
answer can surely be given, and it may in fact be a strength that
most of the newcomers are accustomed to a tradition differing
from that of the host region. At the same time, this creates further
problems, which the linguistic revival could contribute towards
overcoming. But no culture lives or thrives in isolation; in essence,
a people does not, or need not, differ from an individual, so that
external contacts must provide an invigorating stimulus while
leaving the main substance unchanged. When folk culture, or
any other cultural sphere, is concerned, one essential basis for
this to bear fruit is a knowledge and real understanding of the

inherent socio-intellectual background. Traditional folk culture expresses the intelligence of the folk, an attempt to explain or come to terms with a puzzling and difficult environment, and it deserves respect.

The work milieu of those living from mining and fishing, Cornwall's main traditional pursuits, probably exceeds that of all other major occupations in uncertainty and disagreeableness. Hence the innate conservatism and traditional attitudes of these groups, a characteristic which they share with their kin elsewhere. It is interesting that Cornish fishermen preserved, in a purely ritual form, Celtic numerals which, so it is generally believed, were customarily used by certain English and Lowland Scots shepherds – a job which again is lonely and often unpleasant. The origin of these numbers is obscure, and has been discussed by other authors, but they were recorded until quite late over wide areas, though never in proximity to Cornwall, and are said to originate specifically in a sheep-counting tally. Cornish mackerel fishermen, when they hauled up their nets, cried out on first seeing the fish:

Bryel, ha mata, tressa, peswera, pympes, wheffes!
All a-scrawl, all along the line-o!

The Cornish words mean ' A mackerel, a fellow, a third, a fourth, a fifth, a sixth'. Though probably coincidental, it is striking that the shepherd's tally used in south Cumberland closely resembles Cornish. Among all the numerous Celtic tallies recorded, only Eskdale and Scawfell repeat the Cornish six, the relevant numerals (three to six) there being *teddera, meddera, pimp, hofa. Meddera* [four] seems far from Cornish *Peswera*, but *peddera*, used in Dunnerdale and Millom, a dozen miles distant over Black Combe, is phonetically close. The sense of *ha mata*, taking the place of ' a second ' in the mackerel count, appears in Wasdale, where ' anudder' is recorded, but here it replaces four. All these Cumbrian tallies were noted down about a century ago. One recent commentator, Michael Barry, tentatively suggests a link between the tallies and migrant miners, though he rightly associates the majority of numerals with a likely Welsh original. But his basic point is perhaps worth noting, in view of Cornwall's mining past.

Cornish tin miners, traditionally subject to special jurisdiction and privileges, were the heirs to customary rights the origins of which are not known. Their parliament – it was so called – appears to have a very ancient history. Twenty-four Cornish Stannators were elected to this Stannary assembly, and a Speaker was chosen. The formal terminology is from Cornish *stéan* [tin], deriving in turn from Latin *stannum*. In the earliest times of which any account exists, the parliament met at Hingston Down, on the Cornish side of the Tamar, and was a joint assembly for miners of Cornwall and Devonshire. The place is said to take its name from Hengist, the same semi-legendary figure who, with his companion Horsa, is credited with defeating the Cornish here in the fifth century; a better authenticated defeat is that by the Saxon Egbert in 838 on the same spot. A joint parliament persisted until the time of Edmund, the ninth earl, when it was divided. Devon miners thereafter met at Crockern Tor on Dartmoor, within the large slice of south Devonshire made over to the Duchy of Cornwall, while the Cornish Stannary parliament was held at Truro.

The last parliament met there in 1752, but the Stannary courts were not finally abolished until 1896. A titular link with the Stannary administration still exists in the Lord Warden of the Stannaries, a member of the Duchy's council and one of its officers. A dignitary carrying less official status is Lord Protector of Cornwall, though this year a gentleman so styling himself has received some publicity during an attempt to revive the Stannary parliament. The Queen was petitioned for this purpose, a traditional right claimed to derive from Charles I's grateful acknowledgement of the Duchy's support. A Cornish privilege which resulted was direct approach to the Crown. Alas, a privilege may exist without the means of implementing it, and the Cornish effort will probably suffer the fate of the representative Irish peers, who, it was conceded in 1966, have the putative right to sit in the House of Lords, but lack the machinery for being elected to do so. The Lord Chancellor added quaintly that, since there was no longer any such place as Ireland – an argument based on the use of different names for the state since 1921 – peers could not sit in the Lords ' on the part of ' that country. At least such constitutional mysteries cannot be advanced against Cornwall.

The Duchy itself, which included the Isles of Scilly, was established in 1337, after the insignificant tenures of the tenth and eleventh earls, Piers Gaveston and John of Eltham, during the first part of the fourteenth century. It was the first duchy instituted in Britain, set up for the support of the king's eldest son, and to which he succeeded by inheritance. At the same time it is, therefore, the senior royal duchy. Edward, Earl of Chester, better known as the Black Prince, was the first duke, and played some part in running his domain, but from the latter part of the fourteenth century onwards the royal overlords have seldom been there. Nevertheless, it is in the sixteenth century that one of the trappings which help give the Duchy its present identity is first mentioned. In about 1540 we hear of the Duchy flag, a black field with 15 bezants. Bezants are golden discs, and they are arranged to form an inverted triangle so that, horizontally, they are in rows of 5, 4, 3, 2 and 1. A similar flag was carried at the funeral of Queen Elizabeth I in 1603, and the same device, probably dating from some 50 years later, is cut into the wall of the Old palace buildings at Lostwithiel. An earlier representation is on the tomb of the first duke at Canterbury, though the bezants exceeded the present number. In fact, they seem to have been standardized at 15 fairly recently, evidently on stylistic grounds.

In its present form the old Duchy flag has been used officially since 1932, when the late Duke of Windsor was Duke of Cornwall. It flies on all Duchy offices on 17 March, the anniversary of the original Duchy Charter, and is used on other appropriate occasions. A pennant in the same design flies on the Duchy launch in the Isles of Scilly, and the Red Ensign with, in its fly, the bezants on a black shield surmounted by a crown, is used by the Royal Fowey Yacht Club.

Folkloric elements often influence heraldry, and the Trevilian arms, described below, apparently stem directly from a widely believed local legend. On the other hand, in that particular example it is difficult to know which came first, the arms or the legend. Heraldic design, in any case, reflects many other factors, such as name-punning and sheer charm of appearance. This last, nothing more, may well account for the Cornish bezants, 22 of which originally made up the surround of a silver shield bearing a red lion, used by Richard Plantagenet, eighth earl. Some practical symbolism linked to the county may, of course, have existed, or a fanciful tradition, like that which attempts to explain them as representing the sum for which Richard Coeur de Lion was ransomed in 1194. This has no foundation whatsoever. The process by which they were detached to become a flag simply is not known either, though since Richard ruled the Earldom from 1227 to 1272, an origin long predating the flag's first recorded use could be looked for. But all that one can reasonably assume is that it arose from the dignities of an earldom which, as Charles Henderson put it, had a quasi-Palatine character. In practice, at least, this appears scarcely as an overstatement.

Though defeated by Egbert a century earlier, until Aethelstan's victory in 936, and soon after over the last Cornish refuge in the Isles of Scilly, the south-western Celts were subject to England more in name than in reality. Aethelstan it was who banished them beyond the Tamar, though he retained the Cornish King Howell as his viceroy, and the Church remained Celtic. But during the next century the manorial system was set up, an alien form of administration imported and sustained by the Saxons. Large quantities of coinage from Aethelstan's reign and that of his successors have been found in old tin workings and in districts where the mineral was exploited, evidence that extensive mining was going on at the time. If one were to hazard a guess, it might be that, because of their importance in contemporary trade, the miners were allowed some forms of immunity from the alien Saxon regimen, and hence the Stannary system arose. Be that as it may, by the time of Edward the Confessor nearly all land belonged to men with English names, and of this about 90 per cent passed into Norman hands after the Conquest.

It is sometimes supposed that the numerous Cornish giant legends may originate from the Anglo-Saxon, and later Norman, overlordship. In fact, the giants' graves of the Scillies and western Cornwall are long barrows, but it must be added that Cornishmen are relatively small, and the foreign invaders probably loomed large by comparison. From this the tales such as Giant Bolster and Jack the Giant Killer could conceivably have sprung. An example which may parallel this is the Lappish cycle of *Stallo* legends, in which a stupid giant is repeatedly outwitted; the Lapps, another short-statured race, have also suffered from physically larger, politically and economically dominant neighbours – the Russians, Scandinavians and Finns. In Cornwall, to add substance to the legends, a giant is said to have been dug up in 1761, when tin miners unearthed a coffin at Tregony. The box was 11ft long and, while the remains inside crumbled to dust, a tooth measuring 2½in., supposedly the only surviving remnant of the corpse, was shown in evidence.

The complex of racial succession constructed around legends of this type cannot, of course, be treated with enough caution. Writers sometimes like to suggest that the ' little people ' of British tradition are the defunct or assimilated prehistoric and early peoples of these islands, changed by the folk imagination into diminutive inhabitants of an imaginary and often subterranean world. Cornish lore, too, has its folk tales about piskeys and spriggans, beings in this category, and in parts of Bodmin Moor it is still said that someone who has lost his way is ' piskey-led '. For the fanciful, this may seem to derive from memories among the Cornish Celts about predecessors of a different race, fitting into a scheme whereby the English in their turn came to see the Celts in similar transmuted form. But all that can sensibly be said is that Cornwall was inhabited before the Celts arrived, and that, for a period at least, its inhabitants seem to have belonged to the type known as Mediterranean.

The Celtic pale set up by Aethelstan at least provided the Cornish with a compact and well-defined region, not unsuited to cultural survival. For one thing, it was remote – Truro, for example, is 100 miles further from London than Cardiff – and, in addition, the Tamar provides a natural frontier. For practically all but the four miles from its source to the Atlantic coast, the 61 miles of the River Tamar separate Cornwall from Devonshire, almost turning it into an island in fact as well as in spirit. The sparsely inhabited regions of central Devon did not encourage extensive contacts with England proper, and records from Lancastrian times imply that foreign outsiders probably outnumbered any English residents. There is even a belief, with no apparent substance, that some two centuries earlier, in the decades before Edward I expelled the English Jewry (1290), the tin industry was ' in the hands of the Jews and not doing well '. Though a few Jews probably lived west of the Tamar, the nearest community was at Exeter, and it was not large.

A brief account of the last two earls with more than a titular interest in their domain seems to shed some further light, as well, perhaps, as helping explain the odd frequency of Jews in Cornish folklore. The Norman Earldom of Cornwall had been established just after the Conquest in a grant to Robert, Count of Mortain, King William's half-brother. In 1216 Henry III came to the throne, and nine years later he in turn gave the county and tin mines of Cornwall to his brother, Richard, then aged only 16. Two years later Richard was created Earl, he and his son, Edmund (Earl from 1272–99) being the last holders of the title to live in the county.

Richard, in fact, bent his energies to Cornish affairs in about 1265, seven years before his death. An ambitious politician, he had in 1257 succeeded in becoming King of the Romans, an ultimately sterile honour for which, however, he obtained recognition in considerable parts of Germany. Though disappointed abroad, he was both wealthy and influential at home and by 1265 had been closely associated for at least 15 years with Abraham of Berkhamstead. Abraham, one of the richest members of his community, had apparently unscrupulously profited from the misfortunes of his fellow Jews. After an eventful career, he was granted to Richard in 1255 and empowered to lend money. That Richard was comparatively well disposed for the period towards the oppressed English Jews, but also fully prepared to exploit them, is clear from various accounts.

The year 1255 saw not only Abraham of Berkhamstead in particular, but also the whole of English Jewry under Richard's aegis, by way of a mortgage against the king's debts – a pledge in human form. Nor was this the last time the English monarchy mortgaged its Jews to Cornwall. Richard again received them in pledge about a year before his death, and the process was repeated under Earl Edmund.

A belief exists that Richard, once the Jew's were at his mercy, put them to work in the Cornish tin mines. No evidence supports this improbable tale, though it would accord better with the position of hazard and penury in which most of English Jewry existed at the time, than other quite contrary accounts. Hunt, for example, retailed as ' historical fact' that the tin mines were then being farmed out to the Jews. In fact Jewish merchants seem to have little to do with the tin trade. Among others, they are mentioned as buying it in Prague three centuries earlier, but there is no hint that their activity exceeded that of purchasers, and it need not, incidentally, have been British tin.

Almost contemporaneously with Earl Richard's birth, the first initiatives towards the Hanseatic League took place in Lübeck and Hamburg, and, quite contrary to popular tradition about the Jews, it was the Hansa which, in Henry III's time, came to dominate commerce in tin. By the time Richard turned his attention to his Earldom, the two German towns had an agent at Falmouth.

As John Hatcher explains, during the thirteenth century an economic and social system based on pre-industrial capitalism became dominant in the Cornish tin industry, and even non-working shareholders existed. Oddly enough the Stannary privileges, originally evidently a kind of immunity, may well have contributed to this. At any rate, the same system was to dominate tin production through the ensuing centuries, economic precocity which is the more striking the earlier the period under review. That its initiation coincided exactly with a period when English Jewry was linked to the Cornish earldom, an era which culminated in the Jews' notorious expulsion from the country, may help account for their peculiar place in local tradition. It is worth speculating, therefore, whether the equivocal attitude of Cornish folklore towards the Jews stems from their having been made whipping-boys, as has so often happened since, for the perennial anti-cosmopolitanism of the exploited. The general attitude towards Jewry in thirteenth-century England is well illustrated by a caricature of 1233. Drawn in the margin of a public document, it has a negative fame as the earliest such caricature to survive. In it, Isaac of Norwich, a slightly older contemporary of Abraham of Berkhamstead, is shown together with his wife and some of his household. Though evidently a philanthropic Jew, vicious horned demons are preparing to drag him and his companions down to hell.

The knocker legends apart, quite a number of other terms exist apparently linking Jews to the tin mines. A particular type of disused smelting works is a Jew's house, and the bits of tin found in disused workings generally are Jew's bowels. Larger blocks are Jew's tin, while tin mixed up with mine refuse is Jew's leavings. Old mine workings are Jew's works or Jew's whidn, and the refuse found beside them is Jew's offcast. A scattering of other terms, while they have no connection with mining, are recorded in the immediate vicinity of Cornwall, if not in the county itself. These include a Jew's eye for something of great value, and ' to Jew ' as an offensive verb to describe cheating. Both of these were once widespread terms, not exclusively from the south-west. Jew's ear for a type of red fungus also occurs in Cornwall, but is not peculiar to that area.

It is figures of speech which are specifically Cornish that are really interesting. Besides those connected with tin mining, apparently unique to Cornwall except for some usage among the Devon miners, there are two more. Jew's fish was a name for halibut, supposedly because it was among Jewry's favourite delicacies, and a type of beetle was termed ' Jew ' on the grounds that it exudes a pinkish froth. This appears to be connected with the infamous blood libel, since there was a practice of holding it in the hand and calling out: ' Jew, Jew, spit blood.'

A number of antiquarian accounts exist of how Jews, as well as Phoenicians, are supposed to have traded with Cornwall in ancient times. More interesting is the curious notion that Joseph of Aramathea came specifically to Marazion to purchase tin, and that it subsequently became a Jewish settlement. In popular etymology the name means Market Zion, and it is further said that, in earlier times, the place was known as Market Jew or Jew's Town. Marazion actually derives from two Cornish words, *marchas* which is indeed ' market', and *bichan* meaning ' small '. Market Jew itself did exist, but appears to have been a separate place just outside Marghasbighan, as was the contemporary (fourteenth-century) spelling for Marazion, and it was then known as Marghasdiow. ' -diow ' is probably from the Cornish word *dyow* [south]; equally, it might possibly hark back to *Yow*, Cornish for Thursday, supposing that the market was once held on that day. *Yow* is sometimes corrupted to Jew, though in the toponomical context here this last word seems to have appeared late.

Another Cornish expression, Market Jew Crow, was the local name for a hooded crow, given this name, so Polwhele said, writing in the early nineteenth-century, because the species frequented that particular neighbourhood. The bird not only has a poor local reputation – St Neot had to impound the whole species every Sunday, because people were absent from church scaring them off the crops – but its appearance is unattractive, so that any racialist undertones may seem unhappy. But that is not necessarily so. There is a widespread notion, which probably has its origin in popular belief, that King Arthur's soul inhabits a Cornish chough, and this too is a type of crow, though sadly it is now on the road to extinction. It was, however, respect for the king, not support of nature conservancy, that caused a Marazion man to be reproached for firing at a chough, this within living memory. Certainly, then, by association at least, the crow species appears in quite a favourable light in the county. When the Celtic Congress was held at Truro in 1932, R. Morton Nance wrote a play in Cornish in honour of the occasion, choosing for his subject and title *An Balores* (The Chough). The same bird was adopted as emblem of the Federation of Old Cornwall Societies, accompanied by a Cornish motto of which this is the translation: ' He is not dead, King Arthur.'

' He shall come again ' – that is the title, in English, of the Cornish song sung each year at the *Gorsedd*, and this is the meaning of the last two lines:

Where shall we find King Arthur? His place is sought in vain,
Yet dead he is not, but alive, and he shall come again!

The *Gorsedd* is the meeting of Cornish bards, taking place each
year early in September, at a suitable historical spot, with the
proceedings held in Cornish. It resulted from the success of the
Old Cornwall Societies and Pedrog, Archdruid of Wales, was
invited to conduct the inauguration. The Nine Maidens, the name
of the standing stones at Boscawen Un, the site chosen for the
ceremony, are traditionally said to be girls, petrified for dancing
on the Sabbath. The omens for the *Gorsedd*, however, proved
good, since in 1974 it celebrated the 46th anniversary of its
foundation.

Arta ef a dhe [He shall come again] – so sing the bards; the
song is modern, but the notion is ancient. Indeed, sleeping heroes
are a widespread folk motif, and the belief about King Arthur
as such is not unique to Cornwall. Yet for the Cornish this rallying
cry served, for a thousand years of national extinction, to help keep
alive the county's sense of separate entity. For other counties – the
stalwarts of Rutland for example – 1 April 1974 was a bitter
defeat, the formal annulment of a reality to which, for at least
eight centuries, their forebears had owed loyalty. In 1958, when
regional ' rationalization ' first seriously loomed, Cornwall, already
in some fields an administrative appendage of Plymouth and
Exeter, seemed similarly threatened. Not so, however, and to
those who, with whatever historical accuracy, still boast allegiance
to King Arthur, must go some of the credit for the county's confirmation, on 1 April 1974, within its traditional boundaries.

In Gerennius, sometimes identified by antiquarians with Ger-
aint, Knight of Arthur's Round Table, Cornwall possesses a
second sleeping hero. Dingerein, an earthwork between Gerrans
and Carne, is said to have been his castle, and there is a local
tradition that when he died he was rowed in a golden boat across
Gerrans Bay to his burial place, a barrow called Carne Beacon.
There, in full regalia, his sword clasped in his hand, he was
buried, the golden boat with him, ready for the day when he will
rise again to claim his lands. Excavations at the barrow in 1855
proved fruitless, and Gerennius' identity is, in any case, obscure,
though he may be none other than St Gerent to whom the church
at Gerrans is dedicated, also giving his name to the village. The
saint is generally identified either with a Cornish king named
Gerentius, who died at the end of the sixth century, or with a son

of Erbin, King of Damnonia (Devon), named Gerend. He supposedly died in 508 fighting the Saxons.

Legend makes St Just, whom Catholic authorities equate with a boy martyr named Justin of Beauvais, into St Gerent's son. But the likely dates belie this, since Just would have died over two centuries earlier than his parent – a situation as perplexing as the local conundrum, which claims ' more saints in Cornwall than in heaven '.

It is not only inconsistencies of this sort which make Cornish hagiography confusing. More than one saint is often, in tradition or in fact, associated with a particular locality, obscuring and muddling the respective details connected with them. St Ia, after whom St Ives is named, had, for example, one brother named St Erth, who apparently post-dates her by a century, and another, St Ewin, whose identity is lost among the saintly complexities of Uny Lelant. The village's first name is a version of Ewin, but Lelant, on good documentary evidence, derives from St Anta. Uny's feast day is locally recognized, while at the same time tradition brings in yet another figure, Lanent, one of the 50 saintly children of good King Brechan, after whom the village is reputedly named.

Saintliness in the religious is no surprise, but some of the holy men who came to Cornwall showed amazing skills. St Piran arrived floating across the sea on a millstone, and then discovered tin. His doing so is commemorated in the *Mebyon Kernow* flag, used nowadays by Cornish nationalists : its white cross, in the same proportions as the flag of St George, symbolizes tin, while the black field is the ground out of which it is dug. Perhaps because they share the same feast day and originated from the same country, St Piran is often wrongly confused with St Kieran, ' first born of the saints of Ireland '. St Keverne, also incorrectly sometimes identified with Piran, possessed Herculean strength, while St Petroc was a Welsh chieftain who gave Padstow its ancient name *Sancte Petroces stow* (AD 981).

Stow is an Old English word meaning, in this context, ' church '. Though English was evidently the language east of Truro from an early date, only in the north-east of the county are English place names common. The reason for this is not established, but some ecclesiastical influence from Wessex evidently began to affect the south-west before it was subdued. At least 20 years before 708, when the Saxon King Ine began his architectural embellishment of Glastonbury, his compatriots had a monastery at Exeter. But it was Glastonbury which remained a great focus for Saxon and Celt alike, perhaps linking alien religious contacts more closely to the southern shore of the Bristol Channel. St Neot, according to many authorities a priest from Glastonbury, died in Cornwall in about 880. He had the pleasant facility of charming animals, and several scenes in which he does so appear on one of the beautiful windows at St Neot Church. Dating from about 1600, the stained glass portrays traditional scenes from the saint's life, and starts with the discredited story that he was Alfred the Great's elder brother, shown abdicating the throne of Wessex so that he could follow a spiritual calling.

St Petroc, of course, was a Celt, and his influence dates from three centuries earlier; the history of his deeds in Cornwall is scanty, and his memory is perhaps overshadowed by the famous celebration on May Day in his name town. The Padstow rituals are not reminiscent of Celtic tradition, but any firm assertions about their possible origin would be rash. Apart from the interest of the day's events, one can only be thankful that Padstow preserves one of the finest May carols in existence.

Of Cornish music, lay or clerical, not a great amount survives. In the 1950s, Peter Kennedy discovered at Cadgwith, a fishing village on the Lizard, some fine songs and shanties, one of them known locally as ' The Cadgwith Anthem ' :

> Come fill up your glasses and let us be merry,
> For to rob bags of plunder it is our intent.

Entitled ' The Robbers' Retreat ', this must represent those anthems defined as profane. In the eighteenth century church music came very much under the influence of the Wesleys, after the success of John's evangelistic work in the county. In fact Methodist hymns won a place in Cornish folklore, and today form the cheerful, though unlikely, chorus in a pub almost as often as in church.

In spite of regrets for the passing of traditional music, one cannot but admire the Wesleys' work, and in Cornwall they provided the people with an ecclesiastical dignity which they probably had not felt since the Cornish diocese was submerged in Exeter. A separate clerical identity in fact disappeared soon after the loss of political independence, to be exact in 1018. From that year until 1877 no Cornish diocese existed. Fifty-six years after the diocese was re-established, the first Cornish-language church service for 250 years was held at Towednack, on the initiative of the *Tyr ha Tavas* [Land and Language] movement, itself founded in 1933. Three miles from St Ives, the church at Towednack has a squat, unadorned tower, and the devil is credited with breaking off its pinnacles. That the devil is an Englishman is probably a much later idea, since we have it only in a late Cornish play where Lucifer and his Angels speak English. *Gwreans an Bys* [The Creation of the World] dates in its extant version from 1611, nearly three centuries after Towednack Church, when the Reformation, with its clerical anglicization, was making renewed inroads into the Cornish language. Indeed, there was no Cornish prayer book for the 1933 service, an occasion which was subsequently repeated annually at different places. R. Morton Nance had to translate the Anglican evening service specially for the first ceremony, and the whole event, inspired by a youth movement (*Tyr ha Tavas*) which itself grew out of the Cornish revival, provides an interesting link between the bards and the Church. Moreover, it is no exaggeration to say that, through the centuries, King Arthur had been regarded with quasi-religious enthusiasm.

This was not an exclusively Cornish phenomenon. William of Malmesbury, for example, writing in the twelfth century, not long before Geoffrey of Monmouth, spoke of Arthur, of whom ' the Britons rave wildly today '. At about the same time, when some monks from Laon visited Bodmin, in 1113, a riot was prevented only with difficulty when one of them suggested that Arthur was dead. This is evidence enough that Arthurian legend flourished, apparently strongly, in medieval Cornwall, and at almost the same period the Welsh romance *Culhwch and Olwen* had Arthur rest in Cornwall after hunting the boar into the sea. To this day, when the wind howls over Goss Moor, below Newquay, the old king's hunting horn can still be heard as he chases a spectral deer – an example of a notable figure in legend becoming attached to a common folk motif. Some say that Dozmare Pool on Bodmin Moor is Excalibur's last resting place, but this seems to be a recent idea.

While the medley of tradition now presented as Cornish Arthurian legend appears to stem mainly from the writing of Geoffrey of Monmouth (*c.* 1135), Sir Thomas Malory (*c.* 1470) and of Richard Carew about a century later, they cannot be dismissed as a worthless farrago. The old man from Pendeen living in Robert Hunt's time, or his forebears, had personalized as

Arthur the nameless hero who vanquished Cornwall's giants. Though a Cornish Arthur may owe much to Geoffrey of Monmouth, Arthur as a folk hero certainly predated the *Historia Regum Britanniae*. Geoffrey it was who, more than eight centuries ago, arbitrarily made Tintagel, newly constructed by Earl Reginald, natural son of Henry I, into Arthur's stronghold. But nobody can now say when this concept was appropriated by the folk.

In the bewildering concoction which he presented as history, Geoffrey evidently paraphrased the episode of Zeus and Amphitryon's wife, having Uther Pendragon sire Arthur on Igerne, widow of a Cornish duke. This was Gorlois, in whose shape Uther Pendragon appeared to the trusting woman, a subterfuge assisted by Merlin. In his role as a soothsayer, Merlin is locally credited with prophesying the Spanish invasion of Cornwall in 1595:

There shall land on the Rock of Merlin
Those that shall burn Paul, Penzance and Newlyn.

Paul is near Mousehole which, along with the other two places, was duly sacked by the invaders, and in the vicinity there is a rock still known as the Rock of Merlin.

Much of this suggests a picturesque, romantic, outmoded antiquarianism. So, too, does the pseudo-scientific pedigree that has grown up around Castle Dore. Carhurles, nearby, is said to be ' The Castle of Gorlois ', Geoffrey of Monmouth's, Gorlois, spouse of Arthur's mother. Kilmarth, in the same district, is interpreted as ' The Grove of Mark ', that same King Mark who features in the Tristan romance. For Tristan, too, came to form an element in Arthurian legend – though only in versions deriving from Malory, who wedded the two tales in the late fifteenth century.

But any good story, whatever its origin, can find its way into folklore. The wealth of the subject lies in the constant transformation of realities presented to it, and every accretion enriches, if not for itself, then for the underlying psychology. First one must note the absence of any real evidence for Tristan and Iseult being represented in the old traditional lore of Cornwall. The pre-Norman Welsh literary version was edited and refined by francophile court poets before returning to its native shores, and never caught the popular fancy again. Yet one aspect, itself an interpolation, survives.

Historical research, whether it concerns a real person or a legendary figure, generally places the origin of the Tristan tale much further north. But even in the early literary versions, he appears as child of a Cornish princess. He is born on a ship returning from the land of Lyonesse (Loonois), and this appears over four centuries later in Camden's *Britannica* (1586), as an actual appendage of Cornwall. Camden drew on the manuscript of Richard Carew, a Cornish antiquarian, whose own work, *Survey of Cornwall* (1602), repeated the assertion. A notion became widespread that Lyonesse had consisted of the populous, western part of the county, today submerged beneath the ocean as the result of a great tidal eruption. Only its mountain peaks, now the Isles of Scilly, remained visible. The Trevilian family bears arms showing a horse emerging from the sea, and this, it is said, was the steed bearing their ancestor away from the disaster. By the grace of his swift, white mount he reached the present Cornish mainland seconds before the waves overwhelmed him.

It is interesting that King Gradlon, legendary founder of Quimper in Brittany and ruler of Is, then capital of the district still known as Cornouaille, escaped in similar circumstances. This was, so the story goes, in the sixth century, when Gradlon's daughter, Dahut, fell in love with the Devil. He persuaded her to steal from her father the golden key with which sluice gates, protecting Is from the sea, were locked. He then opened them, inundating the whole city, Gradlon himself barely making his getaway on horseback with Dahut seated behind him. As the waves threatened to overtake them, the king threw his daughter into the water, answering a command from heaven to sacrifice her. The sea receded and the rest of Brittany was saved, though Is itself remained submerged. An addenda to the account, as quaint as some of the details attached to the Lyonesse legend, claims that Paris received its name since it alone was as fine as Is — *par* [equal to] Is.

Carew's seemingly factual, but actually highly imaginative, account has readily taken seed. In days of foreign overlordship and cultural disarray it provided a standpoint from which to look back on a glorious, territorially richer Cornish past. More practically, support could be drawn from St Michael's Mount, whose monks had imported from the parent house in Brittany a well-substantiated story of a submerged forest in the bay beneath the monastery. Again, the changing sand dunes of the Cornish coast have from time to time genuinely engulfed constructions of one sort or another. Two churches of St Piran were submerged near Perranporth, though one has now been excavated. Previously these attracted tales of bells ringing beneath the sand, and visions of holy buildings, the first probably an embroidery of the second, itself no doubt a result of the perennial reappearance of the churches in the shifting dunes. Indeed the soaring dunes are credited with having swallowed a whole city, Langarrow, or Langona, overcome in punishment for its greed and dissoluteness. A place of great wealth and importance, according to Hunt, it was also used as a penal settlement, and eventually the local girls intermarried and interbred with the criminals, bringing about the complete degradation of the local stock. After a sandstorm of three days and nights, no trace was left. This was near Crantock, and similar stories of a sandy inundation are told at Lelant, while Trewartha Marsh on Bodmin Moor is supposed to conceal a place named Tresillern.

Edith Oliver, at one time Mayor of Wilton near Salisbury, and an extremely credulous observer of magical events in her own county, reported seeing on two occasions a mass of towers and other buildings, from a vantage point at Land's End. This she presumed to be Lyonesse. Tennyson placed Camelot itself ' in the lost land of Lyonesse, where, save the Isles of Scilly, all is now wild sea '. Another popular theory, which even finds a qualified assertion in sober guide books, has it at Castle Dore, alongside the supposed domains of Mark and Gorlois. A stone found in the same area, and erected near Fowey, now goes by the name of Tristan Stone. *DRVSTANS HIC JACIT CVNOWORI FILIVS* [Drustanus here lies the son of Cunoworus] reads its inscription; Drustanus is equated with Tristan, and Cunoworus (or Cunomorus) is said to have been King Mark. Yet Tristan in the popular romance is Mark's nephew, and in the Welsh versions his father was Tallwch.

Every culture and every region has its pseudo-history, its legends in historical guise. Cornwall, through the romanticism and extent of its adopted Arthurian history, shows folklore's role in national revival. Flint arrowheads found at Boleigh in Penwith become mementoes from Arthur's championship of Cornwall against the Saxons; actually this was probably the site of Aethelstan's victory over the Cornish in 936. At the battle of Vellandruchar, Arthur and the Seven Cornish Kings overcame the Danes. Not a single Viking escaped, and the mill-wheel giving its name to the battle turned with blood flowing seawards. Then Arthur and his men worshipped at Sennen Holy Well, before feasting on a huge rock called Table Mên. The Norsemen never returned to Cornwall,

C

and when they eventually do, so Merlin predicted, a still greater number of kings will gather at this same rock table to witness their advent. All this will coincide with the end of the world.

To what historical events this tale can refer, if any, is obscure. Those early sources which imply that Arthur, or someone like him, really existed, suggest that he could have flourished during the first third of the sixth century. This would make St Sennon, who died in about 560, a greatly younger contemporary of his. Even this is doubtful, as it is not certain that Senan – to whom this date is attributed – and Sennon were one and the same, though the early spelling Senames and Semane for the two names supports their identity. In any case, Sennen Holy Well may well have been venerated before it became linked with the saint, a possibility often suggested regarding Cornwall's numerous holy wells. The Danes are a more puzzling element. Viking domination of parts of the county appears, for a time, to have been well established. This was their Bretland, and there is no suggestion that they relinquished it as result of a sudden major defeat. But all this was about 400 years later. A legend that Olaf Trygvasson was converted and baptized in the Scillies (St Helen's) is not accepted as true, but it is possible that he was known there, directly or by repute. We do know that he was confirmed at Andover in 994, and probably spent about five years from 990 in Britain. His compatriots had been harrying the south-west for at least a century prior to that; indeed, they were installed in Ireland from 795. There the *Ostmen*, as they were called, remained a distinct community until the latter thirteenth century, a period coincidental with the fall of the Manx Scandinavian dynasty. These appear to have been the centuries when Arthurian romance was blossoming and taking root in folk belief.

The ninth-century Danes carried a red banner bearing the emblem of a raven, so history tells us, but Puffin Island, or, in Scandinavian, Lundy, is the best-known relic of Scandinavian influence in the south-west. The name is descriptive, not symbolic; it is interesting, though purely coincidental, that the Cornish have occasionally seen both these birds as containing King Arthur's spirit, alternatives to the chough. In either of these forms, he visits the places with which he was associated during his lifetime. Whatever the traditions about the Viking defeat in the south-west, Lundy probably long remained a base for Scandinavian marauders, as it frequently has in later years, both for pirates and felons. Recorded history first mentions it in the twelfth century when, under its present name, it belonged to the Norman de Mariscos, a period when they were in trouble with the Crown and were using it as a refuge. Later, after a period as Crown property, a Cornish family named the Grenvilles became proprietors in the sixteenth century. Historical events created a curious pattern for Lundy and the Scillies in the seventeenth century, for in 1647 Parliament sold Lundy to Lord Saye and Sele, but two years later the Grenvilles were back in the islands, with Sir John holding the Scillies for the king. After the Restoration he was rewarded with the Lord Wardenship of the Stannaries, and later became Earl of Bath. Lundy also returned to Grenville overlordship, and in 1748 the family leased it to Thomas Benson, a smuggler who was also a Devonshire MP.

During the passion for administrative uniformity which has overtaken England within the past two decades, Lundy and the Isles of Scilly have again suffered a common fate. Following its acquisition by the National Trust in 1969, Lundy lost its freedom from all taxes, customs duty, and from British jurisdiction. Previously the only constitutional link with the mainland was the owner's personal allegiance to the Crown. This unique situation is now changed, and the island has been annexed to Devonshire, a fate which Cornwall foresaw in 1958 as a real possibility for itself.

Lundy, virtually uninhabited, was not perhaps a great issue, though in these stereotyped days the disappearance of a harmless historical anomaly must be regretted. That the Scillies where, except again in matters of taxation, the common writ of Westminster has long run, suffered an eclipse not comparable to Lundy's is partly the result of the efforts of the Scillonian community, partly to the tradition, steadily if not dramatically upheld during the past 50 years by local patriots, that Cornwall and the Isles are with England but not of England.

Most Cornish people on the mainland probably think of the Scillonians as little different from themselves. The dialect spoken now is virtually the same, the Scillies' historical links have long been largely with Cornwall, and the county is the natural mainland focus for the islanders. Nonetheless, the Scillonians undoubtedly do see some distinction between themselves and the mainlanders. The life pattern on the islands differs, and always has, from that in Cornwall, and isolation has created a spirit of independence quite usual in island communities. This, together with the divergence which certainly does exist between Cornish and Scillonian history, justifies the situation today, when, to use the same phrase, the Scillies are with Cornwall but not of Cornwall.

As early as the fourth century, the islands seem to have had strong ecclesiastical links, Sulpicius Severus, writing about 20 years later, speaks of *insula Sylina quae ultra Britanniae est* being used as a place of exile for heretics in 380. Two dissident bishops, Instantius and Tiberianus, were banished there. A number of Welsh clerics, often those with known continental associations, are commemorated in the islands, which would indeed have made a useful staging post between Wales and Brittany. What establishment existed, providing hospitality for travellers, is of course unknown, but the Irish, too, seem to have come there. St Warna, apparently an Irishman, landed in the fifth or sixth century at the present St Warne's Bay on St Agnes. The islanders still recall the legend of his arrival over the ocean, sailing in a little wicker-covered boat covered with raw hide.

No such saint is recorded, and who he could have been is unusually obscure. St Barrfhionn, etymologically indistinct from Warren, was a sixth-century Irishman and evidently a traveller, since he is credited with having visited America – though not, presumably, in a coracle. Or, on similar grounds of verbal mutation, St Ibar (Ivor) might qualify. But little can be based on names when dealing with such uncertainties. Ibar, a fifth-century saint, was among the missionaries who evangelized Ireland, and Donald Attwater, the Catholic historian, says of one of his co-workers, St Ailbe: '. . . his recorded life is a confusion of valueless legends and contradictory traditions '. From the historical point of view, this is true, but as folklorists we must concern ourselves as much with human mental processes as with actual events. An aspect of our study, and one of paramount importance, is the philosophy of the folk. An understanding of ' valueless legends ' and ' contradictory traditions ', as expressive of thought patterns, is an essential contribution to human self-awareness. In the sense that everyone forms part of the folk, and that not one of us is, in the broadest sense, a truly rational being, we must recognize the inescapable role of folkloric activity in human development. Particularly as regards the aspect of society in which the specialist viewpoint interplays with that of the masses – and the specialist in one field belongs to the mass in another – that which is posited by experts must, if it is to have social impact, be transformed into a reality of general acceptability. This is most notably the case when the trained thinker is concerned, the compatability of his idiom with the folk idiom involving an interpretative activity on the part of the folk which remoulds the material presented to it, and which can only be understood within the pattern of folklore. Within this scope, to return to the original example, fall the legends connected with St Ailbe and the other saints.

Evidently the Celts became well established in the Scillies, probably under clerical leadership, for apparently a recognizable Celtic community survived alongside the Danish base which was later set up there. At any rate, when mainland Cornwall fell to Aethelstan in 936, the remnants of Howell's army apparently withdrew there. The Saxon king pursued and defeated them, taking the opportunity to eliminate the Scandinavians too, though the Olaf Trygvasson legend suggests that this may have been temporary.

In 981, 13 years prior to Olaf's confirmation, Tavistock Abbey was founded. We next hear that part of the archipelago belonged to the abbots there, though when this came about is unclear. The grant to them existed in the twelfth century, and about this same period the other islands were obtained by the Blanchminsters, a Norman family. In the next century, a few years before Edward I expelled the Jews from the mainland, a curious local custom is reported in existence, as a method of punishing a felon. He had to be placed ' with two barley loaves and a pitcher of water ' on a certain rock, there ' to leave him until he was drowned by the flowing of the sea '. Thirty-five years later, in 1319, the Blanchminsters successfully obtained a separate coroner for their domain, refusing to acknowledge the official from Cornwall. At that time a coroner was the Crown's legal representative in each county, so this was an important gain.

The service in exchange for which the Blanchminsters held the Isles in the fourteenth century was set at 300 puffins, due to the Earldom of Cornwall – a kind of tribute. On another occasion, this was stated as 600 puffins, or 6s 8d. Puffins seem an odd form of rental. Carew, in his *Survey of Cornwall* (1602), described them as ' reputed for fish, as coming nearest thereto in taste'; reputed they may have been, but he is wrong about the flavour, as they are good to eat. Whether or how they have been used in this way in the Scillies and Lundy is not recorded, though the monks of that other Puffin Island, off Anglesey, thought them a delicacy. In medieval times they were literally regarded as fish, and therefore would have been particularly useful if delivered to the earldom in Lent, as well as for fast-day food. Gesner, the sixteenth-century naturalist, says of the *Puffinus anglorum*: ' It is eaten in Lent because in a measure it seems to be related to the fishes, in that it is cold blooded . . . a bird fish.' His English correspondent, John Caius, added. ' It is used as fish among us during the solemn fast of Lent: being in substance and looke not unlike a seal.'

In 1599, Nash took up the same idea in his burlesque panegyric of the red herring, *Lenten Stuffe*: '. . . the Puffin that is halfe fish, halfe flesh (a John Indifferent, and an ambidexter betwixt either).' Writing more seriously, Thomas Mouffet paraphrased Gesner in his *Health's Improvement* (1655), classing them as ' birds and no birds, that is to say birds in shew and fish in substance . . . permitted by Popes to be eaten in Lent'. Pope, or sometimes pipe, is, by coincidence, the name for a puffin right along the south-western coast, from Hampshire through Dorset towards Cornwall and the Scillies.

In the Scillies, the Church Lands, apparently consisting of the north-eastern islands, must have passed to the Crown at the time of the Dissolution, though they were not thought significant enough to be mentioned. The Blanchminster moiety also passed to the Crown, in 1549, on the attainder of Sir Thomas Seymour who had purchased it two years earlier. Twenty-two years later, the Isles were leased to the Godolphin's at a rent fixed not in puffins, but in pounds – £20, as against the figure of 6s 8d mentioned earlier. A Cornish family, their name evidently derives from a local place name meaning ' evil stream', and Godolphin House, near Helston, was built in the mid-sixteenth and mid-seventeenth centuries as a seat suitable to their standing. They were a wealthy tin family, and for their seal – used on the ingot from their mines – they used an obvious punning emblem, the dolphin. During the Elizabethan era, an estate manager of theirs was John Coke, who succeeded in appropriating a good proportion of their tin for himself. These stolen ingots he marked with a cat, taken from his own arms, and a joke among the employees was that more cats than dolphins left the mines.

However, sufficient dolphins were produced to pay the Scillonian rent, and it is a historical oddity that, from the Blanchminsters with their ' bird-fish' the islands went to the Godolphins with their ' fish-flesh'. Shakespeare, in *Pericles* (1609), was paraphrasing a common sailors' tradition when he wrote: ' Nay, master, said I not as much when I saw the porpoise, how he bounced and tumbled? They say they are half-fish, half-flesh! a plague on them. They never come but I look to be washed.' Seamen regard the dolphin (porpoise) as it plays through the waves as a harbinger of storms, though in legend it was, like Piran's millstone, quite often a saint's vessel. Among those it carried ashore was another enigmatic saint, St Arlan, of whom the little-known Allen, giving his name to the parish of St Allen in Cornwall, is possibly the double. Thought to have been either Cornish or Breton, Allen is claimed hagiographically for the school of evangelism stemming from St Samson. The latter, a Welsh saint who carried the gospel to Brittany, is commemorated in the Scillies by the island named after him. St Ismail, listed as an associate of Allen's, was a disciple of St Teilo, Samson's close friend. Scillonian legend places Teilo's grave in the islands, but when he died in about 580 he was Bishop of Llandeilo Fawr (Llandaff) and there, in all probability, he was buried.

On St Helen's, the legendary site of Olaf Trygvasson's baptism, are the remains of a church thought to be the oldest in the Scillies. Once fanatically venerated, conceivably this was the burial place of St Elidius, mentioned by William of Worcester (1415–82) as being laid to rest in the Isles. At least nominal support is given to this idea by the local name of the shrine's patron, Lides. Popular etymology likes to equate both Helen and Lides with Teilo, but this involves a most tortuous pattern, leading from Lides through Elidius–Felianus–Thelianus to the Welsh bishop, and also from Lides to Dillan and Helen. A sixth-century Bishop of Llandaff mentioned by Giraldus Cambrensis (1146–1220) as Eliud is also cited to prove that Elidius and Teilo are one and the same, but the only comprehensible notion to be derived from this jumble is that several different saints are involved. An identity between Elidius and Lides does not seem too far fetched, but St Allen, or possibly the saint referred to in the life of St Breaca as St Ia's companion, Elwin, would parallel Helen more satisfactorily. A transition from Elwin to Teilo, the bishop being the more distinguished personality, is not impossible on calendrical grounds, since their feast days are near together.

Consideration of this type of possible permutation is inevitably inconclusive, but not necessarily fruitless. It can throw light on the manner in which the folk make use of their logic, not necessarily the logic of actual fact, but the logic of finding a supernatural patron suitable to their aspirations. Allen is an obscure sixth-century saint who may be Cornish or Breton, or in the variant of

Elwin, he is a still hazier figure, a fifth-century associate of St Ia, or possibly even among the saints who accompanied St Breaca himself to Cornwall a century later. Teilo was a sixth-century bishop, famous for his work in Carmarthenshire, Elidius a Welsh luminary about whom no reliable historical detail survives, except that he was, perhaps, associated with Montgomeryshire in the seventh century. Of Helen–Allen and Lides–Elidius it could be suggested, on the scant data available, that they must genuinely have been associated with the islands. Otherwise such apparently inconspicuous figures would probably not survive even nominally. Somehow, so it would seem, this nominal survival has become attached to the reality of Teilo, fictional, so far as can be seen, in his actual presence in the Scillies, but well known through his own deeds and his association with St Samson and St David; possibly, through his links with St Samson, even a transient visitor to the Isles.

With St David he shares the symbolism of the leek, though the connection, very likely the result of nothing but an almanac-maker's inspiration, is certainly unsubstantial. Whatever the reason, the vegetable, known in Cornwall as an *ollick*, marks his feast day, and in the west country it is used as a cure-all at that time of year:

> Eat leekes in Lide, and ramsines in May,
> And all the year after physicians may play.

This is quoted in Aubrey's *Wiltshire*, collected in the years following 1656. Ramsine was once a common name for garlic, and Lide, not the Lides of St Helen's, but a west-country name for March. Earlier it was the late-winter month, covering part of February and March, and, incidentally, taking it close to Teilo's feast day.

Elwin and Allen, the candidates for possible original identity with the Scillonian St Helen, are celebrated on 22 February and 12 January. Despite this, Allantide, with its coincidental similarity, is sometimes dragged into Celtic hagiography. *Avallen*, Cornish for an apple tree, is adduced as further evidence of the word's Celtic origins, because an *aval* (apple) plays a ritual role at this season. Allantide, in fact, is our Halloween, and it is true that the Cornish use apples then for divination, besides which there is a suggestion that they had some special significance in St Allen village. But similar customs occur widely in Germany and France, and also among the Slavs, though they generally take place on St

Andrew's eve, four weeks later. In these cases, divination is usually concerned specifically with love-making and matrimony, and so too in Scotland. The Scots, using the apple rather differently, consult the oracle at Halloween, and in northern England, too, where much the same is done, the date is shared with the Cornish. The truth is that Allantide has nothing to do with *aval* or St Allen. It is a corruption of Middle English *Alhalwen-tyd*, [All Hallows' Tide] and Cornish Halloween customs are variants of those found over a very broad area.

Regardless of which candidate was the real patron of the old church there, St Helen's was evidently once the main spiritual focus of Scillonian life. As times have become gradually more secularized, people have come to regard St Mary's, the administrative capital, as more important. A pleasant, but not particularly distinguished island, its name is nonetheless rather notable. A striking feature of Cornwall is the infrequency of dedications to the Holy Virgin, and a survey of over 200 churches showed only nine named for her – about 4 per cent of the whole. Indeed, against 117 dedications to British saints, only 34, apart from St Mary, were to well-known Church figures.

During the Godolphin period, 260 years from beginning to end, St Mary's was a bleak and poverty-stricken place. The Lord Proprietors had the Scillies on a rent which eventually increased from £29 to £40, and as it went up, so their interest in the islands went down. They seldom lived there, and from 1742, successive heads of the British military establishment acted as lieutenant-governors on their behalf. Wesley paid a visit in September 1743, and called on the Governor, ' with the usual present, viz. a newspaper ' – a commentary on the boredom of the place. The feelings of the forgotten troops who, according to a half-serious Cornish belief, were stationed there by Charles ɪ and have been there ever since, can be imagined.

Robert Heath, resident in 1744, described how the garrison passed the time. During the New Year period a carnival took place, known as ' goose dancing '. The term apparently derives from guising, but the event sounds more like a fancy-dress party, with transvestism a major feature. Here, presumably, lies the origin of the transvestite masquerade, held in the Scillies. Much the same took place at Penzance. Heath also described Scillonian administration of justice, in the hands of a Court of Twelve. The standard sentence was evidently the ducking chair, an improvement on the drowning ritual of Edward ɪ's time. Substitution of one watery punishment for another may not have been entirely by chance.

The lieutenant-governorship was established in the time of Francis, second Earl of Godolphin. He had at that moment just given up his appointment as Lord Privy Seal, after holding various offices under George I and II. Apart from Lord Proprietorship of the Scillies, the Godolphins and their close relatives the Boscawens, whose name derives from Boscawen village (*bos* meaning 'house', *scaven* 'elder tree'), controlled many of the more than 40 Cornish parliamentary seats. Francis Godolphin, for example, before entering the Lords sat for both Helston and East Looe from 1702–10, and for Tregony from 1710–12; while his cousin, later Viscount Falmouth, was MP for Tregony 1702–5, for the County of Cornwall 1705–10, for the county capital, Truro, 1710–13, and for Penryn 1713–20. In addition, the families held several other seats and in 1708 Hugh Boscawen was appointed Lord Warden of the Stannaries. No doubt their many other interests and their prominence in national politics explain the Lord Proprietors' lack of interest in the Scillies, but it resulted in the islanders being fleeced by unsympathetic stewards and reduced almost to penury.

The Godolphin Lord Proprietorship continued to be vested in a lieutenant-governor until the lease ended, and there was then an interregnum from 1831–4. But the lieutenant-governernorship went on for a few years, and Major-General J. N. Smyth, the last to hold the post, died in office in 1838. Four years earlier, the Crown had granted a new lease to Augustus Smith, a Hertfordshire squire. This family continued as lessees until 1933, when St Mary's, St Martin, St Agnes and Bryher, the only inhabited islands apart from Tresco, were surrendered to the Duchy of Cornwall. Tresco was retained on a fresh lease of 99 years.

During the nineteenth century various attempts were made to bring greater prosperity to the Scillies. In 1812 the islands were exempted from salt tax, which was proving crippling, and there was also a scheme for a government-aided fishing company. But although at one time sufficient fish were caught for everyday needs, as well as to salt down for the winter, the islanders had an apparent antipathy towards fishing on a larger scale. However, soon after this potatoes became a major crop, and supplying the early market became a successful trade until it was taken over by the Channel Islanders.

Concurrently with potato-growing, the Scillonians did well

from the construction of small vessels, with which they engaged in the Mediterranean trade. This continued until metal-hulled ships became the rule, the result, as it happened, of the vision of a Cornishman: Richard Trevithick not only invented the original steam locomotive, but foresaw the possibilities of iron in ship-building. He was commemorated on Cornish postage stamps pre-pared during the 1971 postal strike, for the second centenary of his birth, and showing his locomotive, a map of the county and the St Piran flag.

A Scillonian saying revolves around the word ' scad ', this possibly being from a Celtic stem, and evidently a local variant of shad, and ' tate ' which means, potato:

> Scads and 'tates, and scads and 'tates,
> Scads and 'tates and conger,
> And those who can't eat scads and 'tates,
> Oh, they must die of hunger.

With the early potato trade gone and their sea-going industry eclipsed, it seemed that, once again, this was the fate with which Scillonians were threatened. But the second of the Smith Lord Proprietors, T. A. Dorrien-Smith, tried sending to Covent Garden market a box of Scilly white narcissi, a variety indigenous to the Isles. From this example stemmed the daffodil trade, which has remained the backbone of island life.

Covent Garden no doubt found the white narcissus a pretty curiosity. An attractive local name attaches to the more usual yellow and white variety – ' butter and eggs ', though it is also recorded elsewhere. Daffodils were known as Lide lilies, again nothing to do with St Lides, but a name taken from the similarly titled month.

Lide, in fact, is from Anglo-Saxon *Hlýd*, and survives as a calendrical term along the southern shore of the Bristol Channel, stretching slightly inland at its northern end, along the Avon and towards the Cotswolds. *Hredmônath*, from which it derives, seems once to have been in more general Anglo-Saxon usage, *Hlýd*, of course, stemming directly from *Hred*. This in turn appears in the Germanic *Redmanot*, the month preceding *Ostermanot* (*Estor-mônath*), the two months originally spanning between them the mid-February to mid-April period. Just as *Ostermanot* honoured Eostre, discussed in my book, *An Egg at Easter*, so the preceding month was named for *Hrede* (*Hreda*). If any link were to be adduced between Lides of the Scillies and the ancient *Hrede*, it could only be an entirely chance, seasonal, one, in that Teilo, identified by the Scillonians with Lides, celebrates his feast day near the outset of *Hredmônath*.

Subject though they periodically were to Viking rule and incursions, Nordic terminology of this sort must be a comparatively late arrival in Cornwall and the Scillies. So, too, the 99-year period of tenure, beloved of English lawyers. Not that the lease under which the proprietors continue to hold Tresco lacks ancient associations, but, so far as Scillonians are concerned, it is an import acquired with the English legal system. Ninety-nine, as a magic number, does, however, have connections with Nordic tradition, as for example when an early Danish sacrifice consisted of 99 humans, 99 horses, and innumerable dogs and chickens. But it is more likely from Christian practice that 99 entered into legal reckoning, for in some early manuscripts the figures are placed at the end of a prayer. This is because in Greek letters *Amen* adds up to 99, a calculation which no doubt reinforced the respect in which nine and its extensions already were held. In particular, so it is said, since it coincided with the months of the human gestatory period, it symbolized completeness – an added reason, perhaps, why it influenced the term of a lease.

With its 99-year term projecting it well into the twenty-first century, an individual proprietorship, such as that still held by the Dorrien-Smiths at Tresco, may seem an anachronism. Yet Augustus Smith and his successors definitely set the Scillonians on the way towards their present prosperity. Augustus introduced compulsory education, and in 1890 the Isles of Scilly Council was formed. For its first 65 years, the Proprietor was ex-officio chairman, but when Lieutenant-Commander Thomas Dorrien-Smith inherited in 1955, the privilege lapsed. Admittedly this was a democratization the Scillonians would readily have foregone, had they been offered instead continuation of the tax immunity under which they had lived until 1954. The change was a piece of bureaucratic pettiness, comparable to the treatment of Lundy a decade and a half later. Nonetheless, the prize of County Council status, which the fully fledged Isles of Scilly Council came, for practical purposes, to have, is of great value. The traditional link with Cornwall is maintained not only by common ties with the Duchy, but the Duchy, the county and the Isles have the same Sheriff, while, for the last two, this is also true of the Lord Lieutenant. County and Isles also have a few shared services. In the Scillies, English regional government surely reaches its most democratic, with a representation which, if translated to the affairs of Greater London, would mean a London County Council of about 100,000 members. Whatever the administrative appeal of centralization, there are virtues in small units, and folklorists must not ignore the significance of regional political change, or of socio-political activities in general. Welcome though confirmation of the Scillies' status and that of the Cornish mainland may be, many traditional loyalties are overridden by the revised county system recently brought into force, and, gradual though the process may be, this will slowly have an effect on the customary lore of those areas. New allegiances, geographical, social and economic, tend to produce a fresh crop of folkloric activities and attitudes, interesting in themselves, but also obscuring past mores.

It is curious that England, a country which constantly lays claim to a healthy regard for tradition, sometimes shows callous indifference when dealing with the customs and culture of other nations. The courtesy of submitting English laws to the Manx Parliament is no longer observed, and in Wales the modest and reasonable request that street signs should be in Welsh as well as English was allowed to become a major issue. Gaelic has never been given a proper position in Scotland, and the establishment of a Western Isles county as part of local government reorganization is certainly too little, though one may hope not too late. That a local pressure group should have to campaign for signs in Cornish welcoming visitors to the county is a pathetic comment, not on those supporting the idea, but on the authorities. Demands for a Cornish university have failed, yet among the welcome crop of new higher educational institutions, most cater for areas with greatly less cultural distinctiveness. Those most strongly behind both these proposals, different in importance though not in theme, were *Mebyon Kernow* [Sons of Cornwall], founded in 1951.

The history of the name *Kernow* is interesting. It can best be considered alongside that of its English counterpart, Cornwall, and the other terms applied to the area. A popular and widespread belief, sound evidence in support of which is not available, holds that the Cassiterides, the tin isles of the Phoenicians, Greeks and Romans, refer to the Scillies, or perhaps even to the Cornish peninsula. Serious scholars now discount this, though Ictis, mentioned by Diodorus early in the Christian era, does seem to refer to St Michael's Mount. At least on etymological grounds, the

Silures of the Romans could be the Scillies, though the actual origin of the name is unknown. A common belief derives the term from Sol – ' Islands of the Sun ' – but this is just speculation. It is a touching coincidence that St Elidius (Eliud), who may have died in the islands, shared the title, for Giraldus Cambrensis tells us : ' In his old age he was called by the congruous name Elios; for that his doctrine shone like the sun.' This is perhaps Lides, whose memory was once beloved of the Scillonians. *Silya*, the Cornish word for a conger eel, the creature mentioned in the local rhyme quoted earlier, is less picturesquely suggested as a possible root for the islands' name.

Researchers sometimes like to link *Kernow* with another Cornish term, having the sense of peninsula, but all that seems certain is its origin in *Cornovii*, an old tribal name. With a suffix derived from Saxon, this became *Cornwealas* in Old English. Wales, Welsh, have their origin in the same Germanic term, applied originally to outsiders, usually Celtic or Latin speakers, apparently in a rather contemptuous sense. The same root provides Wallonia, Walachia, Valais and numerous other names. Indeed, in Britain place and family names of which ' wall ' or its near equivalents form part often imply a Celtic link. My own is such a name, though here the connection is with the late Welsh speakers of the south-west Scottish uplands – a folk who also gave their name to Wallace, Scotland's hero.

Brythonic speech certainly survived in Cornwall for six centuries after its disappearance in Scotland, and was still spoken around St Ives when Robert Dudley put in there in 1595. Later author of a famous treatise on navigation, he reached Cornwall in the spring of that year, after a privateering expedition to Spain, North Africa, the Canaries and the West Indies. Six months earlier he had sailed from Southampton in the *Bear*, and after an exciting but largely unprofitable voyage, he paid off at St Ives at the end of May 1595. His description of how the voyage ended reads well : '. . . I made for England, where I arrived at S. Ives in Cornwall about the latter ende of May 1595, scaping most dangerously in a great fogge the rocks of Silly. Thus by the providence of God landing safely, I was kindely intertained by all my friends . . .' As a matter of fact, if Heath's comment of a century and a half later applied, there were worse places than the Scillies to be shipwrecked : ' As to the Scillonians, whom a later author has reflected upon for their conduct towards persons shipwrecked on their coast, they are certainly much more known for their services to strangers, in such times of distress, than the Cornish, or any other inhabitants on the coast of England.'

At least one of Dudley's subordinates settled in Cornwall, for, a month after landing at St Ives, John Underhill, a Warwickshire man like his employer, married Honor Pawley of Lelant. The Pawleys were of local farming stock, long established in the district, and John and Honor evidently considered making west Cornwall their home. There are mentions of them in the neighbourhood for a couple of years, but eventually Underhill returned to Dudley's service, taking his wife with him. To me, at least, the story is interesting, since my great-grandmother was an Underhill, and John and Honor were among her ancestors.

The Pawleys' fortune declined throughout the seventeenth and eighteenth centuries, and they are now extinct in Lelant. A curious will of 1721, that of Hugh Pawley who died the same year, gives to his eldest daughter, Prudence, the right to ' Digg Delve Search and look for tyn '. Had she done so, she might have found something more interesting, for in a local legend which is typically Cornish, a whole town lies buried there, in the sands near the church. Even now, local people speak of sandstorms so sudden and so violent that houses could disappear within two or three days. The imagination pictures the present village shadowed by an unseen town, a Pompeii in miniature waiting to be excavated.

Lelant Church possesses various examples of slate carving, a craft which was developed into a fine art in Cornwall, a by-product of local slate quarrying. For carvings on this scale, a specially fine piece of slate had to be selected – two of the carvings at Lelant, for example, are over 6ft in length. The Hollibubber, a character with a title more picturesque than dignified, was a necessary adjunct of each quarry. Not an actual employee, he was a specialized odd-job man, whose chief task was to clear away the slate rubble from beside the mine. He it must have been who often acted as messenger on occasions such as this, when special orders were placed.

Two of the Lelant carvings are seventeenth century, both fixed to the west wall of the south aisle. One honours a member of the Praed family, lords of the manor, famous for the street near Paddington Station called after them. The other is to Stephen Pawley, who died in 1635, and on it is a pleasantly pious eight-line verse, which reads in part:

If teares the dead againe to life could calle
Thou hadst not slept within this earthye balle
If holye vertues could a ransome bynn
So soone corruption has not rapte thee in . . .

Stephen, who was Honor's second cousin, apears in an elaborate carving, kneeling beside his wife and 11 children. The artist shows a touch of realism, giving kneeling cushions neither to Mrs Pawley, nor her six daughters; the two youngest sons are similarly deprived. While demonstrating, perhaps, the spirit of the age, this is also an interesting portrayal of local customs, and a comment on the practical, frugal nature of the Cornish.

A modern story from the depths of Bodmin Moor was quoted to me by Deane and Shaw as an up-to-date example of Cornish thrift and independence. In an agricultural accident just before World War I, a young labourer lost his right leg. During the war, one of his friends lost his left leg in battle. Today they are both still alive, and each year they buy a new pair of boots.

Cornwall is an attractive region, peopled by a folk who are friendly, yet rightly proud and possessive concerning their ancient beliefs and customs. This is true whether one considers Arthurian romanticism, or the physical skill of their unique style of wrestling. The county's traditional lore, permeated with traces of our island's unrecorded past, and coupled with a difficult, yet beautiful and expressive language – an ancient speech which hibernated rather than died – acts as a magnet to many outsiders. Both the authors of the present volume are Londoners. Ten years ago, they began writing together, and among various articles on Cornwall, they contributed frequently to the *Cornish Magazine*. Their published work led to invitations to lecture, and to writing on the county for a famous international publication.

Devotees of Cecil Sharp House will remember them as folk-singers, from their long association with the Cellar Club there. It was as part-time singers in folk-song clubs throughout the country that they first became associated, and their own group, *Legacy*, was disbanded only because Tony Shaw moved to Cornwall. They hope to re-form it soon, as Tony Deane is soon to follow his colleague there.

Why Cornwall? ' A childhood interest ' is their explanation, and that is often as much as any of us can say, to explain our enthusiasms. My own knowledge of Cornish lore does not approach theirs, and, in fact, for much of the folkloric material in this introduction, I must thank them. It is a pleasure to welcome to *The Folklore of the British Isles* series two writers whose first book this is. I hope that it will be followed by others, and that the present volume will stimulate in its readers the same respect and admiration for Cornwall that it has in me. A region as attractive, with so much of historical and traditional interest, will inevitably draw outsiders, but if they are such as Deane and Shaw, Cornwall need have no fears. Their book may help to ensure that this is so.

1 The Life Cycle

LIFE IN OLD CORNWALL WAS HARD. Poverty and hunger were
never far away and a stroll around any Cornish churchyard will
show how rare longevity was before this century. The customs
and beliefs which relieved the monotony sometimes suggest forgotten religions, sometimes fear, but many provided the working
people's only pleasure: moments when the reality of existence
could be forgotten. In later chapters we shall see how certain
beliefs survived in specialised areas and how the annual ' Calendar ' customs played their part in folk life, but here we are
concerned with living and dying: from cradle to grave, with
numerous traditions interspersed between them. Some of the
beliefs, of course, still continue, but mostly they have gone with
an easier living standard. The people themselves must surely
approve of this new comfort, but perhaps they still regret their
lost culture.

> First we bought the porridge-crock,
> And then we bought the ladle,
> And then we bought a little cheeld,
> And had to buy a cradle.

So said a rhyme current only a few years ago. Even then the ' little cheeld ' was starting out on a life filled with tradition. If it were a boy, born during a waning moon, the next child would be a girl, and vice versa; if, though, the birth occurred while the moon was growing, the next child would be of the same sex. A baby born between the old and new moons would have a short life and the unfortunate child with a blue-veined nose would not reach 21 years. No baby's hands were washed in its first year, for its riches would be carried away, and cutting its nails during the same period produced a thief. Hair, too, was allowed to grow until the moon had waned, thus preventing baldness in old age. Children born in May were regarded as unfortunate and, similarly to ' ne'er casting a clout ', to :

> Tuck [short coat] babies in May,
> You'll tuck them away.

In some parts of Cornwall, a cake was made after a birth, called a ' groaning cake ', presumably from the mother's agonies in labour; every caller and well-wisher was expected to eat some of the cake and it was regarded as ill-mannered to refuse.

When a christening party was on its way to church, an essential ingredient was a large currant cake, the ' cheeld's fuggan ' or ' christening crib '. An offering cut from the cake, known as ' kimbly ' was given to the first person met on the road. Sometimes among the really poor, the kimbly was nothing more than a piece of bread, but the belief was always that if the person to whom the morsel was offered accepted it, the child to be christened would avoid any supernatural influences in its later life. The custom continued at least until the 1930s, for in 1932 a christening party on its way to chapel in St Ives presented a total stranger with a biscuit. The kimbly had grown more sophisticated, but still maintained its power. Incidentally, the Celts of the Isle of Man observed a similar custom.

As a child grew up in old Cornwall its life was enriched by various games and songs. A mother would use little jingles to interest her charge. One of these, sung while touching the appropriate parts of the body, has become a ribald pub song in some parts of the county and a rugby song in others:

> Brow-bender,
> Eye-winker,
> Nose-dropper,
> Mouth-eater,
> Chin-chopper,
> Tickle-tickle.

Another would be accompanied by the baby's feet being lightly tapped together:

> Tap-a-shoe, that would I do
> If I had but a little more leather;
> We'll sit in the sun till the leather do come,
> Then we'll tap them both together.

A prayer current in different versions throughout the county was probably more acceptable to children than those of the adult clergy:

> Matthew, Mark, Luke and John,
> Pray bless the bed that I lie on;
> Four corners to my bed,
> Four angels there are spread,
> Two to foot and two to head,
> And six will carry me when I'm dead.

These rhymes were used to keep the children smiling, for, if they frowned, the wind might change direction and their faces remain unhappy.

Cornish nursery rhymes often reflected the children's environment in a lucid and, perhaps, typically childlike way. This verse makes a quick transition from fantasy to reality:

> I would that I were where I wish,
> Out on the sea in a tombey [wooden] dish,
> When the dish begins to fill,
> I wish I was on Mousehole Hill.
> When the hills begins to crack,
> I wish I was on Daddy's back.
> When Daddy's back begins to ache,
> I wish that I was sitting down a-eating currant cake.

The child's matter-of fact outlook is expressed here, too:

> Grandfa Grig had a pig
> In a field of clover.
> Piggie died, Grandfa' cried,
> And all the fun was over.

Girls living in the neighbourhood of Dolcoath Mine many years ago would dry their washing in a local smithy. The smith's name was ' Bullum ' [Plum] Garn, so-called from his garden of plum trees, and, for the young boys of the time, his place was where the girls ought to be:

> Rain, rain, go away, come again another day,
> For little Johnny wants to play.
> Every drop as big as a hop,
> Send the maidens to Bullum Garn's shop.

In Stratton, in north-east Cornwall, the little children sang this song, until quite recently, to the music of the village church-bells:

> Adam and Eve could never believe
> That Peter the miller was dead;
> Locked up in a tower for stealing of flour
> And never could get a reprieve.
> They bored a hole in Oliver's nose
> And put therein a string,
> And drew him round about the town
> For murdering Charles our king.

The Cromwellian element in the second half of the rhyme was echoed in the Devon town of Tiverton, where each year on Restoration Day, 29 May, the local boys would parade through the streets dragging with them a bound ' fool ' called Oliver, who was pelted with refuse by the onlookers. The custom died out in the mid-nineteenth century.

Once out of the nursery, the Cornish children's rhymes and songs were generally used in connection with games, although the St Austell historian, Dr A. L. Rowse, recalls a jingle from his own childhood which appears to have been simply for fun:

Murder in the shoe-box, fire in the spence (kitchen dresser),
I had a little donkey and I haven't seen 'n sence.
Give 'n a little oats, give 'n a little straw,
Gee up, donkey! and away she go.

Riddles have always been popular in Cornwall and a few really old examples still exist in country schools. In Pendeen, a few years ago, a ten-year-old girl described a grindstone as:

> . . . a thing behind the door,
> The more you feed it, the more 'twill roar:

and we heard this gruesome description of an orange from a Gorran boy:

> I met a fellow clothed in yellow
> Upon a cloudy day;
> I picked him up and sucked his blood,
> Then threw his skin away.

An almost identical rhyme appeared in a book written in 1890.
Blind Man's Buff, or 'Blind buck-a-Davy', was a popular Cornish game, and here is a typical dialogue to begin it:

How many horses has your father got in his stables?
Three.
What colour are they?
Red, white and grey.
Then turn about and twist about and catch them when you may.

The children of Looe played a linked-hands game punctuated by a song:

> How many miles from this to Babylon?
> Three score and ten!
> Can we get there by daylight?
> Yes, if your legs are long and strong.
> This one's long and this one's strong,
> Open your gates as high as the sky,
> And let St George (or the King) pass by.

An interesting game was played with marbles, where a boy

would take a handful of them from his pocket and ask his opponent: 'Ship sail, sail fast – how many men on board?' If the
second boy guessed below the correct number he would hand
over sufficient marbles to correct his guess; if he guessed above
he would take the excess for himself. An accurate guess reversed
the roles of the players. Today, a variant of this game, called
'Riding the Pony', is played for money in many Cornish pubs,
but the youngsters seem to have lost it.

Counting-out rhymes pose interesting problems, and in Cornwall an especially picturesque example is:

> Hewery, hiery, hackery, heaven,
> Hack a bone, crack a bone, ten or eleven,
> Baked, stewed, fried in the sun,
> Twiddlelem, twiddlelem, twenty-one.

Another, still current, rhyme recalls the more familiar 'eeny-
meeny-miny-mo':

> Ena, mena, more, mi,
> Pisca, lara, bora, bi,
> Eggs, butter, cheese, bread,
> Stick, stack, stone, dead.
> O – U – T spells out!

From schooldays and the rhymes of childhood it is a short
step to early courtship:

> Saturday night is courting night,
> I wish the time was come,
> For my house is swept and sanded,
> So all my work is done.

Young women tried various charms, especially on Halloween,
to divine the names of their future husbands. Men's names were
written on separate pieces of paper and the scraps then screwed
up tightly and pressed into little mud balls; these were immersed
in a bowl of water and the first one to open revealed the true
lover's name. A wedding ring was suspended from a line of cotton
and held between a girl's thumb and forefinger, accompanied by
the command: 'If my husband's name is to be . . ., let this ring
swing!' Obviously, the girl subconsciously made the ring move

when her favourite's name was mentioned. Even the husband's occupations were foretold by their determined suitors: melted lead poured through the handle of a front-door key proved the profession or trade by the shapes it assumed. This rather odd tradition possibly embodied an indistinct recollection of the sexual connotation of the lock and key, common through British folklore and song.

Rhymes, too, were used by young girls anxious to be married. An apple pip flicked into the air indicated the lover's home, so long as this verse was used:

> North, south, east west,
> Tell me where my love does rest.

While the moon was new, a piece of herb yarrow placed under a girl's pillow was a reliable prophet:

> Good night, fair yarrow,
> Thrice good night to thee;
> I hope before tomorrow's dawn
> My true love I shall see.

If a marriage was due, the girl saw her sweetheart on the following morning. On St Valentine's Day the first man seen by a girl – or a man of the same name – would be her husband, but a delightfully practical couplet from Bodmin Moor puts this into perspective:

> O proper maid, if you'll be mine,
> Send me back some binder-twine.

The men were exhorted to be good lovers, but faithful husbands:

> Come all you young men with your wicked ways,
> Sow all your wild oats in your youthful days,
> That we may live happy, that we may live happy,
> That we may live happy when we grow old.

This honest advice provided a good basis for marriage.

The Cornishman's insularity turned any attempt to choose a marriage partner from outside one's own village into a crime. Many a man who tried to seek his wife in a neighbouring township was 'arrested' by his own villagers and forced to ride in a dirty wheelbarrow. One story was told of an elderly woman from St Keverne who was found weeping, and, when asked about her trouble, explained that her daughter intended to marry a foreigner. Questioned further, she added that he was far worse than a Frenchman or a German – he was a Cury-man, from about eight miles away. This attitude still continues to some extent and another strange custom survived in Morvah until the early part of this century. On their wedding night the unfortunate newly-weds were visited by their friends and relatives, who pulled them from bed and beat them with a sand-filled sack. Afterwards, a furze bush was placed in the bed and the intruders left. While the crowd must have considered this great fun, one wonders at the effect on the victims. Other west Cornwall practices survived until more recently. One involved the men of the village felling a young tree, trimming it of its branches and placing it at night against the wall of the house in which the bridal pair were staying; known as ' propping the house ', this act was supposed to symbolize the need for strength in the marriage partnership. Another superstition demanded that the final part of the wedding feast should be a ' dance around the candles '. Here, candles were placed on the floor in brass holders and the new couple pranced around them, finally jumping high over the flames, to ensure good luck and fidelity – the higher they jumped, the more certain of their fortune.

If there was a discrepancy in the ages of newly-weds, or any rumour of immorality, they might until recently have been subjected to a ' shallal '. This serenade of music played on tin kettles and pans lasted all night and one writer considers that in many cases the custom provided a convenient excuse for any rowdies who had a grudge against the couple. This custom was fairly widespread and known elsewhere as Rough Music or Skimmington. The expression ' a regular shallal ' is still occasionally used in Cornwall to describe a loud noise. A similar practice to the shallal was the ' riding ' or ' mock hunt ', where two villagers impersonating the pair were driven through the streets and jeered at by the crowds; direct reference to the victims was always avoided to evade the slander laws. In 1880 six people from Stoke Climsland, near Callington, were charged with holding a mock hunt. Their defence counsel pleaded that the ceremony was ' older by far in the counties of Devon and Cornwall than any Divorce Court ' and the six were discharged with a nominal fine.

In 1967 the authors received two letters from a 79 year-old

man in Camborne who described himself as an ' ex-rabbit-trapper and horse-breaker '. Our elderly correspondent said he started work at 12 years of age and was obviously rather proud of his writing, which, for an unschooled man, was not at all bad. His stories, he said, came to him from his mother and so on, and he described them as ' God's truth '. One of his tales concerned wife-selling, which we know from contemporary newspaper reports to have taken place in Cornwall during the last century. One man from Redruth would sell his wife to the highest bidder at a local fair. She would then wait until her purchaser was asleep, kill him and steal his money, before returning to her husband. No one knew how often the pair succeeded with their evil game, but eventually the wife was killed by the daughter of one of her victims. We were told, too, of an old tinker, Elizabeth Dunstan, with a drunken husband, prone to bouts of crockery-smashing. One day, after a particularly violent night, he opened his lunch-time pasty to find it filled with broken china, or ' sherds ' in the Cornish dialect. Thereafter, his drinking decreased and his wife became known as ' Lizzie Sherdy '.

The old man wrote of a well in Sithney parish, near Helston, where the water made women barren. They came from miles around, until the local parson heard of it and had the well filled in. It happened about ' 200 years ago ' and, over a period of five years, only three babies were born in Sithney.

His longest story was very gruesome. An old woman, presumably a charmer, told a newly married couple from Wendron the secret to a long life of happiness and prosperity. They must buy a young girl from the market, fatten her and then kill her, preferably by strangling. The body must then be salted, placed in a barrel, and a piece of it eaten each day for six months. Finally, the remains were to be buried in the couple's garden and an elder tree planted on the grave. The newly-weds obeyed their instructions completely, but a neighbour saw them burying the body. They were arrested and locked in the Iron Cage on Hangman's Hill, near Troon, to starve to death, but the man killed his wife by cutting her throat with a sharp stone and then took his own life in the same way. Their bodies were covered with tar and burned at the crossroads on Hangmans' Hill. Our informant added, ' I have seen where the Iron Cage was '.

Most of the traditional rhymes and customs suggest that marriage in old Cornwall was a generally acceptable state. If a couple wanted a large family they had first to rock an empty cradle, for to :

> Rock the cradle empty,
> You'll have babies plenty.

The wife's traditional role is stressed by the following rhyme:

> Rock the cradle, tend the table,
> Blow the fire and spin,
> Take your cup and drink it up,
> Then call your neighbours in.

Tending table is never easy when money is scarce, but the Cornish housewives used their meagre resources to good effect. Although the pasty is now regarded as Cornwall's national dish, the county was remarkable for the variety of its pies. A cottage in St Merryn was held for many years on the rent of a pie filled with limpets, figs and sweet herbs, an apparently delectable concoction! Compared with fish, meat was a rarity in Cornish pies until fairly recent years, but ' nothing ', says the writer, ' was too big or too small, too tough or too greasy' to provide the ingredients. Pilchards were used, mackerel, conger and bream, and strictly vegetable pies contained potatoes and leeks. The less common meat fillings, usually of lamb or pork and offal, satisfied many a hungry miner; giblets were used regularly, together with nattlin (the entrails of sheep or calves) and muggety (pigs), usually flavoured with parsley, pepper and salt. Taddago pies were made from prematurely born sucking-pigs, or ' veers ', and lammy pies from still-born lambs. One of the strangest pies, however, contained the ubiquitous pilchard: it was wasteful to cover the uneatable fish-heads with pastry, and, as the rich oil would be lost if the heads were cut off, it was better to cook the fish whole to enable the oil to drain back into the meat; so the pie was cooked with the fish heads poking through the pastry, hence the name ' starry-gazy '. This somewhat grotesque dish is still cooked in Cornwall, although infrequently, and is usually served with a sauce of sour cream. When pilchards are pressed in bulk, a squeaky noise is made by the air bladders bursting. This is said to be the fish ' crying for more ', and another full net will be the result.

Sweets, when included, were as practical as the main course. Saffron cake, which, according to custom, should only be eaten indoors, remains a Cornish speciality. Here is a typical recipe:

4½lbs flour	½lb sugar
6oz mixed peel	½ nutmeg
2lbs currants	2oz yeast
1½lbs butter and lard	milk
⅛oz saffron	salt

Well mix dry ingredients, put in yeast, leave till light and bake for 1¼ hours.

Figgy obbin, a currant pudding, was another popular food, nicely described in this rhyme:

Rolly-polly in the bag, pudden' in the basin,
If you'd a'been where I have been you'd surely look to taste 'n.

Possibly the most widespread Cornish sweet, though, was 'fuggan', or 'heavy cake', a rich confection made with 2 cups of flour, 2oz of fat, a handful of currants and a pinch of salt; these ingredients were then mixed with sour milk and rolled into an inch-thick oval shape. The cake was always scored with a knife, criss-cross, and baked for half an hour, before serving, often accompanied by sloe gin or parsnip wine.

Local drinks such as these were also important in the county's traditional fare. Cornish mead, probably weaker than in the past, remains a popular liquor. The inns and drinking-shops, or 'kiddlywinks', complemented their ordinary beers with lambs wool, a spiced ale with apples floating or beaten up in it, and mahogany, a mixture of two parts gin and one treacle, was drunk by fishermen.

Cornish food is described as:

Gurty milk and bearly-bread no lack,
Pudden-skins an' a good shaip's chack,
A bussa o' salt pelchers, 'nother o' pork,
A good strong stummick an' a-plenty o' work.

Basic though some of the meals were, grace was usually spoken before and after eating. 'Lord, make us able', the prayer would begin, 'to eat what's upon table'; and, when the food was finished, 'The Lord be praised, our stummicks be aised.' Table manners could be rough. Less than a hundred years ago there was a popular saying in Newlyn: 'Fingers for fish, prongs for mait'.

Despite their basic diet and tough working life, the people of old Cornwall found energy and time for diversion. Among the few surviving sources of written Cornish are the cycles of Miracle Plays, dating from the fourteenth to the sixteenth centuries. These religious dramas written for the layman were performed in playing places, or *plan-an-gwary*, some of which still remain, notably at St Just-in-Penwith and Gwennap. These plays, while didactic, never lost their sense of entertainment and generally concluded with music and dancing. The *Life of St Meriasek*, for example, written in 1504, ends with a song, translated as follows:

> Drink ye all with the play,
> We will beseech you,
>   Before going hence.
> Pipers, pipe ye at once!
> We will, every son of the breast,
>   Go to dance.
> Go ye or stay,
> Welcome shall ye be
> Though ye be a week here.

The Cornish love of play-acting has long outlasted the Miracle Plays and, as we shall see later, mumming is not dead in some parts of the county. Perhaps even the fine Minack Theatre on Land's End echoes the old traditions.

Virtually every town and village in Cornwall has its fair or feast day, although the festivities are now tame compared with earlier times. The fairs presented opportunities for tradesmen of every sort to display their wares and for local sportsmen to test themselves at wrestling, ' kooks ' (a form of quoits) and other games. The background of Cornish fairs will be considered in another chapter, but the enthusiasm of the participants is nowhere better illustrated than in the song *Crantock Games*, where a young man, William Coombe, is shot and killed by a rival:

> Crantock and Newlyn men all in one room,
> The first gun to be shot it proved my doom.
> My name is William Coombe, just twenty in my bloom,
> Just twenty when they shot me at Crantock Games.

Singing is very much a part of Cornish life and some traditional songs are still sung, either as part of an annual custom or purely for pleasure. In a few country inns, Saturday night is still characterized by spontaneous singing and instrumental music. Hunting songs vie with sea shanties and there is often a local accordionist to help the evening along, but the music is not always raucous. A beautiful version of the riddle song, *Scarborough Fair*, was sent to us from St Columb and would certainly silence any pub audiences:

> Can you plough me an acre of land?
> Every leaf grows many in time.
> Between the salt water and the sea sand?
> And you shall be a true lover of mine.

If traditional singing is in decline in Cornwall, competitive bell-ringing has almost disappeared. Until quite recently, however, it was a popular and lucrative pastime. Many villages provided teams of dedicated ringers who would travel great distances to test their skills and perhaps the best known came from Egloshayle, near Wadebridge; a song dating from about 1810 describes them:

> There's Craddock the Cordwainer first, that rings the treble bell,
> The second is John Ellery, and none may him excel;
> The third is Pollard, carpenter, the fourth is Thomas Cleave,
> Goodfellow is the tenor-man, that rings them round so brave.

All five men lie buried in Egloshayle churchyard and their memorials are still standing. At least two other Cornish churches bear witness to the old ringers, with sets of rules in St Marnack's, Lanreath, and these in St Fimbarrus's, Fowey:

> Hark how the Chirping Treble Sings Most Clear
> And Covering Tom comes rowling in the rear,
> We ring the Quick to Church, the Dead to grave,
> Good is our Life, Just Usage let us have.

The ringers' bells rang 'the Dead to grave' and in old Cornwall, as elsewhere, there were many superstitions concerning death, some of which survive today. A cock crowing at midnight salutes the Angel of Death passing overhead, while a church clock may 'chime sadly' if someone is dying. A woman would never use a gate when there was a stile nearby, for to:

Go through a gate when there's a stile hard by,
You'll be a widow before you die.

Earlier this century a nurse attending a dying farmer saw the man's wife wring the neck of a black cockerel. She explained that the cock would accompany her husband's soul to the gates of Heaven, where it would remind St Peter of his own sins and thus make him merciful enough to let the sinner enter.

A hearse should never travel to church by a new road, nor should it stop en route, or more deaths would follow; further tragedy would also occur if a body were left unburied over a Sunday. A soul could not ' pass ' peacefully if it lay ' athurt the planshun ', that is, across the line of the floorboards, and, following a death, indoor plants were draped with black crepe to prevent them from dying too. In the Helston district, up to the time of World War I, a penny, a candle, a hammer and a pinch of salt were always placed upon a coffin to assist a soul on the way to its destiny, while an even older belief stated that the distribution of bread and salt at a funeral protected the mourners against sorcery. Rain falling on a coffin is proof that its occupant's soul has arrived safely, but the souls of those who die through accident or suicide are thought to ' walk ' after death, in the parish where they meet their doom. One writer tells of a strange incident in which a man fell down an unmarked mine shaft in the parish of Perranuthnoe, but, as the shaft ran at a slant, his body landed beneath St Hilary. To accentuate the problem, the corpse was brought to the surface by a different route, emerging in Breage. Here, surely, was a very confused ghost.

Until the early part of this century, many Cornish funerals were accompanied by the mourners singing ' burying tunes ', usually in a minor key and very slowly. The overall effect of melancholia was, perhaps, not unlike the atmosphere created by marching jazz musicians at New Orleans funerals. The final chapters of many men's lives are written by the stonemasons who carve their epitaphs. Cornwall's churchyards contain some fine examples of this art. In Boscastle, this touching verse recalls a past priest and his lady:

Forty-nine years they lived man and wife,
And what's more rare thus many without strife,
The first departing, he a few weeks tried
To live without her, could not, and so died.

Less serious, this piece can be seen in Mylor:

> His foot it slipt
> And he did fall.
> Help, help, he cried,
> And that was all.

And this, from St Buryan, an example of the widespread distrust of lawyers:

> Here lie John and Richard Benn,
> Two lawyers and two honest men.
> God works miracles now and then.

Finally, the summation of the Cornish life cycle appears in this epitaph from Zennor, the story of one man and of many in old Cornwall:

> Hope, fear, false-joy and trouble
> Are these four winds which daily toss this bubble.
> His breath's a vapour and his life's a span,
> 'Tis glorious misery to be born a man.

E

2 The Tinners and their Legends

CHUN CASTLE, NEAR ST JUST-IN-PENWITH, was built in about 200 BC. In 1925 several small smelting pits were discovered at this ancient earthwork and a piece of metal slag found in them. The slag was proved to be tin and so confirmed a pedigree of well over 2,000 years for the Cornish metal industries.

It is quite possible that trade existed in pre-Christian times between Cornwall and other parts of Europe. The Romans played their part in the commercial use of tin, and later when the Saxons penetrated east Cornwall they exploited alluvial tin. The Greek writer Herodotus referred to the Cassiterides, those ' Islands of Tin ' which some Cornishmen like to equate with the Scillies, and the story of Ictis, the island *entrepôt* of the tin trade widely held to have been St Michael's Mount. In the seventh-century *Life of St John the Almoner*, the tale is told of a sailor from Alexandria who came to Cornwall with a cargo of corn to relieve a famine. He returned home aboard a ship laden with tin, which magically changed to silver on the way. If there is any historical basis for the story, the cargo was presumably silver from the outset. Still, the miraculous superstructure suggests a contemporary awareness of Cornish tin in the east Mediterranean.

Huge gaps were left by the historians and these provided ample scope for the people to produce their own legends. The Phoenicians' trade with Cornwall is still current in popular imagination, although Phoenician, Jew and Saracen appear to be synonymous. In Elizabethan times derelict mine workings were known as *attal Sarsen*, or 'Saracens' offcasts', while up to the early part of the twentieth century traces of medieval smelting works were called 'Jews' Houses' by the tinners. Even the brasswork in King Solomon's Temple was supposed to have been wrought from Cornish tin. The Bible, in fact, plays a major role in the old stories. The Rev. H. A. Lewis quotes from a Cornish mine captain: 'One of these (traditions of metal workers) is that St Joseph of Arimathea, the rich man of the Gospels, made his money in the tin trade between Phoenicia and Cornwall . . . and that on one occasion he brought with him the Christ Child and His Mother as passengers and landed them at St Michael's Mount.' Creeg-brawse Mine, between Chacewater and St Day, is the centre of the Christ legends. Jesus and Joseph were said to have preached there and a similar story connects the place with St Paul; a neighbouring hamlet is called Salem. Gwennap Pit, near Truro, an old mine working where Wesley preached, may have been adopted by the Methodist leader because Christ was said to have used this site too. Joseph of Arimathea's name also appears in a tinners' song:

> Joseph was a tin man,
> And the miners loved him well.

The miners' own story of the discovery of tin in Cornwall is an attractive legend. St Piran was an Irish saint who came to Cornwall when his lawless countrymen tired of his good deeds and threw him into the sea, a millstone chained about his body. As the stone touched the water it became miraculously buoyant and Piran was able to sail upon it to Cornwall, where he landed on a wide stretch of sand, later to be named Perranzabuloe – 'St Piran in the Sands'. There, from his newly built oratory he began exploring his new surroundings. One day, while preparing a meal, he used a large piece of black stone for the fireplace. As his fire grew hotter he was amazed to see a stream of pure white metal flowing from the flames: he discovered tin. The local people, with whom Piran shared the discovery, were overcome with joy at their new-found prosperity, and held great feasts in celebration of it. The phrase ' As drunk as a Perraner ' passed into oral usage as a result and, even today, Piran's emblem, a white cross on a black background, said to represent tin against the base rock, remains the standard of the Cornish nationalist movement, *Mebyon Kernow.*

As St Piran was not born until the fourth century AD, his part in the finding of tin must be regarded as a fable, but when one comes to the later, well-documented era of the metal industry, the truth is often as exciting as fiction. This is not the place for a detailed history of mining, but a brief recollection is necessary to understand the tinners' traditions and customs. Until its decline in the early part of the twentieth century, the industry maintained a vital role in British economics. One authority offers the twelfth century Pipe Rolls as the starting point for documentary history and points out that, before the 1400s, Cornish mining as such was unknown, the tin being extracted from alluvial deposits in streams, a process known as ' streaming '. This may be why Cornish metal workers are commonly referred to as tinners, rather than miners.

Beginning in about 1200 the workers were organized under a Stannary system, with their own laws and courts of justice. Helston, for instance, was a Stannary town and Coinagehall Street remains there today. The men had special privileges and were free of the usual feudal laws between master and serfs. Although they were allowed onto enclosed land only with the owners' permission, they could take their choice of all other land to search for tin; they knew this as ' bounding ', the tinners' oldest right. Courts were set up to deal with those men who chose to abuse their privileges, justice meted out by their fellows. Thus the tinners enjoyed an odd, if only slight, independence among the ' tied ' community and this singular existence generated a richly individual vein of folklore.

The miners, like members of most esoteric societies, were very superstitious. Even today, swearing and whistling underground are frowned upon, although possibly the original objection that they displeased the mine spirits has been forgotten. An old tinner recently observed that ' the first thing I was told when I went below grass was that I should have me skull bate in if I cocked lip [whistled] under the adit level '. Fishermen, however, believed that whistling on board ship would bring a favourable breeze: nonetheless, many superstitions were shared by the mining and fishing communities. In fact, families often contained workers in both trades and miners from the maritime districts around Lelant, St Ives and St Just-in-Penwith frequently owned shares in fishing boats; they would go to sea in fine weather and underground in bad. In the early eighteenth century the historian Lhuyd collected an old Cornish rhyme in St Just:

> *Sav a man, kebner, tha li, ha ker tha'n hal;*
> *Mor-teed a metten travyth ne dal.*

Translated it says:

> Get up, take breakfast, and go to the moor;
> The sea-tide of the morning is worth nothing.

The method of streaming for tin was known as ' going to the moor '.

Beliefs about the supernatural significance of certain animals and birds were common to miners and fishermen. Miners, in particular, were afraid of mentioning creatures by their proper names; secret, evocative words were substituted and an owl became a ' braced farcer ', a fox ' long tail ', a hare ' long ear ', a cat ' the rooker ' and a rat ' the peep '. Rats, although rare in mines, were believed to warn the miners of rock falls by their shrill screams. Toads are equally rare, but good luck was said to follow them. One tinner stated that ' I saw a toad jump out from behind some rubble; 'pon that I goes to the cap'n [overseer] and, says I, I'll take that end of tribit [tribute] for six months.' They agreed a price, and the man had his best-ever strike of tin. Snails and spiders were also prophetic. A miner on his way to work was dismayed to see a snail and appeased it by offering it a crumb from his lunch or a piece of tallow from the candle on his hat to guard against a mishap in the mine. Spiders, however, brought good luck. Several mining families considered that their fortunes had been made by a spider alighting on the nose or cheek of one of their number. Magpies, too, were prophetic. In Cornwall, as elsewhere in Britain, the chattering of these birds was supposed to foretell great disaster and the miners had their own ritual to accompany the rhyme:

> One [magpie] is sorrow, two is mirth,
> Three is a wedding, and four is death.

To counteract the birds' power, this couplet had to be chanted slowly while spitting towards the offending creatures.

More practical than their animal fantasies was the miners' attention to fire. They carefully watched the burning of a candle: the colour of a flame could foretell the future; so too could sparks emitting from half-extinguished embers. These things, of course, were vital to life – or death – underground and, as such, they retained a mystical significance on the surface. The minerals themselves engendered certain beliefs. Natural gases in the mines produced weird, flickering lights which the workers insisted were lamps held by spirits to show the way to rich lodes; these ' Jack o' Lanterns ', or ' Tin Lanterns ', commanded great respect among the men and often proved useful guides. Technical proverbs became part of the miners' language, among them ' Capel rides a good horse '. Capel is a form of schorl which accurately indicated the whereabouts of tin. It was said, also, that only ' a wise man knows tin ', a truism confirmed by the many varieties of the mineral found in Cornwall.

The mine workings even provided their own folk medicines. The historian, Hals, wrote in 1730 that the tinners would apply a solution of mundic (iron pyrites) and water to a wound in the certain belief that an immediate cure would be effected. Such notions were probably necessary to combat the absence of any real medical attention for the miners. Similarly, with conditions underground and low pay precluding any hope of an easy life, charms for producing gifts were plentiful. Showing money to the new moon was supposed to result in a present of the coin's value before the night ended. An itching palm was an omen of imminent wealth, as was the appearance of white specks beneath the thumb-nail. When the specks grew under finger-nails, however, trouble was at hand and if both thumb and fingers were speckled, the tinner did not know whether to be glad or sorry.

An even more peculiar tradition survived amongst the miners of St Just until the late nineteenth century. When a man became a father for the first time, his hat was burned, to ensure a long life for the child and, so some say, to signify the end of his old, free life and the beginning of his new one, tied to the family. Another belief of the Cornish miners, common also to those of Northumberland and Durham, was that it was fatal to return and fetch anything that had been forgotten. A man, for instance, who had left his lunch or pipe in his coat pocket while changing to go underground would recall this rhyme:

> Forget, return and there remain,
> Or bad luck follows in your train.

However much time was at his disposal, he would rather go hungry than chance his luck.

If the tinners were superstitious, they were also – and still are – musical and fond of rhymes. Cornwall is a land of choirs, especially mining ensembles. Nowadays such groups as the Skinners Bottom Glee Club are mostly concerned with hymns and popular songs, but old favourites like ' Camborne Hill ' still have their place in the repertoires. At St Hilary, in West Cornwall, the Tinners Arms inn once had this verse inscribed above the door:

> Come all good Cornish boys, walk in,
> Here's a brandy, rum and shrub, and gin;
> You can't do less than drink success
> To copper, Fish and Tin!

Again, one can see the obvious sympathy between mining and fishing folk. A clergyman, formerly of Gwennap parish, recalls the following rhyme as being still current in the twentieth century:

> Up Poldice the men are like mice,
> And tin is good and plenty,
> But Cap'n J. Teague, a man from Breage,
> Will give 'ee ten for twenty.

To be ' like mice ' indicated a lack of labour problems, for, when the men were being unfairly treated by the mine owners, their cry was, ' Are we men or mice, to put up with it.'

Songs specifically concerned with mining, however, are less frequent, but one old tune had these words:

> Here's to the Devil, with his wooden spade and shovel,
> Digging tin by the bushel with his tail cocked up.

Certainly, this was a drinking song, but now, sadly, it has vanished from common usage. During the mid-1950s, though, the folksong collector, Peter Kennedy, heard a fine song in Redruth:

> O the Farmers go around and fill their bags tied up with straw,
> The miners they go underground and never miss a blaw,
> O a-mining we will go, my boys, a-mining we will go,
> With picks and shovels in our hands, a-mining we will go!

It was sung to the tune used by Parson Hawker of Morwenstow for his ' Trelawny ' ballad, possibly originating from the traditional French *Petit Tambour*. This air was also used in Cornwall by Christmas mummers:

> O a-mumming we will go, will go, O a mumming we will go,
> With bright cockades all in our hats, we'll make a gallant show!

as well as by the tinners for several songs, among them ' Wheal Rodney '. *Wheal*, incidentally, is old Cornish for ' mine-working ', while *bal* means ' mine ':

> Now I and Cap'n Franky got up to go to bal,
> We started for Wheal Rodney where there was work for all.

Hawker's ' Trelawny ' with its ' twenty thousand Cornishmen ' knowing the reason why, is often thought to be traditional itself, but the good parson probably adapted it from an earlier miners' song concerning Napoleon and with this final verse:

> And should that Boney Peartie have forty thousand still
> To make into an army for to work his wicked will,
> And try for to invade us, if he doesn't quickly fly –
> Why forty thousand Cornish boys shall know the reason why!

A version of another song ' The Streams of Lovely Nancy ', was collected by the Rev. Sabine Baring-Gould in 1889. This piece is still current and is sometimes known as ' Come All You Little Streamers ', an obvious reference to early tin mining. Indeed, Anne Gilchrist, suggests that ' Nancy ', or ' Nantsian ' as it is sometimes written, could be a corruption of Marazion, the town overlooking Mount's Bay and St Michael's Mount. Miss Gilchrist adds that the couplet:

On yonder high mountain a castle there does stand,
It is built with ivory near to the black sand.

sounds remarkably like a description of the Mount, which is built of white quartz and stands amid seaweed-covered sand.

Mining communities throughout the world have attracted fairy stories and in Cornwall the little people who lived underground were known as ' knockers ' or ' nuggies '. The Cornish writer, A. K. Hamilton-Jenkin, describes them as ' withered, dried-up creatures ', apparently the size of a one- or two-year-old baby; their heads, though, were large and ugly, with old men's faces and their arms and legs ungainly. Their origin is explained in two ways. One view is that they derive from a long-lost tribe which inhabited Cornwall before the Celts, their spirits being too good for Hell, but not good enough for Heaven. Thus they were condemned to haunt the underground and, although at one time of reasonable height, began to diminish at the birth of Christ, ultimately to disappear altogether. The more common and distastefully antisemitic explanation is that the knockers were ghosts of the Jews who encouraged the crucifixion of Jesus, and were sent to the mines as a penance. This is, of course, inconsistent, since they were said never to work on the Christian festivals, Christmas Day, Easter Day and All Saints' Day, as well as Saturdays, the Jewish Sabbath. The tinners themselves were wary of working at those times for fear of offending them. On Christmas Eve they held midnight mass in the deeper levels of the mines and miners have claimed to hear them singing carols to the accompaniment of organ music. A possible side issue of the Jewish theory is the miners' aversion to the sign of the cross. Robert Hunt recalls the story of a tinner who was walking through a complicated series of adits with his colleagues. As he intended to return alone, he scratched a cross on the wall to mark his route, but his companions were shocked and demanded that he alter it to another symbol.

Although the miners were afraid of the knockers – as, indeed, they still are in the far west – they knew them at times to be friendly. They only worked around rich lodes of tin and William Bottrell quotes a tinner from Balleswidden Mine, near St Just, as being ' in good heart, because for every stroke of my pick, I heard three or four clicks from the knockers, working ahead of me '. This man maintained that he had seen a group of the little people busily working at their various trades, one of them a smith with a tiny anvil between his knees. The song ' Wheal Rodney ' extols the knockers' eye for a good strike:

> Now we had luck at last, boys, the knockers showed us where
> To shut the rock and raise the tin, that started us off fair.

But while they were useful, the knockers could also be extremely spiteful if their wishes were not respected.

Tom Trevorrow was a tinner from St Just, working in the Ballowal Mine. One day, Tom heard what he took to be the knockers and, being sceptical of their powers, told them to be quiet and go away. He was immediately struck by a fall of small stones, but still unconcerned, continued working. After a while he heard the sprites again:

> Tom Trevorrow! Tom Trevorrow!
> Leave some of thy fuggan [Cornish heavy cake] for Bucca,
> Or bad luck to thee tomorrow.

Bucca is a Cornish word meaning ' imp ', but Tom ignored the warning and cried ' Go to blazes, you cussed old Jews' sperrats, or I'll scat [knock] your brains out!' Then the knockers spoke again, but this time their tone had become hard and threatening.

> Tommy Trevorrow! Tommy Trevorrow!
> We'll send thee bad luck tomorrow,
> Thou old curmudgeon to eat all thy fuggan
> And not leave a didjan [little piece] for Bucca.

When Tom arrived at work next day he found that a rock fall had buried not only his precious tools, but also the pile of rich ore that was to provide his month's wages. A confirmed sceptic, he was still not entirely disheartened, but his ill-luck persisted until he was forced to leave the mine and seek work as a farm labourer – a terrible fate for a tinner.

Like poor Tom Trevorrow, a miner called Barker, from Towednack, scoffed at the power of the knockers. He believed that they were the figments of imagination, of dreams or of drunkenness and paid them no attention whatsoever. Barker was a lazy man and when his associates protested at his scepticism, he suggested going to a local mine reputed to be alive with knockers and, lying in the sunshine at the mouth of the shaft, to watch for them. But the knockers detested being spied on and Barker was soon to pay for his curiosity. After some while he heard the little men chattering below him and learned that they worked eight-hour shifts, after which they hid their tools until the next time. Barker determined to find the hiding-places and steal some tools for himself, so he listened even more carefully to the knockers' conversation. At last, he thought himself lucky. ' I shall leave my tools in a cleft of the rocks ', declared one knocker, ' And I shall leave mine under the ferns,' said the second. The third was more explicit. ' I shall leave mine on Barker's knee!' he cried and, at that instant, Barker felt a massive weight smash onto his left knee. His screams were answered only with laughter from the mine shaft and, to his dying day, he walked with a limp. ' As stiff as Barker's knee ' is still a current phrase in Cornwall and, al-though it probably refers to rheumatism caused by dampness in the mines, the tinners prefer to believe otherwise.

Another story concerns a man named Trenwith, who, with his son, saw the knockers working at the Ransom Mine in west Cornwall. He offered the fairy miners a bargain, suggesting that, if they would let him work their tin, he would leave them one-tenth of the best metal each day. To save themselves toiling over-night, they agreed, and soon old Trenwith was wealthy, although he never forgot to leave the knockers their daily share. After he died, however, his son, a greedy man, decided to keep all the tin for himself. Immediately, the lode failed, and the young man was unable to find alternative work. He drank away his father's fortune before dying a beggar: further proof of the knockers' power.

The knockers were by no means the only spirits to haunt Corn-wall's mines. The shafts and levels were filled with wraiths of every imaginable shape and a few stories are still told by old tinners. In the mid-1960s an ex-miner from St Agnes recounted a tale of the nearby Baldhu Mine. A shaft from this working can still be seen in the garden of the Railway Hotel in St Agnes and, on odd occasions, the ghost of a witch leaves this shaft, enters the inn and moves a picture on the wall. The story, though un-remarkable in itself, is perhaps a survival from the legend of Dorcas.

Dorcas was an old lady who lived in a cottage near Polbreen Mine at the foot of St Agnes Beacon. She tired of her lonely life and, one night, threw herself into a deep shaft at Polbreen. Her body was recovered by a miner and buried with as much ceremony as suicide would allow, but her spirit lived on in the mine. The phantom rarely appeared, but its voice often broke the silence of the mine to call a miner away from his work. Indeed, any tinner on piecework who contributed a poor return was said to have been ' chasing Dorcas '. On one occasion, though, Dorcas's ghost forgot her mischief, and did a good deed. Two miners were at work in Darkey's (Dorcas's) Shaft when they heard one of their names being called. They stopped working and listened and again the name was called, louder than before. The man dropped his hammer and went off to find the caller, but he had gone only a few yards when a mass of rock fell onto the spot where he had been standing. He swore thereafter that Dorcas had saved his life, for no other person could be found who admitted to calling his name. Hamilton-Jenkin, writing in 1927, stated that, although the old tinners of St Agnes still remembered the story of Dorcas, none owned to seeing or hearing her spirit.

Other ghosts have been responsible for saving lives in the Cornish mines. In a pit near St Austell, a tinner working in a particularly treacherous area was killed by a rock fall. Some time later one of his former colleagues was approaching the scene of the accident when he was startled to see a cloud of smoke suspended a few feet above the ground. The man's curiosity changed to terror as the smoke assumed the shape of his dead friend. He fell back in horror, just in time to avoid another fatal fall of rock. On yet another occasion, John Lean, a member of a wealthy mining family, was examining a rich lode in Wheal Jewel, a mine at Gwennap. Suddenly, he heard a distinct voice calling: ' You are in the winze [shaft]!' Knowing that no other person was near him, he still had the sense to throw himself flat on his back. When he sat up he discovered that he was only inches from the verge of a deep shaft. Had he not been warned he must have died. Even the famous Dolcoath Mine, the largest pit of all, was not free from spectres. Eight men who were entombed there in 1893 were warned of their peril by ghostly cracklings in the rock.

Hunt relates another strange tale, of Wheal Vor, near Helston. A young miner made an error in charging a hole with blasting powder and he and an older comrade had the unenviable task of removing the powder. Tragically, the charge exploded and men nearby saw the two unfortunates blown into the air. When the bodies were brought to the surface, they were found to be in such a terrible state that one of the onlookers picked them up on a shovel and threw them into an engine furnace, to save the feelings of the men's families. The keeper of the engine house thereafter swore that the place was haunted by a troop of small black dogs and that, although few tinners would speak of the apparitions, none liked to work in the vicinity. Another black dog, according to the eminent Cornish folklorist, William Paynter, also appeared on the main road between Bodmin and Launceston, near Linkinhorne: it was said to be as big as a calf, with eyes as large as saucers and a foaming mouth. Some believed it to be the spectre of a miner killed in an accident at the Marke Valley Mine, but, although traces of the mine can still be seen, the dog has fortunately not manifested itself for many years.

A disembodied hand has appeared at many mines in Cornwall, always prophesying disaster. The hand usually carries a miner's tallow candle and those who see it should fear for the future. At Wheal Vor, a white hare is also said to spell doom to the seer. Ghosts even followed the migrant tinners, for one night, asleep near Pachuca in Mexico, a Cornish miner dreamed of his beloved daughter at home in Cornwall. She lay a cold hand upon his brow, repeating the words, ' Oh, father!' He learnt later, almost without surprise, that she had died that night. The miners' belief in the unworldly is understandable in view of their environment, but the *West Briton* newspaper of 31 January 1840 reported a spirit ' in the shape of the Devil ' seen underground. Five brave men went to investigate – and found a fox.

The Cornish tin miners had little enough time for recreation, yet they managed to maintain certain dates as ' feast days '. Carew wrote that the tinners had ' more Holy-Dayes than are warranted by the Church, our lawes, or their owne profit ' – but Carew had never experienced the dangers that lay behind such excess. Neither had a writer in 1710 who castigated the tinners of Germoe as ' crazy folk, without fear of God and the world '. At their leisure, the miners would wrestle – sometimes against teams of fishermen – play at hurling, kailles (ninepins) and kooks and, of course, drink and fight. The Monday after Saturday pay-day was known as ' Maze Monday ' or ' Bad Monday ', from the riots that typified it. Beer and illicit ' moonshine ' were held to blame for the destruction, but perhaps it was actually the environment.

The tinners' year really began on 23 January, the eve of St Paul's Tide. This was known as Paul's Pitcher Day and Jonathan Couch of Polperro described it as the ' first red-letter day in the tinners' calendar '. Said to commemorate the discovery of tin smelting, the celebrations included a strange ritual. A water pitcher was set up at a chosen spot among the tin works and the miners would pelt it with stones until it was completely destroyed. They would then leave work and go to the nearest inn, where they bought a replacement pitcher and used it to keep themselves in beer for the rest of the day. In part, the ceremony was regarded simply as an expression of rebellion by the tinners against the mining rule that only water could be drunk during work. It was also current among the fishermen of Padstow, perhaps as a copy of the miners' custom, or possibly having a common earlier origin in some ritual of renewal. The young men of Bodmin took the performance a stage further; as late as 1896 they would parade through the town throwing the broken pieces of earthenware against the door of each house, crying:

St Paul's Eve,
And here's a heave!

St Piran's Day fell on 5 March and was a miner's holiday. St Piran, as well as being the patron saint of tin mining, was apparently something of a tippler. Indeed, he was said to have died drunk. Like Paul's Pitcher Day, St Piran's feast was in memory of the first tin smelting and the miners enjoyed it. Hamilton-Jenkin quotes from a cost book of the Great Work Mine for the years 1759–62, in which an allowance for St Piran's Day was stated. At ' Perrantide ' the men were allotted 6d each and the mine captains 1s. The inns and ' kiddlywinks ' did a marvellous trade. The Colorado Folklore Society situated in a mining area of the United States, still holds a dinner of traditional Cornish fare on the eve of each St Piran's Day. *Lide* is an Anglo-Saxon word for the month of March and the First Friday in Lide provided another tinners' rest day. The men would send a young miner to the top of the highest ' bound ' or hill on the works and there he would lie down and sleep for as long as he possibly could, a period which was taken as a measure for the men's afternoon break over the following 12 months. It is worth mentioning that the Cornish climate in early March is hardly conducive to a lengthy open-air slumber. The archaic word *Lide* survived among the miners and one of their proverbs suggested that ' ducks won't lay till they've drunk Lide water '.

An important day in any folklore calendar is Midsummer. In west Cornwall, poles surmounted by sycamore bushes were set up on the highest points of every tin works, with flags hoisted from the engine houses. All the men stopped work at midday and were given 1s each for their entertainment. At night great bonfires of furze collected from the surrounding moors were set alight to blaze away across the landscape. Cavities were dug in granite outcrops and charged with gunpowder. When these ' Midsummer holes ' were set off, the country reverberated to the sound. In the eastern part of the county, the festivities were less spectacular but poles and bushes were still erected on the highest hills.

The last big day of the mining year occurred on the second Thursday before Christmas. In some parts of Cornwall the occasion was known as *Chewidden* (White Thursday) and, again recalled the discovery of tin smelting – hence the ' White '. Money was given to the men but, as usual, the real beneficiaries were the innkeepers. Elsewhere the day was called ' Picrous Day ', after a man named Picrous, who apparently found tin. Many explanations have been suggested for this name but perhaps the least implausible is that it is an obscure corruption of Piran. In the Blackmore Stannery especially, Picrous Day was regarded as a great feast, with supper for all the workers. As Picrous Day and *Chewidden* fell at the same time and, earlier, St Piran's Day and the First Friday in Lide almost coincided, it seems likely that there were originally only two holidays. Local habits probably split the celebrations and time wiped out their connections. The miners benefited by extra free time, but this might be considered scant reward for working underground.

We have seen the tinners' love of superstition and should hardly be surprised by it. These men spent the greater part of their lives far below ground, their only lighting the untrustworthy flicker of tallow candles – until Davy invented his lamp. On the surface, too, the mining country was gaunt, sparsely vegetated, broken by jagged hills and angular engine houses. Even in this electronic age, the night-time silhouettes of derelict ' Cornish castles ' are a grotesque sight. The tinners lived always in fear of death and poverty; they saw their comrades crushed, their families made destitute. What wonder then that they turned inwards by way of escape. The stories which sprang from their own imaginations cast some light onto a very dark world.

To the Cornish miners, work was truly a way of life: they knew no other and, for all its hardness, wanted none. Even the children grew up on nursery rhymes like this:

> Balance-bob works up and down,
> Pumping the water from underground,
> Over the while the engine do lash,
> Scat the old man back in the shaft.

Thus they grew, like their fathers, to 'know tin', to work underground and perhaps to supplement their meagre earnings by scavenging from wrecks along the coast or stealing the odd sheep from a local squire. Once, this little verse was left on a farm gate in Gwennap parish:

> Dear Sir William, do not weep,
> We've had one of your fat sheep;
> You are rich and we're poor,
> When this is done we'll come for more.

Here surely is a pleasant reminder that, while the tinners may have felt driven to crime, not all of them were totally illiterate.

The slow passing of the miners' old ways began in the eighteenth century with the coming of John Wesley and Methodism. With little religion other than their fanciful legends, the tinners were easy targets for Wesley's proselytizing. He gave the men something to cling to in their dangerous situation and they responded eagerly. Lay preachers like Billy Bray and Richard Hampton were from the mines themselves: they brought with them biblical tracts to replace the oral tales, rousing corrective hymns instead of country songs. It would be churlish to deny Methodism's beneficial effect upon the miners; Wesley and his successors virtually wiped out organized crime among the men and gave them an object in life other than work. But, sadly, this old 'burying song' might also have rung the death knell for the tinners' own culture:

> . . . bear me gently to my grave,
> And as you pass along,
> Remember, 'twas my wish to have
> A pleasant funeral song.

Today, speculators are hoping for a great revival in Cornish mining. The old beliefs, though, have mostly gone forever.

3 The Sea

Here's a health to the Pope, may he never know sorrow,
With pilchards today, and pilchards tomorrow.

THE PILCHARDS ARE NOW IN SHORT SUPPLY off Cornwall's coasts,
but for centuries they provided both income and staple diet for
the Cornish fisherfolk. Indeed, a rhyme explained that:

Pilchards are food, money and light,
All in one night.

Cornwall's fishing fleets are today reduced to little more than a
handful of boats and even these generally supplement their earnings by transporting tourists to the diminishing fishing grounds.
As with tin and copper mining, fishing in Cornwall has lost out
to foreign competition and much of the folklore associated with
this tough career his died with it. Not all though, and, as we
shall see, a tradition of song struggles in parts of the county
against todays' electronic music, while a few old beliefs are fixed

F

in the seamen's minds. The sea is never more than 25 miles away in Cornwall and, not, surprisingly, the folklore connected with it is wide and varied. Here, we shall look first at the fisherman's work and songs, then at his traditions and the supernatural elements of sea lore – the monsters and the mermaids – and finally at the very human world of smugglers and wreckers.

The Cornish pilchard season coincided roughly with harvest-time on the land, as a rhyme explains:

> When the corn is in the shock
> The fish are on the rock.

Seine fishing provided the main method of catching pilchards: sets of three boats were arranged with vast nets hanging between them to await the fish, whose appearance was signalled from the shore by men known as huers, from the French *huer,* to shout. Strange little houses still stand on the cliffs above Newquay and St Ives, the last remnants of these iron-lunged men who would watch for the fish, then, when they saw them, scream directions to the fishermen waiting below. ' Hevva, hevva!' was their introductory cry, possibly a corruption of *hesva,* the Cornish for ' shoal '; then shouting and waving bunches of sticks – ' bushes ' – they would lead the boats to their prey. Seine nets could be a quarter-mile in length, so the amount of fish taken was enormous on a good day. In St Ives, when the catch was completed, the town crier in his high-pole hat would walk through the streets announcing which inn the men from each boat should attend to collect their payment: much of it no doubt remained in the taverns.

Hamilton-Jenkin describes the launching of the seine fleet as ' a joyous occasion '. The children crowded onto the beaches as the boats were launched and sang:

> A laky [leaky] ship with her anchor down,
> Her anchor down, her anchor down,
> A laky ship with her anchor down,
> Hurrah, my boys, hurrah!
>
> We're loaded with sugar and rum, my boys,
> And rum, my boys, and rum my boys,
> We're loaded with sugar and rum, my boys,
> Hurrah, my boys, hurrah!

But the claustrophobic excitement in the little towns is perhaps better described in this poem from an anonymous St Ives poet:

> Pilchards are come, and hevva is heard,
> And the town from the top to the bottom is stirred.
> Anxious faces are hurrying in every direction,
> To take a fine shoal they have no objection.
> The women now gathered before the White Hart
> Their hopes and their fears to each other impart.
> ' What stem have you got?' ' A first to the lea,
> And look! our men are now going to sea.'
> We see the huer with bushes in hand,
> Upon the White Rock he now takes his stand.
> While ' Right off ', ' Win tow-boat ', ' Hurray ' and ' Cowl
> rooze ' (cast net)
> Are signals no seiner will ever refuse.

Smoked pilchards were known as ' fumadoes ', from the Spanish word *fumade*, or smoked. This the Cornish easily corrupted to ' fairmaids ', making sense of a fine little song collected during the last century by Baring-Gould:

> The cry is ' All up! Let us all haste away!'
> And like hearty good fellows we'll row through the bay.
> > Haul away, my young men,
> > Pull away, my old blades,
> > For the county gives bounty
> > For the pilchard trades.
> 'Tis the silver fairmaids that cause such a strife
> 'Twixt the master seiner and his drunken wife.
> She throwed away her needles and burnt all her thread,
> And she turned him out of doors for the good of the trade.

Song has always been an integral part of life in the Cornish fishing communities, and today well-organized fishermen's choirs make beautiful music throughout the county. Traditional song, too, has flourished among the fisherfolk, who often produce harmonies unlike any other ' folk ' styles in Britain. Here is a survival from Elizabethan times, when Carew noted the beauty of ' three men's songs ' – fishermen's catches for three voices and sung in Cornish. In 1698 a St Agnes skipper recalled such a song, a rare example of genuine Cornish folksong:

Ha mî ow-môs en gûn lâs
Mi a-glowas trôs an buscas mines,
Mes mî a-drouvias un pesk brâs, naw ê lostiow;
Ol an bôbel en Porthia ha Marghas Jowan
Nevra na wôr dh'ê gensenjy.

In translation, the song is seen as a riddle, to which the answer is thought by the Cornish to be an octopus, its body forming the ninth ' tail ' :

As I went on a green plain [the sea]
I heard the sound of little fishes,
But I found one great fish, with nine tails;
All the people in St Ives and Marazion
Could never get hold of it.

The cast of the Padstow mumming play includes Tom Bowling, who enters playing an accordion and singing:

Here am I, Sailor Boy, just come from a-cruising,
I'll marry the girl and make her my wife
And go no more a-cruising.

Padstow is the focal point of an area rich in folklore and song and much of the singing involves the sea. In nearby St Merryn, the locals will insist that ' Spanish Ladies ' is ' our song ', although it has been discovered in virtually every port in England.

We'll rant and we'll roar like true British sailors,
We'll rant and we'll roar all o'er the salt seas,
Until we strike soundings in the Channel of old England,
From the Ushant to the Scillies is forty-five leagues.

Falmouth, too, is a ' singing-town ' and its song is a variant of the widespread ' Oak and the Ash ' :

O Falmouth is a fine town with ships in the bay
And I wish from my heart it's there I was today;
I wish from my heart I was far away from here,
Sitting in my parlour and talking to my dear.
For it's home, dearie, home, it's home I want to be;
Our topsails are hoisted and we'll away to sea;
O the oak and the ash and the bonny birken tree,
They's all growing green in the old country.

During this century many shanties and forebitters have been collected in west Cornwall. In 1926 John Farr, a sailor from
Gwithian, near Penzance, sang a whole range of shanties to the
collector, Jim Thomas, and 30 years later, in Cadgwith on the
Lizard peninsula, Peter Kennedy heard the local fishermen who
still sing there today. While their most striking song is ' The
Robbers' Retreat ' mentioned earlier, they have many other fine
pieces; ' The Liverpool Packet ', for instance, is an excellent
version of a well-known naval ballad, ' The Flash Packet ' :

> We were going to sea from the Waterloo Dock,
> And the boys and the girls on the pierhead did flock,
> To give us three cheers with a hearty weigh-O
> She's a Liverpool packet – O Lord, let her go!

Although the Cadgwith fishermen are now probably the best-
known group of traditional singers in Cornwall, they are by no
means unique in their preservation of sea songs. Most of the small
ports along the coastline boast a few men who recall the old
music: one such is Boscastle, the home of Bill Kinsman.

The folk-song collector, Ken Stubbs, heard Bill Kinsman sing
a version of ' Pleasant and Delightful ', a fairly common song
throughout the west country. The song tells the regular story of
a sailor who goes off to sea, leaving his sweetheart behind him,
but vowing to return one day and marry her. In most versions,
the lovers' names are given as William and Polly, but Kinsman
calls the lady ' Nancy ', and presents an interesting parallel with a
west Cornwall legend. Porthgwarra, a tiny fishing hamlet south
of Land's End, was once known as Sweethearts' Cove, following
the romance of Nancy, the only daughter of a rich farmer, and
William, a common sailor. Nancy's parents disapproved of the
relationship and forbade the lovers to see one another, but they
contrived a brief meeting just before William's ship was due to
sail. He vowed that he would be true to Nancy forever, but
for many months no news came from him and the girl grew more
distracted with each day that passed. She watched for his ship
from Hella Point, which local people began to call Nancy's
Garden. Eventually grief at William's absence turned her mind and
she became quite mad, spending all her days lamenting his loss.
One night, though, when she was lying in bed, Nancy dreamt of
William calling to her from the sea; she arose, dressed and
walked down to Porthgwarra Cove. An old woman sitting on the

cliff-top saw Nancy approach the sea's edge, where a young man suddenly appeared at her side. Together, they stepped into the breakers and were never seen again. Word came to Porthgwarra that same night that William's ship had foundered with all hands.

The fishermen, as mentioned already, shared the miners' respect for animals, in particular for hares and rabbits. In Fowey recently a young skipper explained that rabbits must never be mentioned on board ship. If anyone did, the only antidote to the resulting spell is to touch cold iron immediately, an example of the common folk belief in the power of iron. During World War II a motor torpedo boat based in Plymouth was manned by a crew of sailors from Looe and Polperro. An outsider, knowing of the Cornishmen's superstition, placed a rabbit on board, as a practical joke; although under the strictest orders, the men refused to take the boat to sea until the creature had been caught and put ashore. Quite recently, too, a landsman pointed out a rabbit to a sailor actually travelling to his boat to start work; the seaman promptly turned for home and would not put to sea that day. Members of the clergy appear to share the rabbit's attributes. A parson on the quayside is a bad omen, and he must never be discussed on deck; even the church should be referred to obliquely, as a 'bell-house '.

In the district around St Levan, storm winds were said to embody the spirits of drowned sailors ' hailing their own names ' and Newlyn fishermen were reputed to be the last in Cornwall to give up the practice of throwing fish into the sea as offerings to the sea spirits. These spirits were known by the Cornish as *bucca-dhu* [the black spirit] and *bucca-gwidden* [the white spirit], words probably akin to the Irish *puca*, the Welsh *pwca*, both of which apparently derive from the English puck; *bucca* is today applied jokingly to scarecrow, but the farmers who use it are likely preserving a much older terror. The sea, with its strange lighting effects in certain weather conditions, has encouraged many ghost stories. We have heard already of the lovers of Porthgwarra and tales of spectral ships will be told in a later chapter, but here are two stories of drowned sailors from west Cornwall.

A man from St Ives met a seaman and, being sociable, he tried to start a conversation, but could get no response. At last the silent mariner disappeared and his inquisitor realized that he had been speaking to a ghost. He fell ill for six months and during that time all his hair fell out; when he began to recover, though, his hair grew again, thick and brown, as the drowned sailor's. Above the grave of another drowned seaman, near Land's End, a ghostly bell rings from the tombstone at certain hours. A sceptical sailor who visited the grave and, to his horror, heard the bell, put to sea that same night and was never heard of again. Perhaps, neither of these corpses shares his grave with the body of a seagull, for, if so, his ghost would have been laid.

The story of Lyonesse is one of many such legends involving lands submerged beneath freak tidal waves. The legend tells of a prosperous country with fine cities and 140 churches. One night the sea arose and destroyed the entire land, leaving only the mountain peaks to the west, now seen as the Isles of Scilly. Just one man escaped: his name was Trevilian and he rode a swift white horse, reaching high ground at Perranuthnoe seconds before the tide could overwhelm him. It is interesting that the Trevilian family arms still depict a horse issuing from the sea.

Camden, writing in the sixteenth century, told of Land's End at one time stretching far to the west, with a watch-tower on the farthest point to direct mariners; and Carew mentions that the rocks known as Seven Stones were believed to be the remains of a great city, called by sailors ' The Town '. The seamen told of windows, doors and other household impedimenta becoming entangled with their nets while fishing around the Seven Stones and, more mysteriously, how they could hear the church-bells of Lyonesse ringing beneath the waves.

A journalist named Stanley Baron, working for the now defunct News Chronicle, was staying with a family of fisherfolk in Sennen Cove during the 1930s. One night he completed an article for his newspaper and went to bed at eleven o'clock. Two hours later he awoke to hear the rhythmic clanging of bells, which continued until three o'clock in the morning, when he fell asleep again. Later Baron was awakened once more by a distant peal of muffled bells which continued until dawn. His hosts told him that he had heard the bells of Lyonesse. Edith Oliver, once mayor of Wilton, near Salisbury, saw on two occasions a jumble of towers, domes, spires and battlements, while standing on the cliffs of Land's End.

Parts of the Scillies, now submerged, were definitely once above sea level, but are we to believe the fishermen's tales? St Michael's Mount, now separated from the mainland by a causeway, was called, in Cornish, *carreg-luz-en-kuz* [the hoar rock in the wood]. There is a petrified forest around the base of the Mount, under the sea, and an axe factory was discovered in Mount's Bay dating from 1500 BC. These findings support an old legend about Mount's Bay once being a great plain, with churches, fields and woods. However, similar claims are made for Mont St Michel, off the coast of Normandy.

Even today the world under the sea is comparatively unknown and it is therefore understandable that stories of sea monsters should be told. These, of course, exist in all parts of the world, but in Cornwall belief in a huge octopus-like creature still lingers in the district around Godrevy and Portreath on the north coast. Here, the sea-bed shelves steeply and the old sailors explained the sudden depth as a monster's lair. The creatures which are most common around Cornwall's coast, though, are mermaids, or ' merrymaids '. Robert Hunt knew of Cornishmen in the last century who believed that seals were really mermaids, and he tells of the Mermaid's Rock at Lamorna, where a lady with a fish's tail sat with a comb and glass in her hand. The well-known sailors' song, ' The Mermaid ', has been collected in several parts of the county and Seaton, a tiny village near Looe, lost its one-time importance as a major port when a mermaid blocked up the harbour because a local man had insulted her. A similar story is told of the Doom Bar which precludes Padstow's natural harbour from shipping of any great size. Although the harbour was once deep and open, it was a mermaid's playground; one day a villager tried to shoot her and so caused the port's downfall. Hunt also relates the tale of an old man from Cury, who found a stranded mermaid and helped her back to sea. For his kindness, she granted him the power to break evil spells and to comfort his neighbours in times of distress. She also gave him her comb, with which he could stroke the sea whenever he wished to speak to her. The shark's tooth comb, says Hunt, remains in the old man's family.

Cornwall's most famous mermaid is immortalized by a carved bench-end in Zennor Church. Her portrait now forms part of the chancel seat in the transept and, somewhat unflattering, depicts her with waist-length hair and a scaly tail; in her hands she holds the usual mirror and comb. She can also be seen on the dial of the clock, and her story is a dramatic one. For many years a strange, handsomely dressed woman attended service in Zennor Church. She never appeared to age and captivated successive generations of men with her beauty and exquisite voice. Although she had been watched as she left the church and people said that they had seen her pass beyond Tregartha Hill, no one knew where she lived and she had a mysterious air which discouraged curiosity. One day she met Matthew Trewhella, the churchwarden's son, and the finest singer in Zennor; the couple fell in love, left the village and were never seen there again. Some time afterwards a mermaid hailed a ship off Pendower Cove and the captain made for St Ives at full speed. When the Zennor folk heard of this, they assumed the mermaid to be the strange lady in her true form, who had enticed Matthew Trewhella beneath the waves. To commemorate her, they carved her image in holy oak for their church. It is, perhaps, coincidental that two bench-ends in Towednack Church, dated 1633, portray two churchwardens, Matthew Trenwith and James Trewhella.

The Cornish characters most favoured by romantic novelists are the outlaws of the sea, the wreckers and the smugglers, and perhaps the black prince of these was David Coppinger. Robert Hawker, the imaginative vicar of Morwenstow, wrote a colourful account of Coppinger's activities, which owed more to the old droll-tellers than to fact, but nevertheless the story of ' Cruel ' Coppinger is worth recording. In the midst of a dreadful storm in 1792 a foreign ship was wrecked off Welcombe Mouth, near the northern borders of Cornwall and Devon; while villagers watched from the shore, only one man escaped death. He was a massive figure and, after struggling onto the beach, he grabbed a cloak from an old woman and jumped upon a horse behind the rider, a girl called Dinah Hamlyn. Spurred on by the stranger, the horse galloped home, to a farm owned by Dinah's parents, who welcomed their new guest and gave him food and dry clothing. The man proved to be a Dane named Coppinger and he worked on the land until Farmer Hamlyn died a few months later. Then he married Dinah and at first all seemed well; but the match was not a happy one and Coppinger began to show himself as a callous and sadistic man. Eventually, Dinah bore him a son, but this, too, was a disaster. The unfortunate child was an idiot, deaf and dumb, reproducing his father's cruel nature to such a degree that he was said to have been born without a soul.

Coppinger turned back to the sea and forced many of the local people to join him in forming an organized group of smugglers and wreckers. Under the threat of their leader's violence, they showed mercy to neither shipwrecked sailor nor to ship's captain whom they wished to rob, and soon the entire district was terrorized by the Dane's gang. No man dared insult them for fear of being pressed to join in, and even the revenue officers kept clear of Coppinger. At last, though, the forces of law pressured him into leaving Cornwall. On a night as black as the night of his arrival he boarded a strange ship which sailed off into the darkness never to return. While the tale of Coppinger has been greatly romanticized by Hawker and other writers, it seems certain that he did actually exist and, allegedly, the title deeds of a small estate were discovered towards the end of the nineteenth century, still bearing his name. Dinah Coppinger died in 1833, but her husband's memory lived on for many years afterwards in this powerful rhyme:

> Will you hear of Cruel Coppinger?
> He came from a foreign land;
> He was brought to us by the salt water,
> He was carried away by the wind!

David Coppinger, according to the legend, was a totally evil man, with no hint of human kindness, but the Cornish wreckers were in general very different. Their motivation was poverty rather than greed and they regarded wrecks as ' gifts from the gods '; when, for instance, *The Good Samaritan*, bound from Liverpool to Constantinople, ran aground at Bedruthan Steps in 1846:

> *The Good Samaritan* came ashore
> To feed the hungry and clothe the poor,
> Barrels of beef and bales of linen,
> No poor man shall want a shillin'!

Although Crown rights included a claim to all wrecks, people living along the Cornish coast considered it their privilege to gather pickings from any ship that came ashore: as recently as 1936, in fact, an American steamer provided many St Ives's inhabitants with their Christmas fare. The universal idea of a *right* to wrecking is exemplified by the widespread story of a Cornish preacher who commanded his flock to remain in their places while he descended from the pulpit; thus, no one had any advantage in the race to the beach!

To the novelist, of course, wrecking is quite distinct from sophisticated beachcoming. Stories of ships being lured to their doom by lights waved from the clifftops were once commonplace in Cornwall, but it is almost certain that, while such incidents did occur in places, they were far from being everyday events. The area around Mount's Bay, however, was notorious for this type of practice:

> God keep us from rocks and shelving sands
> And save us from Breage and Germoe men's hands.

In the Isles of Scilly, it was said that donkeys were paraded along the cliffs with lanterns slung from their neck as false guides to shipping, but here again – if the stories were true – poverty was probably to blame. Another terse rhyme describes the Scillonian fishermen's dreadful diet:

> Scads [mackerel] and 'tates, scads and 'tates,
> Scads and 'tates and conger,
> And those who can't eat scads and 'tates,
> O they must die of hunger.

Food like this might have driven many a good man to wrecking and, to prove that not all coastal dwellers in Cornwall were vicious barbarians, a writer in 1861 said that:

> When a wreck occurs on the coast, the noble and fearless conduct of the Cornishmen cannot be exceeded. At such times, as indeed, in all times of danger, they show the most heroic courage and risk their own lives to save the shipwrecked mariner.

Here, certainly, is the other side of the coin, and, if less spectacular, it is probably more accurate.

Like wrecking, smuggling in Cornwall was regarded as an honourable profession and the men who practised it were known as ' fair-traders '. The tiny coves along the Cornish coast were perfect for the smugglers: the beaches offered ample landing space, where the cargoes could be ' run ashore ' and the caves were simple but effective hiding-places. These coves are generally isolated and, before the advent of metalled roads, were often accessible only to those with good local knowledge. Thus, the Revenue men – rarely local and ever the common enemies – were at a permanent disadvantage. Robert Hawker wrote of an old man who complained bitterly at the hanging of a Morwenstow smuggler. He thought the punishment very excessive, as the man's crime was nothing more than the killing of an Exciseman. In Talland churchyard, near Polperro, stands a memorial to Robert Mark who:

> . . . by a shot which rapid flew
> Was instantly struck dead.

Mark was a smuggler and his epitaph continues:

> Lord pardon the Offender who
> My precious blood did shed.

The ' Offender ', of course, was an officer in the Revenue service.

The sense of honour among Cornish smugglers was widespread and usually to some extent justified. Richard Pentreath of Mousehole was described by the Collector of Customs at Penzance in 1771 as ' an honest man in all his dealings, though a notorious smuggler ' and Isaac Cocart, a Falmouth fair-trader, was twice mayor of the town and a respected magistrate. Probably the best-loved smugglers in Cornwall were the Carter family of Prussia Cove, where the parents, eight sons and two daughters were actively involved in an illicit spirit trade with France. The Carters' leader was one of the sons, John, and it is he who figures most prominently in their story. As a child in the mid-eighteenth century John dubbed himself ' The King of Prussia ' after Frederick the Great, a contemporary hero, and the title stayed with him throughout his life; the family's home at Porthleah, near Land's End, was, indeed, renamed ' Prussia Cove ', as it remains today. John Carter's exploits are for the historian rather than the folklorist, but one event epitomizes the smugglers' mystique above all others. A consignment of smuggled liquor was discovered by the Revenue men and taken to Penzance custom house for storage. When Carter heard of this he was deeply grieved, for the goods were promised to certain of his clients on a pre-arranged date, and failure to deliver them would damage his honest reputation. So John Carter, with some of his colleagues, raided the custom house and retrieved his property. The excisemen knew the culprit could be none but Carter, for he was ' an upright man and [had] taken away nothing that was not his own '.

Smuggling in Cornwall virtually died out in the late nineteenth century, when penalties were increased and law enforcement became more efficient. Then the fair-traders realized that their heyday was over. However, in 1929 a fragment of a smuggling song was related to the collector Ralph Dunstan and still today the little port of Helford, despite its yachtsmen and painted cottages, recalls Carew's name for it—Stealford.

4 Fairies and Giants

WRITERS IN THE NINETEENTH CENTURY placed Cornish fairies into five categories, but the traditional stories and various personal accounts contradict themselves so much that the field can be narrowed down to three types. The knockers of the mines have already been dealt with in the chapter on tinners, and rare accounts of brownies, said to be the guardians of the bees, and the Small People, spirits of an ancient Cornish race, vary little from the stories of piskies who, along with the spriggans, this section will consider.

The spirits of the hills, rivers and groves, have now become known under their confused generic name, piskey, or ' pisgie '. A hundred years ago they were mischief-makers who took delight in ' mazing ' lonely travellers into losing their way. An old man named Glasson told how he was piskey-led one bright moonlight night. He was returning to Ludgvan from Gulval, but no matter which path he took it led him back to where he had started. At last he turned his coat inside out, the only way to break the spell, and reached Ludgvan without further trouble. Many piskey-led victims have described how they heard the high-pitched laughter of their invisible tormentors – hence the old expression ' laughing like a piskey '. In 1965 a lady who had spent much of her life on the moors around Warleggan told us there were still a number of old people who would not go near the moors at night for fear of being piskey-led by the dancing lights. These strange illuminations are not the products of imagination, but are actual phosphorescent lights seen over marshland and known in Cornwall as ' Jack o' Lantern ' or ' Joan the Wad ', and elsewhere as ' Will o' the Wisp ', *Ignis fatuus*, or ' corpse lights '. They are caused by an atmospheric condition or gaseous emanation from the ground. White, red or blue in colour, they appear to dart away as a person approaches, re-appearing elsewhere :

> Jack o' the Lantern, Joan the Wad,
> Who tickled the maid and made her mad
> Light me home, the weather's bad.

Cornish farmers often found their horses frightened and tired after being piskey-ridden during the night, and on the moors in central Cornwall ponies rounded up for Summercourt Fair had their manes badly tangled and looped up in a manner suggesting stirrups for fairy folk. Many farmers placed pieces of lead, known as ' piskey feet ', at intervals on the farmhouse roofs to prevent the piskeys dancing on them and turning the milk sour. Sometimes, however, the farmers benefited by the piskies' nocturnal visits, as in the story of the Piskey Threshers, related by Thomas Q. Couch in *Notes and Queries*. One morning a farmer was surprised to find that a quantity of corn had been threshed during the previous night. Later he crept to his barn door and saw a small man wearing a tattered green suit working hard with a flail; to show his gratitude, the farmer left a new suit of green for his fairy helper. That night he went once more to the barn door to see if his gift had been accepted and there he saw the piskey admiring his new clothes and singing :

> Piskey fine and piskey gay,
> Piskey now will fly away.

From that day on the farmer received no more assistance from the piskey thresher, presumably because, according to tradition, the fairy helpers prefer to remain invisible to human eyes.

More often than not the piskies were feared rather than loved and in some areas the beliefs live on. A lady told us a story given to her by her landlady when she was staying at Bossinney, near Tintagel, in 1954. Some years previously the landlady and a friend took their children for a picnic. After the meal they started for home, but soon realised that one of the friend's little boys had forgotten to bring his jumper; the child's mother returned to search for it while the others waited. Unable to find the jumper, the mother rejoined the party and they continued homewards. As they descended one side of a valley, they noticed a car run over a dark object lying in the lane which appeared on the other side. They reached the spot and were astonished to find that the object was the little boy's jumper. At home, they told their story to the landlady's mother, who warned them that the place chosen for their picnic was a piskey ring and that what had happened later was a sure sign of death. The boy's mother, worried lest her son should be run over, kept him at home, but a short time afterwards he broke an arm and contracted a blood disease from which he died. Our informant's landlady was deeply superstitious and still carried out the custom of leaving a dish of cream for the piskies, for if they were annoyed the butter would churn against the sun and be spoilt.

It was a general belief in Cornwall that stillborn children became piskies, changing gradually into ants, locally called *muryans*, while some Cornishmen believed that the little people were spirits of the ancient race which once inhabited the far west. Fairy children were occasionally entrusted to human care and at other times mortals were kidnapped and carried off by the piskies. Margery Daw, in the Cornish version of the old nursery rhyme, is an example:

> See-saw, Margery Daw,
> Sold her bed and lay on straw;
> She sold her straw and lay upon hay
> Piskey came and carried her away.

There were also stories of piskey ointments, which, if rubbed on the eye, enabled humans to see Fairy Land. In most cases, though, the seers paid for the privilege by losing their eyesight, if the piskies discovered them.

An old woman highly skilled in midwifery was sitting by her fire one night when she was disturbed by a rapid knocking. She opened the door hatch and saw a tiny man sitting on a large horse. He informed her that his wife was in labour and needed her immediate help; so the old woman mounted behind him and off they went, passing many hidden turnings, until they arrived at a house where the woman was taken to her patient. Later, when the old midwife was washing the newly born dwarf child, she accidentally wiped some of the soap on her own eye and Fairy Land was immediately revealed to her. The woman sensibly said nothing and, her work being done, was sent home by her grateful host. A short time afterwards at a large fair in the neighbourhood, she saw the same little man whom she had helped and asked how the mother and child were progressing. He replied: ' On which eye do you see me?' ' On this one,' she said, pointing to the eye that had been smeared with soap. A blow from the little man's fist blinded her in that eye forever.

It was customary, as already mentioned, for a nurse to carry some cake to church when a baby was to be christened and to give it to the first person the party met on the road; this apparently protected the child against witchcraft and the piskies. In many a cottage home it was also the practice to pin a baby's nightgown to its cot overnight to prevent the piskies from stealing the child and substituting one of their own offspring. Stories of these changelings appeared all over Cornwall and on 14 July 1843 the *West Briton* reported the case of J. Trevelyan of Penzance who was charged with ill-treating one of his children. It appears that the young boy was frequently starved, kicked and beaten by the servants and that at Christmas 1841, when the child was only 15 months old, he had been placed outside on a tree and left to remain in the cold for two-and-a-half-hours. The parents believed that he was a changeling and that their own child had been taken away by the fairies. The case was dismissed for lack of evidence.

The piskies did not always get their own way. In a cottage on the moor near Towednack lived a woman named Betty Stogs with her husband and six-month-old baby. While her husband was out working Betty would leave the baby at home with just the cat for company. The baby, of course, was neglected and, when people asked Betty why she did not wash it more often, she replied that the moor was a cold place and that a good layer of dirt helped to keep it warm. One night Betty returned home to find the cradle empty and no sign of either her baby or the cat which always

G

slept with it. Betty informed her husband who went to get help, but no matter where they searched they could find no trace of the child. The following morning Betty saw the cat and followed it into a brake of furze where she discovered a bundle of old-fashioned chintz. She opened it to find the baby fast asleep. It was wrapped in gay clothes and scented with sweet herbs but its own old garments were nowhere to be seen and for the first time in its life it was beautifully clean. The old folk, when they heard, decided that the baby must have been stolen by the fairies, who intended to carry it back to their own realm. It took them so long to clean it, however, that daylight surprised them and they left it hidden in the furze.

Cornwall has many tales of men, women and children transported to a beautiful subterranean fairy world. Such a story is the Lost Child of St Allen. A small boy was gathering flowers one warm evening, when he was lured by the sounds of music into a dark grove and at length found himself by the edge of a lake. There he met a beautiful lady who led him through into an underground cavern built of pure crystal and supported by pillars of glass. After many days had passed the boy was discovered by his frantic parents, asleep on a bed of ferns. He told them of his meeting with the lady and of how she introduced him into the fairy world. The tale was still current in the district until quite recently.

The best-known case of a fairy encounter appears in letters from Moses Pitt to the Bishop of Gloucester, concerning Anne Jeffries. Anne, who was born in 1626 in the moorland village of St Teath, was bound as a child to the family of a local worthy, Moses Pitt. In 1645, at the age of 19, Anne had her first meeting with the 'airy people', as she called them. This encounter caused her to fall into a fit, the prelude to a long illness, which left her with the power to heal by touch. She could cure broken bones and such diseases as the falling sickness, an ability which she first practised on Pitt's mother. Ann was supposed to have spoken and danced with the fairies and to have been fed by them for long periods. In 1646 she was confined in Bodmin gaol by John Tregeagle, steward to John, Earl of Radnor, and charged with witchcraft. She was starved and treated cruelly, but miraculously suffered no apparent hardship as her fairy friends kept her well-nourished. On her release through lack of evidence Anne went to live with Mrs Frances Tom near Padstow, where she continued curing the sick. Eventually she married a William Warner, bailiff to Sir Andrew

Stanning, and died of old age, taking her secrets to the grave.

The spriggans were a race of warrior fairies, grotesquely ugly and believed by some to be the ghosts of the giants, altering their size at will. The guardians of buried treasure, they were to be found around the cairns, cromlechs and ancient barrows of Cornwall. They were also held responsible for bringing storms, for the destruction of buildings and crops and, like the piskies, for the loss of children.

In the story of the spriggans of Trencrom Hill, a man who believed he knew the hiding-place of a crock of giant's gold proceeded one night to the enchanted hill and began to dig. The sky grew darker and the moor was blotted out by thunder clouds, as howling winds whistled among the rocks. Through the lightning flashes the man saw swarms of spriggans emerging from the boulders and increasing in size as they came. Frightened almost out of his wits, he took to his heels and ran home, where he went to bed and prayed. No permanent harm came to him, but he remained unfit for work for a long time. Another tale tells of a troop of spriggan soldiers in the ' Fairy Revels ' on the Gump, near St Just. They were guarding the fairy fold and dealt with a human intruder by pinning his hair to the ground with the aid of magical cobwebs. As an additional punishment, a small spriggan jumped on his nose until, laughing, he shouted : ' Away, away, I smell the day!' and ran off. At daybreak the man was able to shake himself free and return home.

According to Geoffrey of Monmouth, Cornwall was named after Corineus, who was given the county by Brutus of Troy, after he had defeated the giant Gogmagog, in a wrestling match on Plymouth Hoe :

> For which the conquering Brute on Corineus brave
> This horn of land bestow'd and mark'd it with his name
> Of Corin, Cornwall call'd to his immortal fame.

Corineus, Geoffrey relates, ' experienced great pleasure in wrestling with giants of whom there were far more there than in any other district '.

Many giant tales may have originated in the days of the Celts, who saw the huge stone circles built by earlier settlers and considered them to be the work of some titan race. The Land's End peninsula abounds in ancient earthworks and stones and it is here that the giant-lore is richest. The Iron Age cliff castle at Treryn

Dinas, known as the Giant's Castle, was willed from beneath the sea by the Treryn Giant who lived there. He was supposed to be the strongest of all and skilled in the black arts. In a holed rock in the cliff, called locally the Giant's Lock, he placed a key in the form of a large round stone and prophesied just before he died that if ever it were removed, Treryn and its castle would disappear beneath the sea. In another account, the Treryn Giant was slain by a younger giant, who lived in a cave beneath the nearby Logan Stone; the victor took over both his wife and his castle.

On Carn Brea hill, near Redruth, are the Giant's Coffin, the Giant's Head and Hand, the Giant's Wheel and the Giant's Cradle, all the traditional property of a giant with the unlikely name of John of Gaunt, one of the last of his race. The traditional explanation for all the loose boulders transported by the ice flow in Cornwall is that much of the giants' time was spent throwing them at each other or using them to play the old game of 'bob-button'. The giants of Trecobben and St Michael's Mount used the Mount as the 'bob' on which large, flat stones were placed to serve as 'buttons'. Another pastime among the giants was quoits and the old Cornish called the stone chamber-tombs at Lanyon, Mulfa, Trethevy and elsewhere after them – the capstones of these tombs, of course, resemble the quoits allegedly used by the giants.

Legend says that St Michael's Mount was the home of the giant Cormoran or Cormelian, and it was he who built the Mount out of 'white' rock. The Cornish name for the Mount – *carreg-luz-en-kuz* – is sometimes translated as 'the white rock in the wood' and the greenstone on the Causeway between the Mount and the mainland known as Chapel Rock was dropped there by Cormoran's wife. She was attempting to ease her building tasks by using local greenstone instead of the white, which had to be carried a great distance. Her husband, when he discovered the trick, kicked her in his anger and caused her to drop the stone. This lady was accidentally killed by a blow from a cobbling hammer thrown by the giant of Trecobben Hill. The two giants, after their mourning, buried her body under Chapel Rock, or, some say, under the courtyard of the castle. Bottrell carries the tale a little further, stating that the Trecobben giant died of grief over the death of his friend's wife, but not before burying his treasures deep among the cairns of Trecobben Hill, where it still remains, guarded by a platoon of spriggans.

The giant Bolster must have been among the largest of his clan, for he was able to stand with one foot on St Agnes Beacon and the other on Carn Brea, a distance of approximately six miles. Bolster fell in love with the virtuous St Agnes, following her wherever she went, but Agnes eventually tired of her admirer and asked him to prove his love by filling a hole in the cliff at Chapel Porth with his blood. The giant stretched his arm across the hole and plunged a knife into a vein; roaring and seething, the blood gushed into the opening. Eventually Bolster fainted from exhaustion and his life's blood flowed on until he died. The cunning saint had known full well that the hole was bottomless and opened into the sea. The evidence of Bolster's death still remains at Chapel Porth in the form of a red stain, which marks the track of his blood. A very similar tale was told of another giant from Gorran, with a doctor replacing St Agnes and the nearby Dodman Point, or ' Dead Man ', being so-named after his death.

Richard Carew wrote in 1602 :

> Not far from the Land's End there is a little village called Trebegean, in English the town of the Giant's Grave, near whereunto and within memory (as I have been informed) certain workmen searching for tin discovered a long square vault which contained the bones of an excessive big carcase and verified this etymology of the name.

We learn from Hunt that the giant's name was Trebiggan, a vast man with arms so long that he was able to pluck men from passing ships. The name of Trebiggan was also used by mothers to frighten their unruly children, as it was said that he dined each day on young humans fried on a large, flat rock near his cave.

A giant named Wrath, or Ralph, was once the terror of St Ives fishermen and a large fissure in the cliffs near Portreath, known as Ralph's Cupboard, was to be avoided at all costs. This giant was reputed to watch for any unfortunate sailors who drifted or were driven by storm into his cupboard; they became his diet. The roof of the cupboard apparently collapsed after his death, leaving the open chasm we know today.

It was the giant of Carn Galva who gave Morvah its fair :

> Morvah Fair's a very fine feast,
> Good sport and eatings there for man or beast,
> We're all some proud, the biggest with the least,
> A-riding off to Morvah Fair.

Holiburn, as this giant was called, spent his life protecting the people of Morvah and Zennor and harmed nobody except one unfortunate young man whom he killed by playfully tapping his head. When Holiburn realized the fatal force of his blow he cried : ' Oh my son, my son, why didn't they make the shell of thy noddle stronger?' The giant pined away and died of a broken heart, but his memory is perpetuated by the fair. Another side to Holiburn's character, though, appeared in 1889, when a group from an antiquarian society was told that a large stone near Morvah Church was called the Giant's Grave and that voices from beneath it were sometimes heard. According to their informant, it marked a pit made by Jack the Tinner from an old mine adit. Jack lured the cruel giant into the pit and piled stones on him, crushing him to death. The storyteller added that the event was commemorated by Morvah Feast.

In the old chapbook version of Jack the Giant-Killer, Jack was a farmer's son living in the Land's End district during the time of King Arthur. Hearing of the reward for slaying the giant of St Michael's Mount, who was carrying off cattle either on his back or strung from his belt, Jack dug a pit and covered it with sticks and straw. He then blew his horn and down the Mount rushed the giant, falling into the pit. Jack finally despatched his adversary with a mighty blow from his pickaxe and filled in the pit with earth. For this valiant action he was given a magnificent sword and an embroidered belt emblazoned with a verse in letters of gold :

> This is the valiant Cornishman
> Who slew the giant Cormoran.

Jack then travelled into Wales to gain further fame as a giant-killer.

It is unlikely that the chapbook story originated in Cornwall, but the traditional Cornish drolls concerning Jack the Tinner, or ' Tinkeard ', and his friend, Tom of Bowjeyheer, were collected by Hunt and Bottrell around the middle of the nineteenth century, and Hunt himself remarks on the similarity between the tales he heard at the Ding Dong Mine and the story of Tom Hicka-thrift, the strongman of the Isle of Ely. In the Cornish version, Tom, who lived in the Lelant district, was a strong but lazy young man who spent most of his time wandering around with his hands in his pockets. In the hope of obtaining plenty of strong beer, he undertook to drive a brewer's wain and moved to Market Jew (Marazion) to be near the brewery. One day, returning from St Ives, he found his way blocked by a giant's hedge made from great slabs of rock. Under the influence of three or four gallons of strong ale, he decided to take the short route through the giant's land.

After about a mile, Tom came across the wall to the giant's castle and was greeted by a dog, which began to bark as he approached. Out rushed the giant demanding to know what Tom was doing on his land. ' I am on the road ', said Tom ' and you have no right to build your hedges across what used to be the King's highway and shall be again '. The giant in his fury pulled up a young elm tree about 20ft high, stripped the branches off and started towards Tom. Tom turned his wagon upside down, slipped off a wheel and pulled out the exe (axle-tree): These became his sword and buckler in the fight that followed. Tom killed the giant and took possession of his castle and lands, plus, ' she being a tidy body ', his wife. In the East Anglian story, Tom Hickathrift, like the Cornish Tom, was a strong, lazy young man who took a job delivering beer to Wisbech. Hickathrift also fought and killed a giant with the use of a wheel and axle-tree; he, too, took over the giant's riches, and both Toms met up with tinkers wearing coats of leather.

The Cornish version continues that one day, when Tom was hedging, he saw a Tinkeard (or Tinner) smashing down one of his gates with a large hammer. Tom challenged the man who said he was going to complain to the giant about hedging in all the land. Mistaking Tom for the giant's son, the tinner became abusive and Tom challenged him to a fight. ' Very well ', said the tinner, ' I'll match my blackthorn stick against anything in the way of timber that you can raise on this place '. Tom picked up a bar from a broken gate and they began to fight. The tinner soon gave Tom a bloody nose and two black eyes, but Tom's blows had no effect, as the tinner was wearing a coat as hard as iron made from a shaggy bull's hide. They fought on until they were both exhausted and Tom, feeling hungry and forgetting the dispute, invited the tinner home for dinner. The two men became firm friends, with Jack the Tinkeard teaching Tom the skills of archery and Tom teaching Jack how to wrestle.

Another story tells how Tom of Bowjeyheer was enchanted by Pengersec the Enchanter, who desired his daughter, but Jack came to the rescue, breaking the spell with a blow from his hammer. It was Jack, too, who killed the Morvah giant as we have seen, who destroyed wolves and broke the skulls of sea-raiders. He also discovered rich lodes of tin and married Tom's daughter.

How Cornwall came by its versions of the giant-killing stories will never be known, but it is strange that they seem to be confined to a small cluster of parishes in the Land's End district.

The giants of Cornish legend range in height from Bolster, who could stride across from Carn Brea to St Agnes, down to Tom of Bowjeyheer, who was a mere eight-footer, but Cornwall had its real-life giants, too. Anthony Payne was 7ft 2 ins in height and possessed tremendous strength; once, when asked to find a servant who had gone to fetch firewood, Payne returned with donkey, man and faggots all carried on his massive shoulders. John Laugherne of Truro, 7ft 6in high, was known as 'Long Laugherne'; he fought for the Royalist cause in the Civil War as a lieutenant in a cavalry regiment, and it took more than two strong men to pull his sword from one of Plymouth's gates when the Cornish Royalists laid siege to the town.

A man known as Giant Chillcott, who died in the parish of Tintagel in April 1815, was 6ft 4ins in height, 6ft 9 ins around the chest and weighed about 460lbs. He smoked 3lbs of tobacco each week and one of his stockings held 6 gallons of wheat. Chillcott took great pleasure in addressing curious strangers by saying, ' Come under my arm, little fellow.'

5 Ghosts and Demons

SUPERNATURAL APPARITIONS IN CORNWALL are very varied. There are stories of spectral balls of light, of drowned sailors reappearing, weeping women, horses, dogs and phantom ships, of demons and the Devil. Man has throughout recorded history believed in ghosts, possibly because of a basic human fear of non-existence after death. Ghosts at least offer some assurance of survival, no matter how slight, and it is often amusing to hear a man refuting the suggestion of his eternal existence, only to tell later in friendly conversation some personal experience of ghostly phenomena.

The following account is given in the informant's own words and relates to incidents in the mid-1950s.

> I was about eleven years old and staying at a farmhouse in Bossinney, which was said to be one of the oldest buildings in the area. One morning my sister and I awoke to find that

the large heavy old paintings had been taken down and were standing face to the wall. [The informant's mother added that she and another guest examined the pictures and agreed that neither of the children could have removed them.]

A few nights later my father, who was asleep in the adjoining room, was awoken by the rattle of a pitcher and bowl which stood on the deep window ledge in our bedroom. On entering our room he saw me sitting cross-legged on the ledge, apparently staring out to sea. He asked me what I was doing and I replied that I had seen a little, bent old man, who whispered to me, so I had got out of bed and gone to sit in the window. This remains very blurred to me and all I can remember clearly is my father speaking, picking me up and putting me back to bed. My parents, the following morning, asked the owner if she had been disturbed by the noise in the night. She enquired what had happened and when told said that she hadn't said anything before, because people wouldn't stay in the room, but that it was supposed to be haunted by a hunchback who had lived in the two rooms [ours and my parents'] and that he used to sit in the window, cross-legged and staring out to sea, exactly as I had done.

We stayed in this particular farmhouse for three years running and I am not clear in which year the following event occurred. My mother and sister had gone into Launceston with some friends and as I was terribly car-sick they had left me behind with my father. It was a dull, miserable day and late in the afternoon, feeling fed-up, I went upstairs to my bedroom, where I saw an old man sitting hunched up in a cross-legged position on the window ledge. The whole time I stayed in that house, apart from a couple of nights when I slept in another bedroom, I experienced the most terrifying dreams and had a very real fear of our bedroom whenever I entered it. I was quite unaware of the fact that it was supposed to be haunted until a few years later. [The informant's mother, who verified the story, refused to admit that any unnatural influence caused her daughter's terror and blamed it all on her imagination.]

A non-physical awareness of some presence is experienced by many people and the informant speaks of her real fear of entering the bedroom; sometimes the presence is said to reveal itself through chilliness, a cold patch causing one to shudder on cross-ing the threshold.

Maria St German, the author of *The Bells of St Hilary*, des-cribed how, while renting a house in Cornwall, both she and her friends were troubled by the sound of footsteps at night. She also told of one hot July day, when she was sitting in her bedroom, sewing. Suddenly she heard the heavy tread of boots mounting the stairs and moving past the room. She went to investigate, but found no one there; she did, however, note that the air on the staircase was as cold as ice. The house was formerly owned by a retired sea-captain who had died there and it was apparently well-known in the neighbourhood that his ghost still walked.

Sometimes a spirit makes itself known by moving objects from their proper place, as in the earlier account where the paintings were taken down. The removal of pictures from walls, along with banging in the night, occurs at Dockacre House in Launceston. Dockacre is said to be haunted by the ghost of Elizabeth Herle, who was buried on 28 December 1714. This unfortunate woman went mad and her husband, Nicholas Herle, locked her up and left her to starve to death. Nicholas haunts Dockacre too, and his ghost usually appears in the main hall. He also plays the flute when a death is imminent in the household, although the instru-ment he uses has been blocked up and turned into a walking-stick. There is another tradition at Dockacre that each owner hands on a walking-stick to his successor: there are at present 13, and, if put away in the wrong order, they are supposed to have the power to sort themselves out.

Ghosts are often seen to return and re-enact a crisis scene from their former lives. Some years ago a girl in St Austell was knocked down and killed by a car while stepping off the pavement near a bus stop. Later a driver pulled up at this same stop and offered a lift to a girl standing there, but when he looked again nobody was there. A number of drivers have experienced a similar shock since the girl's death. At other times ghosts will appear seeking proper burial, to complete some task left undone, or to look for something lost. The Lady of the Lantern at St Ives, for instance, wanders up and down among the rocks on stormy nights, carry-ing a lantern and searching in vain for the baby she lost when their ship was wrecked off the back of St Ives Island.

On 12 March 1819 the *West Briton* reported the appearance of a ghost at Padstow: the apparition was seen near a warehouse, where Messrs Ryan and Sheppard were storing bones to be shipped to Bristol. Local people, convinced that the ghost did not wish its bones to be removed, attempted to prevent the ship from sailing. They wished to make sure that no more of their ancestors' remains left their native soil. The ghost of a murdered sailor, who returned to finish his drink at Jamaica Inn on Bodmin Moor, has also been seen sitting on a wall outside the inn by many sightseers. In 1893 the inn became the Bolventor Temperance Hotel. While this transformation was short-lived, the beer-drinking ghost must have experienced a nasty shock.

Another Cornish inn that can boast its own ghost is The Dolphin at Penzance, where an old sea captain, dressed in tricorn hat and laced ruffles, has been seen and, more recently, heard. He may have been a victim of Judge Jeffries, who is reputed to have held court in what is now the dining room, or perhaps a smuggler returning for the brandy casks discovered a few years ago in a cellar hideaway when renovation was taking place. A lady staying at a farm on Looe Island in 1850 was frightened by a tall, aristocratic-looking man with beautiful hands and long fingers, who appeared to her, enveloped by a bluish haze, before vanishing through the opposite wall. The woman heard later that several people staying there had seen blue lights, but never before the ghost itself. Some years afterwards a skeleton was exhumed on the island and found to be that of a tall man with very long fingers. Presumably, in this case, the ghost was seeking a proper burial.

There are many legends about the farmplace of Trewoofe (pronounced 'Trove'), overlooking the lovely Lamorna Valley at Land's End. It is here that the ghosts of two children gather wild flowers by the banks of the Mill Pool. Once the home of the powerful Lovelis family, the great house that originally stood on the site contained a haunted chamber from which came the sound of an old spinning wheel. This belonged to the spirit of a housekeeper at Trewoofe obliged to card fleeces of black wool until they became white, and to spin enough yarn to make herself a shroud. Trewoofe was also the scene of the old guise-dance play of *Duffy and the Devil*. Squire Lovell marries Duffy, believing her to be the best needlewoman in Veryan, only to find that all her fine knitting was really the work of the Devil.

Another Trewoofe legend tells that when Squire Lovelis was out hunting one evening he spied a white hare and, calling to his hounds, gave chase. The hare fled into a large opening in the ground, a Cornish *fogou*, or inland cave. Lovelis led his pack into the cavern, where a dreadful sight met his eyes. The hare had changed into a witch and joined a coven presided over by a demon. The squire recognized the demon as his wife's seducer and cursed him. At once the assembly turned on him and when he finally emerged from the cave at midnight he was quite mad. His dogs followed him out, baying wildly and foaming at the mouths. The *fogou* is still haunted by Lovelis's raving spirit and at nearby Boleigh the name means 'the place of slaughter'.

The last remains of Pengersick Castle still exist at Germoe, on Mount's Bay, Here, like Trewoofe, is a classic example of one location attracting several legends of the supernatural. Pengersick was the seat of the Milliton family and long ago a member of the family seduced a foreign king's daughter. When she and her son followed him back to Cornwall he threw them both into the sea. The boy was rescued by a passing ship, but the lady drowned and her soul slipped into the body of a white hare. One day the hare ran in front of Milliton's horse, causing it to lose its footing and plunge into the sea: both horse and rider were killed. The son then returned to claim his inheritance. Another Milliton married a witch and after the wedding no strangers were allowed to enter Pengersick. Legions of spirits were summoned up and sometimes the demons were so powerful that only harp music could placate them. Local people avoided the castle, but one day a tall stranger appeared, sitting on a rock at the head of Pengersick Valley. Soon afterwards the castle caught fire and the forms of two men and one woman were seen rising above the flames: the stranger was the Devil himself.

Finally, there was the Milliton and his wife who detested each other so much that they committed mutual murder. They were drinking together, when the husband announced that he had poisoned his wife's drink; she replied that they would both die, as she had poisoned his. It may seem strange for so much horror to be associated with one house, but a writer in 1910 supplied a plausible explanation: 'The occupants of Pengersick appear to have had differences with the clergy in old times and the priests generally contrived to blacken the characters of those who became obnoxious to them.'

It has been suggested, somewhat fancifully, that battlegrounds and other areas of conflict maintain an aura of electricity in the air above them, which may produce ghostly phenomena. On 19 January 1643 Cromwell's army suffered a rare defeat at Braddock Down, near Lostwithiel, and on each anniversary of the battle the thunder of horses' hooves can be heard in the district. Comprigney, a field on the outskirts of Truro, takes its name from the Cornish *gwel cloghprenyer* [the field of the gibbet]. Local people still avoid the place after dark because of shadowy figures and rattling chains. Another field, above Tregavarras, near Gorran, has no known history of conflict attached to it but a young, sophisticated man who walked past the field gate at night was seized with panic for no apparent reason and ran for at least a mile along the lane. Some years previously a lady related to one of the authors swore that she had seen the figure of a man sitting on the same gate and experienced a similar fear.

Among Cornwall's most amusing tales are those of clerical ghost-layers. Parson Woods of Ladock was a skilled exorcist. He carried an ebony walking-stick with a silver knob on which was engraved a pentacle, with various planetary signs and mystical figures depicted on the broad silver band below the knob. Bottrell recounts many tales of Parson Woods and his habit of changing demons into animal forms, then thrashing them with his whip, a method also used by Parson Richards, curate of Camborne. A tale once well-known in the Camborne area tells how two miners were crossing the churchyard. They unwittingly interrupted Parson Richards as he was using his whip to lay the ghost of Lord de Dunstanville in the south porch of the church. The parson was so annoyed with the two men that he is supposed to have chased them to Crane, vigorously flourishing his whip. According to Robert Hunt, the Rev. Jago, Vicar of Wendron, was a very successful ghost-layer and it was said that 'no spirit walking the earth could resist the spells laid upon him by Jago.' The Rev. Polkinghorn of St Ives had the reputation of being the most powerful exorcist west of Hayle. Several ghosts belonging to the Harris family of Kenegie were laid by Parson Polkinghorn, including the renowned ghost of Wild Harris, whom he set to the task of counting all the blades of grass at Castle-an-Dinas.

Perhaps the most famous of the ghost-laying parsons was the Rev. Richard Dodge – Parson Dodge – Vicar of Talland, near Polperro, from 1713–47. He is supposed to have put the Devil himself to flight, when he met him driving his sable coach and headless horses. Such was his fame that on his approach evil spirits would exclaim: 'Dodge is come! I must be gone!' It is believed that Dodge was in league with the smugglers and that he spread the story of demons appearing in Bridle Lane, which leads up from Talland Beach to the church, to frighten away unwelcome visitors.

Talland Church has its own story, for local legend suggests that the building was begun well inland, at a place called Pulpit. Each night the stones put up during the day were removed to the present site, near the sea; this stone shifting was accompanied by a mysterious voice which said: 'If you will my wish fulfil, build the church on Talland Hill.' A similar story is told of Egloshayle Church, where the Devil threw a stone at the tower, for, when it was finished, there would be the sound of bells, which he hated. The Devil is also responsible for the lack of pinnacles on the church tower at Towednack, and the Probus Tower, the tallest in Cornwall, was originally designed for Truro Church, but, as it was being transported, Satan upset the wagon and planted the tower where it now stands.

Perhaps the best-documented case of exorcism is preserved in the diary of a seventeenth-century clergyman. On 20 June 1665 Parson John Ruddle, who began his ministry at Launceston in 1663, was invited to preach a funeral sermon at the burial of John Eliot at South Petherwin. As he was leaving the church after the service, Ruddle was approached by an elderly gentleman called Bligh, who invited him to visit his home, Botathan. Therefore, on the following Monday, Ruddle dined at Botathan, where he met a neighbouring cleric who suggested he should see the gardens after the meal. ' First he began to tell the infortunity of the family in general and then gave me an instance in the youngest son; for, says he, the poor boy believes himself to be haunted with ghosts and is confident that he meets with an evil spirit in a certain field about a half a mile from this place as often as he goes that way to school.' Both the boy's parents and the cleric asked Ruddle's advice and, on questioning the boy, Ruddle became convinced of his sincerity. The boy informed him that the ghost was Dorothy Dingley's, who had died about eight years previously: it never spoke, but just passed him by in a field called the Higher Brown Quartils. Ruddle visited the field with the boy and saw the spirit for himself. Some three weeks later, on 27 July 1665, he returned alone and once more saw the apparition.

The following day he returned with the boy and his parents, this time noting that a spaniel who accompanied them became frightened and fled in terror when the phantom appeared. On the third day Ruddle again visited the field and this time spoke to Dorothy Dingley's ghost, which answered in a voice neither audible nor intelligible. After this rather one-sided conversation the ghost disappeared. The Rev. P. T. Palman, Vicar of South

Petherwin, noted in a letter to Baring-Gould in December 1896 that there had been a little path called Dorothy Dinglet's Path running through a field called Higher Brown Park before it was ploughed up and that the local people used to frighten farm apprentices with stories of Dorothy's ghost.

A number of Cornish clerics returned as phantoms themselves and housemaids at a vicarage near St Cleer would never kill a spider, firmly believing that their deceased master, Parson Jupp, had been reincarnated in this form. The Rev. John Penneck, one-time Chancellor of Exeter, haunts St Hilary, flying into fits of rage and causing bad storms, while an eighteenth-century parson named Cole still roams the vicarage gardens at Luxulyan.

Inevitably the sea has played its part in furthering superstition amongst the Cornish, who lived by and worked upon its waters. Cornwall's rugged coastline has been the scene of innumerable shipwrecks, with countless lives lost, so it is hardly surprising that a people who believed in ghosts on land should find them at sea.

At Porthcurno, when evening mists were rising, a black ghostly square-rigger was said to come in from the sea and glide up over the sands to pursue its course across dry land; many people were said to have seen the phantom ship which foretold misfortune. According to marine experts, phantom lights seen at sea and along the coast are due to phosphorescence emitted from the decomposing carcasses of sea birds, but in Cornwall they are known as ' Jack Harry's Lights ' and are regarded as death omens, being the ghosts of drowned seamen. Stories of spectral lights luring men to their death often appear in the Cornish ghost tradition and it was until recently believed that those who perished as a result of German submarine action during World War I returned to lure German ships onto the rocks by means of false lights. The souls of drowned sailors are said to haunt those parts of the coast where shipwrecks have occurred and the ' calling ' of the dead has been heard before the coming of a storm; also many fishermen swear that they have heard the dead ' hailing their own names '. A ghostly bell chiming from a sea captain's grave at St Levan means death to anyone unfortunate enough to hear it.

Legends of drowned sailors returning to visit their lovers are to be found all over Cornwall and the stories of Nancy Trenoveth and Frank Lenine from Boscean and the Lovers of Porthgwarra, described earlier, have their similarities. So does this story from

St Levan. A young girl was waiting to be married to her sailor lover on his return from sea, when she was told that his ship had foundered in a storm. Night and day she cried for her lover's return. Nothing would pacify her, until one night, when a storm swept the coast, she was aroused from her bed, believing that she could hear her name being called above the screaming of the wind. She ran to the window and saw the figure of her lover standing below. He was soaking wet, with seaweed hanging from his boots and hair and his face shining deathly white. She ran out into the night, although her lover was no man of flesh and blood but a ghost returned from the sea. They walked hand in hand down to St Levan cove, stepped into a boat and rowed out over the breakers into the heart of the storm, never to return.

Animal hauntings are not uncommon in Cornwall and, at Looe, a white hare is sometimes seen running towards the Jolly Sailor Inn from the direction of Talland. It is said to be the ghost of a girl who committed suicide and is thought to be a warning of imminent danger. Before the use of auxiliary engines the fishermen of Looe stayed at home if the hare was seen, rather than tempt fate by putting to sea. A white hare also haunts the churchyard at Egloshayle, together with the headless ghost of the hunter who, disbelieving its supernatural existence, tried to shoot it.

This story was given to us by a lady, living in Bradoc, near Lostwithiel. In the parish of Lanreath lived an old rector who had a young and beautiful wife. A new curate who came to assist the old man fell in love with his wife. One evening, after all three had dined, the rector went down to the cellar to fetch another bottle of wine but fell down the steps and died. Whether the tragedy was by accident or design is not known, but the next day a large black cockerel appeared in the village and attacked every man, woman and child that it met. The villagers were unable to catch the bird and believed it to be the ghost of the old rector, returned to haunt them. One day the evil creature accidently flew through the kitchen window of the Punch Bowl Inn and straight into a huge cloam – earthenware – oven. These ovens were oval or square in shape with a slightly domed top, a fire was lit in the oven and left until the right temperature was obtained, then the embers were brushed out and the food put in to cook. The kitchen-maid with great presence of mind quickly shut the door and trapped the cockerel inside. A mason was then called to cement it so that it could never be opened again.

H

A phantom white horse ridden by its dead owner once haunted Porthgwidden beach at St Ives. The horse, a magnificent animal, belonged to a gentleman named Birch, sometime in the nineteenth century. Every evening Birch would ride to Porthgwidden for a swim, until one stormy night he was swept away and drowned; a fisherman found the horse later, patiently waiting on the beach for its master. Sometime afterwards when the animal had also died, local people swore that they had seen Birch riding along Island Road to Porthgwidden beach.

The familiar story of a ghostly black dog appears all over Britain and Cornwall is no exception. An evil spirit in this form once appeared to a group of wrestlers on Whiteborough, a large tumulus on St Stephen's Down near Launceston, as they were finishing the day's sport; the earthwork was once believed to be the burial place of the giants and their gold. The ghost of Vincent Darley, who lived long ago at Battens, a farmhouse in North Hill, appeared sometimes as a man carrying a bundle of sticks, but more often as a black dog. Darley died on 8 February 1764 and his spectre begins its walk at Darley Ford and ends it at Battens. The black dog was seen by many people at Botterell, both at Berriow Bridge and at Berriow, as well as at Battens, where, in more recent years, Darley's ghost has been observed driving his coach wildly into the yard.

Phantom dogs are often demonic, like the pack of hounds who run howling across the Cornish moors. The legend of the Devil and his Dandy Dogs recalls the Norse tradition of the Wild Hunt, when Woden led his pack across the stormy skies, bringing death to all who saw them. The Phantom Hunter appears in northern England, too, but elsewhere he becomes King Herla or even King Arthur. In Devon, he is the ghost of Sir Francis Drake, with his Wish or Yeth Hounds but in Cornwall he is the Devil. Thomas Q. Couch once wrote:

> He was terrible to look at, and had the usual complement of saucer-eyes, horns and tail accorded by common consent to the legendary Devil. He was black, of course, and carried in his hand a long hunting-pole. The dogs, a numerous pack, blackened the small patch of moor that was visible, each snorting fire and uttering a yelp of an indescribably frightful tone.

Thomas Q. Couch goes on to tell of a poor herdsman journeying home across the moors one stormy night when he heard the baying of the Dandy Dogs. The terrified man was chased by the Devil and his hounds until, exhausted, he fell to the ground and began to pray. The power of prayer in this case worked, for immediately the hell-hounds stood at bay and the hunter shouted, ' Bo Shrove!' said to mean ' The boy prays!' The hunter and his dogs then disappeared.

An unscrupulous lawyer who murdered his wife and children, stole the estates of an orphan and sold his soul to the Devil – this was John, or Jan, Tregeagle of Cornwall's most famous ghost legend. His spirit still haunts the moors and rugged coast, doomed to a life of wandering. Tregeagle can be heard howling in the wind, when storms roll in across the Atlantic and angry seas batter the cliffs; someone who is over-boisterous can still be told that he is ' worse than Tregeagle roaring before the storm '. Some accounts have him flapping around the cliffs at Land's End like a giant gull, when the wind is wild; in others he is a gigantic bird which haunts Bodmin Moor, luring travellers to their death. It has been said that John was an historical figure, one of the Tregeagle family from Trevorder, near Bodmin, a wealthy man enriched by dishonest means. This wealth enabled him to bribe the clergy before his death into burying him in consecrated ground in St Breock churchyard. The real John Tregeagle was steward to John, Earl of Radnor, and the same Tregeagle who issued the warrant for the arrest of Anne Jeffries, mentioned previously. But it is the myth rather than the man which has survived in the Cornish memory.

There are many and varied stories about Tregeagle, but they mostly agree on how he first came to be called from the grave. Just before his death he had witnessed the loan of a large sum of money from one man to another. When the moneylender demanded settlement the debtor denied all knowledge of the deal and the case was taken to court at Bodmin, where the late Tregeagle was claimed as the only witness. The defendant, certain of his safety, dismissed his crime with an oath exclaiming, ' If Tregeagle ever saw it, I wish to God he would come and declare it!' In a flash of lightning, the ghost of Tregeagle appeared and addressed the terrified courtroom: ' It will not be such an easy task to get rid of me as it has been to call me!'

The debtor sought to rid himself of Tregeagle with the aid of a parson, who eventually succeeded in binding him to the task of emptying Dozmare Pool with a leaking limpet shell. Dozmare was once believed to be bottomless and some people believe that the early Celts might have thought it a Lake of the Underworld. Tregeagle miraculously completed the job and returned to torment the unfortunate man, who then procured the assistance of another cleric, a powerful exorcist. The priest drew a circle and bade the man stand in it. Tregeagle assumed the appearance of a large black bull and attempted to gore him with his horns, but he remained unharmed while the cleric performed his rite. At length Tregeagle quietened down and, restrained by the exorcist, allowed himself to be taken to Gwenvor Cove. There he was set to weave a truss of sand bound with sand ropes, which, when finished, he should carry to Carn Olva. Tregeagle was unable to accomplish his task, until one cold winter, on a hard frosty night, he poured water from nearby Vellandreath Brook onto the truss; it froze together and in triumph he carried it to the top of Carn Olva.

Immediately Tregeagle returned to pester his wretched quarry, intent on tearing him to pieces. but the man held in his arms a baby, whose innocence warded off the attacker. Once again a priest was called and Tregeagle was bound to weave another sand truss at Gwenvor, but this time he was forbidden to approach water. Defeated at last, Tregeagle remains in constant struggle with the sand and, when a northerly wind comes to destroy his work, his roars can be heard across Whitesand Bay.

This is just one version of the legend and, according to another story, the emptying of Dozmare Pool was not so easily accomplished. Tregeagle was kept at his work, overlooked by a pack of demons, until a particularly ferocious storm blew up. Terrified, he defied even the demons and fled across the wastes of Bodmin Moor, with the evil pack in hot pursuit. At last he reached the hermitage on Roche Rock and thrust his head through the east window, thus gaining the sanctuary of the church. Although his head was within the chapel, his body remained outside, exposed to the full fury of both storm and pack of demons. His screams were heard for miles around and after a few days the incumbent priest could stand it no longer. With the aid of two local saints, he removed Tregeagle to the beach at Padstow, but the local people were not at all happy with the continual screaming and urged their patron saint, St Petroc, to move Tregeagle on again.

Petroc forged a chain with his own hands and drove the spirit to Bareppa, near Helston. There, he was commanded to carry sacks of sand across the estuary of the river Cober and to empty them at Porthleven. He laboured for a long time until one day a demon caused him to drop the sack, spilling the sand across the estuary: the ridge it formed is today known as the Loe Bar. More tales of Tregeagle are found throughout Cornwall and wherever one travels in the county there are reminders of him. A menhir at Porthpean is called Tregeagle's Stick; he got drunk with the Devil in Lanlivery; and a cave near Carne, in Veryan parish, is named after him. Veryan, of course, is also the home of the famous Round Houses, so built to keep the Devil from hiding in the corners!

In 1807 a ballad appeared called *Tregeagle or Dozmare Pool, an Anciente Cornishe legend,* in which Tregeagle sells his soul to the Devil:

> A bargaine! A bargaine! then said he aloude,
> At my lot I will never repyne;
> I sweare to observe it, I sweare by the roode,
> And am readye to seale and to synge with my bloode,
> Bothe my soule and my bodye are thyne!

John Penwarne, the ballad's author, appears to have taken various incidents from different traditional tales and woven them into a story of his own. In one part, Tregeagle captures Goonhylda, the Earl of Cornwall's daughter and holds her prisoner, until he is challenged to a duel by the Black Hunter, who ends his wicked life:

> Then from the black corpse a pale spectre appeared
> And hyde him away through the night!

Tregeagle's phantom has been haunting the night ever since.

6 Witchcraft and Herbal Lore

ALTHOUGH OCCASIONAL LAWS AGAINST WITCHCRAFT had been passed in England since Anglo-Saxon times by both Church and State, the Cornish tended to treat it with extreme indifference. This may help to explain why the death penalty appeared far less frequently in Cornwall than in some other parts of the country, even during the witch-hunting craze of the sixteenth and seventeenth centuries, when hundreds of women and men were executed on the most trivial of evidence extracted under torture. In 1671 a woman from Looe was accused of hindering the English fleet in the war against the Dutch, responsibility for the Queen's barrenness and causing a bull to kill Colonel Robinson, Member of Parliament and Justice of the Peace, because he prosecuted the Nonconformists. The chief evidence given against her suggested that a number of cats had been seen dancing in the air and that she had several marks on her body where the Devil had sucked her. Although she was found guilty she received only a short gaol sentence.

On 27 July 1686 at Launceston an account of a case between John Tonken and Jane Noal, alias Nickless, and Elizabeth, alias Betty, Seeze, undersigned by Peter Jenken, Mayor, and John Grose, Justice, was printed as follows:

One John Tonken of Pensans, near the Mount in Cornwall about fifteen or sixteen years of age, was in April last strangely taken with sudden fits; and on the 4 May 1686, as he lay in bed, there appeared to him a woman in a blue jerkin and red petticoat, with yellow and green patches, and told him that he would not be well before he had brought up nutshells, pins and nails; which the boy afterwards related to several people that were at his chamber though none did see or hear the apparition but himself; soon after the lad was taken with fits of striving, or yoaking, insomuch that two men could scarce hold him, and after several fits, he brought up three pins and half a walnut-shell, and in a few days after, he brought up three walnut-shells and several pins, some of which were crooked. The woman very often appeared to him sometimes in the shape as before; at other times like a cat; whereupon the boy would shriek, laying his hands over his eyes and mouth, and would say with a loud voice, ' She is putting things into my mouth, she will choke me, she will poison me '. At other times he would say, ' I will not be tempted by thee, and in the name of Jesus, I defy thee and all thy works '; for a while he would lie as dead and on a sudden he would spring from the bed three or four feet high, from between two men that usually sat upon the bed by him. On further occasions the youth brought up straw, rushes, pins, nails, brambles and needles, the woman usually appearing to advise him of the nature of the coming vomit. Careful examination of the boy's mouth revealed no trickery. In further visions, he saw a witch take a mouse, and noticed her going out of the window, but she would not tell her name. In his last vision there appeared three women, whereat he cried out, ' What a confederacy! What you old witch, more confederates ', and then she bade him farewell, and said she would trouble him no more and two days after the boy was pretty well again and goes abroad with crutches.

The two women were sent to Launceston gaol, but it appears from the gaol book that only Jane Nickless was indicted. She was found not guilty.

John Wesley, while preaching at Lanzafried in 1746, found that fear of the Devil and belief in the black witches' power was still prevalent, for he met a woman ' whom Satan had bound in an uncommon manner for several years '. The woman had insulted a neighbour who then went to a man famous in those parts, named Francis Morgan, and gave him 14s to do his worst. The next night she knew the Devil was close to her: from that time on she lived in fear, feeling as if her flesh was being torn from her body with burning pincers.

Witches were supposed to have the power of changing shape and resuming it again at will. There are many stories of the hare who baffled the pursuing hounds until, when wounded by a silver bullet, it turned into Old Mother So-and-So, who from that day walked with a limp. As recently as 1934 a family on a motoring holiday in north Cornwall, staying at an hotel, went for a walk on the moors; suddenly they came upon a large hare sitting on its haunches and shrieking. One of the family picked up the animal and calmed it and eventually the creature hopped quietly away. On returning to the hotel they met the landlord and told him their story. The man turned pale and ran back into the house, returning to inform them that he had made a mistake and was unable to accommodate them any longer. When the visitors insisted the landlord relented, but made quite sure that their stay was an uncomfortable one. Tiring of the treatment they had received, the family paid their bill and drove off amid hoots and groans from the assembled villagers. Later they were informed that no-one but a witch could handle a hare as they had done.

A witch was accused of employing evil spirits to destroy crops, of inhibiting sexual relations, ruining health and generally causing ill-luck by laying a curse, or ' ill-wishing '. In a village near Tywardreath in 1841 a woman was held in great dread by her neighbours, and many tales were told of persons actually dying through her incantations. One person who had been ill for some time called for the assistance of a witch-finder, who, on his arrival, immediately pronounced the cause to be witchcraft. The manner of the witch's initiation into the Black Art was in this case by attending the sacrament, repeating the Lord's Prayer three times backwards, consuming the wine, but retaining the bread and feeding it to a toad – which one assumes was the witch's familiar, employed to do her evil work. Initiation could also be carried out in the following manner: ' Go to the Chancel of a church to sacrament, hide away the bread from the hands of the priest, at midnight carry it around the church from south to north, crossing to east three times. The third time one would meet a big open-mouthed toad, feed it the bread; when swallowed he will breathe three times upon you and from that time you would become a witch.'

The police at Falmouth in July 1845 arrested three women named De Freez for assaulting another named Warne. It was disclosed during the examination that the women charged with the assault could have exonerated themselves, but the neighbours who witnessed the affray were deterred from appearing in court because they believed that Warne was a witch and might ill-wish them. In another case a man from Ludgvan parish was brought before the court, accused by his wife of keeping her on bread and water for several days and of physical assault. His defence was that his wife's sister had ill-wished his pigs and he had beaten his wife to make her ask her sister to remove the curse. A common expression still used in Cornwall to a person who appears unwell is ' E me 'andsome, you're looking brer ill-wished.' That is, ' You're looking very ill or pale.' While this does not necessarily show current belief in ill-wishing, it is a survival from recollections of the old fear.

A common way of removing the curse of an ill-wisher was to draw blood from the witch in the belief that by doing so her life force and magical power would be destroyed. Two old women who lived in the almhouses at Morvah hardly ever spoke to each other. During the winter one of them fell ill and became convinced that the other had cast a spell. Determined to remove it, she thrust a rusty nail into her neighbour's arm, causing it to bleed. There was a great outcry and the local vicar had to intervene, threatening the assailant with a summons if she ever tried to repeat the offence. The blood of a bewitched person was also used to combat a witch; combined with urine, hair and nail-clippings in a bottle heated over the fire, it caused an ill-wisher to writhe in agony. One such ' witch bottle ' was found about 40 years ago while repairs were being carried out in the kitchen chimney of an old cottage in Padstow.

Those who believed themselves bewitched but were unable to rid themselves of the curse would consult the local ' peller ', a word possibly originating from ' expeller ', that is, a remover of witchcraft. These were professional conjurers and herbalists who made a living recovering lost or stolen property, selling love philtres and countering the black witches' curses. The pellers, known otherwise as ' cunning men ', ' conjurers ', ' white wizards ' or ' charmers ', practised their craft openly and if they were unable to cure sickness by magic and herbal charms they would diagnose witchcraft. The peller was often responsible for barbaric cruelties inflicted upon animals. In 1865 a farmer from Portreath burnt a calf alive for the purpose of removing a disease. Another farmer who had lost a number of cattle, and believed them ill-wished, visited a conjurer who lived near the Lizard Point. The conjurer told the farmer to bleed the next animal that fell ill and to catch the blood upon straw, taking care not to lose any. The blood-soaked straw had then to be burnt and the farmer would be sure to see the witch pass through the smoke. The gullible farmer carried out the conjurer's instructions and, seeing an old woman who through curiosity had entered the field, jumped upon her and cruelly ill-treated her.

The peller often wore an allegedly magical ring made from a blue stone with a yellow, twisted line running through it. The stone was known as an ' adder stone ' or ' millpreve ', from the Cornish *mylpref* [a thousand snakes]. It was held to be an unfailing remedy against snake bite from the popular belief that hundreds of adders gathered together to produce the stone by hissing on a hazel wand stuck in the ground. Famous among the pellers in Cornwall was Tamson Blight, or Tammy Blee, and many stories involving magical cures were told of her. On one occasion a woman, whose child suffered a mysterious sickness, and who believed him ill-wished, visited Tamson demanding the name of the person responsible. This was refused, but she described her in such detail that the woman immediately knew who it was and returned home determined to break the spell. A few days later, when the supposedly guilty party passed the woman's door, she rushed out and dug her nails into the woman's arm and made it bleed. From that time on, we are told, the child began to get well.

From Robert Hunt, quoting from the *West Briton*, we learn that Tamson married a man named James Thomas from Illogan, who tried unsuccessfully to make a living as a conjurer himself. Tamson, who came from Redruth, parted from her husband and moved to Helston where she became famous for her cures. One night when she was very ill a farmer came and asked if she could cure his horse, which he said would die unless helped.

As she was too ill to move, she called her little boy to her side and touched him saying certain words. She then informed the farmer, 'If you can carry my child to where the horse is, his touch will cure it, for I have passed my power on to him for this occasion.' He did as he was told and the horse recovered. This last story about Tamson Blight shows the old belief that magical power is hereditary, handed down from male to female and vice versa. Tamson stated herself that she was of the real peller blood.

The white witch also provided charms to ward off evil; one such charm written on parchment and hung round a person's neck was composed of a magic square made up of five words, each appearing four times as the rows were read from top to bottom:

S	A	T	O	R
A	R	E	P	O
T	E	N	E	T
O	P	E	R	A
R	O	T	A	S

This charm has been found inscribed on ancient drinking vessels, a column at Pompeii and at Cirencester where it is presumed to date from the Roman occupation in the third century AD. It has been recommended for finding witches, for colic and against pestilence. It could be an early Christian spell, possibly forming an anagram of Pater Noster with the letters A and O twice repeated, containing the first two words of the Lord's Prayer with Alpha and Omega, the first and last, a symbol of Christ. Whatever the meaning, though, the charm has survived and retained its magical importance.

Often, when a charmer was consulted, a sheep's heart stuck with pins was roasted before the fire while the assembled people chanted:

> It is not this heart I wish to burn,
> But the person's heart I wish to turn,
> Wishing them neither rest nor peace
> Till they are dead and gone.

Blackened animal hearts riddled with pins have been found in many old Cornish cottage chimneys under renovation. Another charm widely used by the Cornish conjurer demanded a piece of hangman's rope, which, together with magical incantations, was used to cure the ' Kings Evil ', scrofula. At an execution in Bodmin in August 1845 it was noticed that there was an active demand for pieces of the rope which the executioner sold at a shilling a length. Sometime later, when a local surgeon was dressing a wound in a patient's back, he found a small chintz bag suspended from the man's neck. He asked what it contained and was told that; ' It was a bit of rope the man was 'anged with a' Badment ' and that ' o'other bit' was buried and as the rope rotted, the wound hailled '. The village charmer would attempt to cure rheumatism, alleviate snake bite, and remove warts. A charm for whooping cough was given to Canon Hammond of St Austell : ' Take a mouse, tes a clean eatin' animal, sure! kill un and roast un as black as a coal; then put un in a pessle and mortar and pound un up and put milk to un an' clunk [swallow] et down, an et'll cure 'ee.' The medical use of mice seems fairly widespread and was used for various ailments, such as measles and bedwetting.

A lady who wrote to the authors in January 1972 gave this cure for ringworm :

> When I was at school, this would be 1922 or thereabouts, all our calves became afflicted with ringworm. My mother who fed them with milk in buckets soon developed them on her arms. A few weeks later I, too, had them. Between us we had dozens, I can't remember when we went to the doctor, but we did have treatment and they only increased. We were told of a family called Pryne who lived at Rosenannon, St Wenn, who charmed ringworm. After a couple of visits here, stopping all medical treatment, the ringworm faded away, also the calves were cured too!

She goes on to tell in another letter how the cure was effected :

> We saw an old lady and were shown into a small front room with a round table on which stood a large book, most likely a Bible. I don't remember seeing anyone else; she touched all our ringworms and muttered something. We made about three visits, and we took some strips of sheeting. The bandages were placed between the pages of the Bible,

perhaps from one visit to the next. We wore the bandages until the ringworm died away, which they very soon did from the centre.

Jimmy Moore, a present-day charmer from the St Tudy area, who heals both ringworm and warts, is still called in by local farmers to cure their cattle when all normal methods have failed. Jimmy believes that his healing powers were a gift from a grateful gypsy woman whom he befriended 50 years ago. He explained that the gypsy wrote something on a piece of paper and told him to learn it and then destroy it. He believes that ever since that day he has had the power.

A small village in west Cornwall boasted a rat charmer, who, like the Pied Piper, was employed to rid the village of rats; this he undertook by whistling to them, producing a hypnotic effect and causing them to crawl to him or, if running away, to stop. A wart charmer in the Helston district used to cure warts by placing a table knife lightly over them while muttering incantations, then cutting a strip of bark from an ash tree. She assured the patient that, as the bark withered, so would the warts. A Devonshire man told the authors about his father-in-law who was Cornish:

> My wife's father would put away warts; he would rub a penny over them, then he would bury it in the earth and within a few days the warts would be gone. One time he did it when his son was with him; some days after when they were going to work his son said he was a penny short for an ounce of tobacco, so he was going to dig up the penny. His father said, 'Don't do it or your hands will be covered with warts.' But his son did and the next day his hands were covered.

These charms show the type of sympathetic magic apparent in many of the old Cornish healing charms. A cure for snake-bite transcribed from a manuscript volume kept by a charmer ran as follows: ' " Bradgty, bradgty, bradgty, under the ashing leaf," to be repeated three times, and strike your hands with the growing of the hare. " Bradgty, bradgty, bradgty," to be repeated three times nine before eight, eight before seven, etc., down to one before every one, three times for the bite of an adder.'

The hand of a dead man held great healing powers if passed

seven times over the afflicted part of the body – seven is generally regarded as a magical number. A tomcat's tail rubbed on the eye was sure to remove a stye, and this charm healed strains:

> Christ rode over the bridge,
> Christ rode under the bridge,
> Vein to vein, strain to strain,
> I hope God will take it back again.

To staunch blood, charmers in the Gwennap district read from Ezekiel 16:

> Then washed I thee with water,
> yea I thoroughly washed away thy blood from thee,
> and I anointed them with oil.

If the sufferer were male, a woman had to say the lines and vice versa. Another remedy for staunching blood was suggested to one of the authors by a resident of Portloe when his young son fell and cut his head. Unable to stop the bleeding he enquired at the Ship Inn for the whereabouts of the local doctor. Overhearing the conversation a lady exclaimed, ' Poor mite, rub 'en with a gold ring, that'll stop 'en.' Gold has long been considered a cure-all by country people.

The Cornish charmer also made great use of herbs and plants. Polwhele, writing in 1826, states: ' There are some plants which are disallowed or neglected by botanists, but whose qualities brought into action by some church-town crony will sometimes cure a disease which has been given up by her betters as irremediable.'

A story about Billy Bray, the evangelist miner, tells how one day he was sent to the doctor to fetch medicine for one of his children. Walking through a field on his way back, the cork came out and he lost some of the contents of the bottle. Billy noticed a pat of cow dung, the centre of which had filled with brown water; feeling sure that it had a herbal base, he filled the empty space in the bottle. Apparently the child did not die.

The Cornish believed implicitly in the power of the old remedies and were more inclined to visit the village wise woman than perhaps travel many miles to see a doctor whose fees they could rarely afford. Hamilton Jenkin writes, ' They were firm believers in the old adage that there is a doctor in every hedge.'

A lady from Lostwithiel gave the authors the following remedies which have been in her family for many years:

For a cold
Pick elder flower and angelica leaves, steep in boiling water
for ten minutes and strain, adding sugar to taste. The flower
of the elder (*Sumbucus nigra*) infused and taken in the form
of a tissane is used today to ease hay-fever and catarrh.
Angelica, apart from any therapeutic properties, was the
strongest protection against witchcraft.

Ointment for bruises
Gather some mallow leaves and bruise them up well, mix
with pig's lard, put into a jar and cover. Smear on bruises,
strained joints, ulcers, etc. It takes out heat and pain. The
mucilage of the common mallow (*Althæa officinalis*) is still
used to relieve diseases of the chest, intestines and kidneys.

For ague
Put a handful of groundsel into a small linen bag, pricking
the side next to the skin full of holes; wear it at pit of
stomach and renew every two hours until well. An infusion
of groundsel (*Senecio vulgaris*) is used by modern herbalists
to cure jaundice, and to relieve obstructions from the bladder
and kidneys.

For corns
Apply bruised ivy (*Hedera helix*) leaves daily and in about
a week corns will drop out.

Sciatica
Boil nettles until soft, strain off liquor and apply nettles
as a poultice or carry a potato in your pocket until it withers.
Nettles (*Urtica dioica*) are used today for gout and nettle
rash.

For wounds
Bind the leaves of ground ivy on the wound, quickly heals
cuts and draws out thorns and splinters. The berries of the
ivy are used in febrile disorders and a vinegar of these was
used during the London Plague.

Clubmoss (*Lycopodium clavatum*) was considered good for eye
diseases if cut on the third day of the moon, when the thin crescent

is seen for the first time. The knife for cutting the moss was shown
to the moon while a charm was spoken. Crowfoot was known as the
' kenning ' herb and was used as a cure for ' kennings ', or ' ken-
nels ', the Cornish word for ulcers in the eye. For a head cold, a
draught of mugwort (*Artemisia vulgaris*), made by pouring boiling
water over a handful of the herb, was swallowed hot and sweetened
with treacle. Coltsfoot (*Tussilago farfara*) was smoked by the
Cornish miners as a precaution against lung diseases and is still
used in herbal tobacco. Camomile (*Anthenis nobilis*) flowers,
gathered when ' full faced ' and in ' high sun ', then dried, can
be used as an aid for rheumatic tendencies, when steeped in boiling water either by drinking or bathing and the flowers made into
a ' plaque ' to bind around the inflamed joint; another cure for
rheumatism was to carry a piece of ash wood (*Fraxinus excelsior*)
in one's pocket. This was also used as a charm against witchcraft
and to ward off snakes, for a single blow from an ash stick meant
instant death to an adder; struck by any other stick, the reptile is
said to remain alive until the sun goes down.

Scabious (*Kanutia arvensis*) was known in Cornwall as 'Devil's
Button ', or ' Devil's Bit ', and the root was used to cure all kinds
of ailments. The Devil was afraid it would banish all illness –
at least that is what people thought – so he bit off the end of the
root leaving only its present shortened stump.

An infusion of burdock (*Arctium lappa*) was taken by the
Cornish sailor as a cure for scurvy and is still considered to be
one of the finest blood purifiers. The healing power of the dock
leaf for nettle sting is well known, but the rhyme that once used
to accompany it has now disappeared :

> Out nettle,
> In dock.
> Dock shall have
> A new smock.

The Great Plague was said to have been introduced to the
parishes of Tregony and Veryan by an infected handkerchief
accidentally dropped in the district. The dreadful disease wiped
out numbers of people from whose graves in Veryan churchyard
sprang the ' pestilent wort ', or ' plague wort ' (*Tussilago petasitis*),
which was useful during the time of the epidemic. In 1790 a
blacksmith, Ralph Barnes, was supposed to have cured himself
of a cancer by taking immense quantities of the juice of hemlock

(*Conium naculatum*). Hemlock is a highly poisonous plant often associated with the Devil and witchcraft, but used nowadays as a sedative for spasmodic affections such as epilepsy. It should be administered only under medical supervision, as overdoses produce paralysis. One must therefore assume that Mr Barnes was very lucky. In many parishes the minister combined his religious functions with the practice of medicine and his methods sometimes differed little from those employed by the charmers of the day. A successful practitioner like Hugh Atwell, Rector of St Ewe from 1559 to 1615, could easily gain the reputation of being a magician simply because his cures actually worked.

Thomas Q. Couch, writing in 1855, states: ' The belief in witchcraft holds its ground very firmly and of all superstition it will probably be the last to die out.' Despite the advances in modern technology and medicine during the past century, his statement still holds true today. In 1973 a national Sunday newspaper carried the report of a field at Lower Harlyn Farm, overlooking the sea near Padstow. The story begins back in the days when Padstow was an important fishing port. A large cargo of pilchards that the Italian buyers had declined to purchase because of the price was dumped on the field and the near starving villagers were refused permission to take it. People said that Mother Ivey, a witch who gives her name to a local bay, then intervened. She lay a curse on the field, declaring that if anyone ever again tried to cultivate it the death would surely follow of the eldest son of the resident family. On a later occasion an eldest son was thrown from his horse and died in the field, adding weight to the legend.

During the last war, when the whole nation was being urged to ' dig for victory ' and every patch of land was cultivated, the local War Agricultural Committee was persuaded to leave the field lying fallow, although the Home Guard dug some slit-trenches in it. Shortly afterwards the present owner's father, then who was the eldest son, was killed. Mr. Hellyar, the owner, states in the newspaper article that he would need a very good reason before he touched the field and that nothing about the curse has ever been written down, the facts having been passed down from father to son. Recently attempts have been made to break the curse by Mrs Mary Rees, the joint owner of the field, who consulted a wise woman. She stuffed pieces of rag into a tin, spoke some strange incantations over them and told Mrs Rees to bury the tin in the infected field. But Mr Bennett, the tenant farmer, still insists: ' I wouldn't plough up that field, not for any money.'

Mr Hellyer, Mrs Rees and Mr Bennett would, we feel, be interested to learn that the mystery of their field is not unique, even in Cornwall. Near Mullion, a similar patch of land, once a local burial ground, is never tilled for the same reason.

7 Animal, Vegetable and Mineral

THE REV. SABINE BARING-GOULD WROTE the following paragraph in his *Book of Cornwall*:

> The Quakers in Cornwall have, as elsewhere, their Monthly Advices read to them in the meeting-house, wherein are admonitions against various sorts of evil. Among these is one against ' vain sports '. Now, just about hay-making time, a newly-joined member heard this injunction and he timidly enquired whether ' making sweet hay with the maidens ' came under the category. ' Naw, sure,' was the answer, ' that's all in the way o' Nature '.

This chapter will investigate the ways of nature in Cornwall: stories of birds, beasts and plants, some of which overlap from the previous chapter, rhymes and superstitions concerning the Cornish climate and the miraculous powers of Cornwall's rock formations, some natural, others man-made.

After mining and fishing, farming provides Cornwall with its third natural industry. The Cornishman's involvement with his surroundings is typified by the three most beautiful sights and the three most ugly, given to the authors by a lady from Lostwithiel:

> A woman with a child,
> A ship in full sail,
> A field of corn waving in the wind.

Here we have the real countryman's delight in birth, freedom and the land, and here his disgust in the squalid and the unnatural:

> A fat slovenly woman,
> A poor lean horse,
> An old scat bal [disused mine].

There is an unpleasant story of how a horse, not necessarily a lean one, became an ugly sight to a woman of St Martins' – this not much more than a century ago. Believing that her sheep had been bewitched, she travelled from her home in the Isles of Scilly to visit a charmer in Penzance. He advised her that an old mare kept in the same field as the sheep was possessed by an evil spirit. Following his instructions she returned home and, while her equally credulous neighbours watched, surrounded the poor horse with faggots and set them alight. Other sacrificial practices to ward off witchcraft are mentioned in the preceding chapters and animals cruelly suffered in this way until quite recently. Instances of cows being burned alive were quite common, and Jim Thomas, a Camborne miner and amateur folklorist, tells of a live toad roasted to break an ' ill-wishing '. A nasty game played by boys had no obvious magic intention: a live fowl was tied to stakes set in the ground, then chased and beaten to death with bats. Cock-fighting was a popular pastime and the last recorded bull-baiting took place in 1811, near Ponsandane Bridge in Penzance.

Animals used to be credited with human characteristics and were subsequently treated as human. They were often put on trial and executed in the Middle Ages, though this was more usual on the Continent than in England. A strange story is told of the fisherman of Mevagissey who caught a monkey washed ashore from a wrecked French ship and hung it as a spy.

If the francophobia of former times lends credibility to the monkey story, romanticism must account for recollections among Ludgvan's inhabitants – or their not too distant forebears – of the last wolf roaming through Rosepeath Park. Wolves became extinct in England nearly five centuries ago. More plausible is the account current among elderly people around Truro until at least the 1930s, of the last wild stag in Ponsanooth Valley.

Stray cows, unlike wolves, were evidently a nuisance within comparatively recent times and Lake, writing about a century ago, describes an elaborate ritual in St Austell for disposing of them. They must be impounded for a given time, then displayed at the Mengue Stone for a number of market days after which, if no owner had come forward, they could be sold. The Mengue Stone is set in the pavement of St Austell and from here all important proclamations were formerly read. A witch, so it is said, was once burnt alive on the stone.

St Austell's church, Holy Trinity, contains many splendid carvings, including one of a bench end, which shows a fox preaching. Fantastic animals on the bench ends in St Columba's at St Columb Major have a curious history. The woodcarver who made them, so the story goes, had been so impressed by the performing animals in a passing show that he perpetuated them in his work.

We have already heard of many animal ghosts appearing in Cornwall. The hare, in particular, was feared throughout the county, as it was generally regarded as either a witch's familiar or even the embodiment of the witch herself. Later, rabbits acquired a similar reputation and the writer, Daphne du Maurier, recalls one occasion when a boatman from Lantic Bay, near Fowey, turned for home when she mentioned rabbiting aboard his boat. In the early part of this century there was a story in the village of Mylor of a terrifying black bull that rushed through the street breathing fire and ' roaring something terrible '. No farm reported the loss of a bull and it vanished as mysteriously as it had appeared. A headland near Mylor is called Tarra Point, a name reminiscent of the Cornish word *tarow* [Bull]. The story in Zennor that a cow ate the bell rope and deprived the village of its Sunday alarm becomes less whimsical when one considers the sparse vegetation in the vicinity. The unfortunate animal swallowed the rope to avoid starvation.

In St Neot, as elsewhere, kittens born in May were doomed to be drowned as they were believed to attract adders and other vermin indoors. A saying in West Cornwall explained the situation: ' Kittens born in May bring adders to the door in August.' This is basically true, as kittens learning to hunt stalk moving things and adders enjoy the August sun. In fact, cats are good adder-killers and the people of St Neot probably did themselves little good by destroying their May kittens. Dogs are said to be useless for the job as the snakes are able to bite the soft flesh around their noses. Another superstition from St Neot insisted that extracted teeth must be burned immediately. If they were thrown away, a dog might eat them and dog's teeth would grow in the late owner's mouth.

Animals, of course, appear frequently in children's songs and rhymes. In Cornwall, the bat is known aptly as an ' airy-mouse ' and this rhyme was popular among the children of Polperro during the nineteenth century:

> Airy-mouse, airy-mouse, fly over my head,
> And you shall have a crust of bread,
> And when I brew or when I bake,
> You shall have a piece of my wedding-cake.

Two riddles are worth quoting here, if only for their simple charm:

> Two lookers, two crookers,
> Four upstanders and a whizabout.

Surely here is the most perfect definition of a cow, unequalled by any dictionary! The man milking her is similarly treated:

> Clink, clank, under the bank,
> Ten dragging at four.

A widespread nonsense song, ' The Frog and the Mouse ', was very popular among Cornish children and ' Old Daddy Fox ' remains a great favourite:

> When he got home to his old den,
> Out came the young ones, eight, nine, ten;
> The fox and his wife ate the grey goose then
> And the young ones picked the bones-O!

While 'The Old Grey Duck' and 'The Sweet Nightingale' are the two best-loved traditional songs in Cornwall – the latter surprisingly so, as nightingales do not appear in the county – they are too well known to repeat here and so we will concentrate on the strange superstitions attached to birds: even their eggs were not exempt as bad luck followed them if they were carried indoors. Witches would stuff a dying man's pillow with wild birds' feathers to ensure him a long and painful death and if ravens croaked over a fit man's house, he soon became ill. The almost universal fishermen's belief in the supernatural powers of the albatross is echoed in Cornwall, where seamen will not kill gulls as they imagine them to embody the souls of their shipwrecked comrades. A scolding woman was dubbed a magpie and this bird was always greeted with the doffing of a hat, a gesture which turned away anger. A proverb declared that 'a whistling woman and a crowing hen are two of the unluckiest things under the sun', and Robert Hunt knew of hens being killed for it. One strange belief mentioned by Carew and surviving until quite recent years concerned migratory birds: they were thought not to fly to foreign lands but to spend their winters in caves hundreds of feet underground.

The cuckoo has attracted a complete mythology all of his own:

> In April, come he will,
> In May, he sings all day,
> In June, he alters his tune,
> In July, he prepares to fly,
> In August, go he must.

If the first cuckoo of spring utters his cry 12 times, a year of prosperity will follow for the local farmers, but if a person hearing the cry is looking at the ground, an untimely fate awaits him, As in Ireland, it is lucky to hear the cuckoo from the right-hand side and unlucky from the left. Jonathan Couch heard one of Britain's oldest folk songs in Polperro:

> The cuckoo is a fine bird, he sings as he flies,
> He brings us good tidings, he tells us no lies;
> He sucks the sweet flowers to make his voice clear,
> And when he sings 'cuckoo' the summer draws near.

The Wise Men of Gotham, in Lincolnshire, incidentally, built a hedge around the cuckoo in an attempt to preserve eternal spring; so, too, did the men of Gorran, Towednack and Zennor.

There was a once-popular game in Cornwall called ' Robin's Alight '. The players would sit round a fire and pass a stick, twisting and burning, between them; the person holding the stick when the flame died would be forced to pay a forfeit. A similar game was played in Scotland and it might in some way echo an old French belief in the ability of the robin to turn and roast itself when spitted. This last superstition also applied to the wren and it is the robin and the wren who are the main characters in Cornish birdlore. Once they were regarded as sacred birds and anyone who killed either of them would be shunned by his fellows. A writer in the early part of this century knew of parents who banned their children from playing with such a boy and abnormally small children were often accused of having killed a robin or a wren, or of destroying a nest, causing their growth to be stunted:

> Kill a robin or a wran,
> You'll never grow to be a man.

Lack of growth was just one misfortune that resulted from the heinous crime. One man who killed a robin as a boy held the small body in one of his hands – it shook to the end of his days, a constant reminder of the couplet:

> Strub a robin or a wran,
> You'll never prosper, boy nor man.

The power of the robin was held in some awe by the Cornish people and if one managed to get into a house, especially through a window, a resident was bound to die. The robin's red breast derives from Jesus's friendship with the little bird. When He was a child He fed it each day with crumbs, and years later, when the Crucifixion procession neared Calvary, the robin saw a thorn in Jesus's forehead. The bird picked it out with his beak and blood from the wound flowed onto his breast, staining it for ever. It was added that the robin joined with the angels in singing the Resurrection Song and this is probably why in west Cornwall the robin or, by its old name, the ruddock – was known as ' the saint '. A rhyme from Madron ran as follows:

Robin, St Ruddick, take care of your nuddick,
Against the cold winter comes on.
' I care not,' said he, ' how cold it may be,
I'll creep in somewhere and keep myself warm
And put my bill under my wing.'

As well as being saintly, the robin was thought to be a glutton, eating twice his own weight every day. A rhyme with the concluding couplet:

He ate the church and then the steeple,
And if he wasn't shot he'd 've ate the people!

perhaps offered an excuse to the brave man who chanced to kill him.

Although the wren has been equated with the robin in later years, the bird was once the object of a brutal ritual. The ceremony of Hunting the Wren still survives in Wales, Ireland and the Isle of Man, and in Cornwall it continued until this century as a general ' bird-shoot ', on St Stephen's Day, when it was unwise to be out in the lanes, with guns being fired indiscriminately. It was explained as punishment for the wren, because he woke St Stephen's guards as the saint was about to make his escape from captivity. A second explanation is that when St Paul was converted, the evil side of his character took refuge in the body of a wren. Since then the birds have become so vicious that, unless they were killed, they would destroy every creature smaller than themselves.

Cornwall also has its superstitions about these ' victims ' of the wren – insects, spiders and snails. When moths are flying, news may be expected and when fleas bite the dangerously ill they will recover their health. The first butterfly to be killed each year brings ill luck to the killer, but crickets around a house carry good fortune with them; when they leave, though, the householder should beware.

Concern about earwigs is commonplace and the Cornish kill them at every opportunity, since they are alleged to drive a man insane if they get inside his ears. Luck will follow if a swarm of bees settles near a house: the owner may throw a handkerchief over them and claim them as his own. To sell bees, however, is unlucky, but a swarm in May will mean a new lamb is to be born. The insides of beehives should be scrubbed with elderflowers to prevent a new swarm from leaving and honey must be collected on the feast day of St Bartholomew, the patron saint of bees. Ants, or *muryan*, embody either the souls of unbaptized children or those of transformed piskies, and a piece of tin placed in their nests at a certain phase of the moon is supposed to change to silver.

In some parts of Cornwall, spiders were never killed, as one was believed to have spun a web over the baby Jesus to hide Him from Herod. Elsewhere, though, they were not so lucky. In Redruth, for instance, to cure whooping-cough, the unfortunate spider was tied inside a nut-shell and suspended from the suffering child's neck. As the spider's life ebbed away, the disease diminished.

In an earlier chapter we noted the Cornish miner's respect for snails. This feeling though, was by no means restricted to the mining community and snails were generally regarded as lucky charms. Children would greet them with a rhyme:

> Snail, snail, come out of your hole,
> Or I will beat you black as a coal.

If the snail condescended to appear, he would be picked up and wished upon. Particularly lucky was a variety of snail with a striped shell, possibly an edible species known to the Romans. When found, it was thrown backwards over the finder's head, accompanied by this rhyme:

> Lucky snail, lucky snail, go over my head
> And bring me a penny before I go to bed.

It is worth mentioning in this connection a dance performed by the villagers of Roche, in central Cornwall, until early this century. The dancers followed the village band and pranced in a decreasing circle, until the band cleverly swung around to unravel the knot. The dance was called ' The Snail's Creep '.

We now turn to flowers and trees. At one time, all tasks of great importance were prefaced by invocations. As the Christian faith gained ground, these pleas to the spirit world were replaced by Latin prayers: *In nomine Patris et Filii et Spiritus Sancti.* In Cornwall, the old incantations became known as ' nominys '. Here is one:

Old man Dumbledeed
Tilled his garden full of seed,
When the seed beginned to grow
Like a garden full of snow,
When the snow beginned to melt
Like a garden full of silk,
When the silk beginned to fly
Like an eagle in the sky,
When the sky beginned to roar
Like a lion at my door,
When my door beginned to creak
Like a stick put 'bout my back,
When my back beginned to smart
Like a penknife through my heart,
When my heart begins to bleed
That's the time for sowing the seed.

Many plants possessed strange qualities. Arum – or ' trumpet'
– lilies were known as ' Devil's Candles ' and were thought to be
very unlucky, perhaps because of their association with funerals.
Blackberry stains could not be washed out until the season was
over, but a good crop of berries foretold a fine herring season.
To bring may-blossom, furze or blackthorn indoors was tempting
fate and as the spikes of a cactus grew so did one's troubles. In
Zennor, a certain cure for blackheads was to crawl nine times
around a bramble bush. Pleasant dreams were the result if myrtle
was placed under the pillow, but to transport barley meant a death
in the family. Following death, as mentioned earlier, indoor plants
would be put in mourning and swathed in black crêpe; otherwise
they too would drop their heads and die.

Around Liskeard and Landrake, young girls arose early on
May morning to pick bracken. Then they walked to the neighbouring farms and, if they had a frond long enough to cover the cream
bowl, they were given slices of bread and cream, after reciting
this rhyme:

Here's a fern
To measure your shern [cream vessel],
Please give me some milk and cream.

Girls believed that their complexions could be improved by
rubbing their skins with leaves of the wild strawberry. This tra-

ditional cosmetic is recalled in a fragment of old folk song collected in 1698, another example of the few preserved in the
Cornish language:

> *Pelea era why moaz moz, fettow teag,*
> *Geu agaz bedgeth twin, ha agaz blew mellyn?*
> *Mi a moaz tha'n venton, sarra wheag,*
> *Rag delkiow sevi gwra muzi teag.*

Sadly, it proves in translation to be little more than a variant
of the widespread English song, ' Dabbling in the Dew ' :

> Pray whither so trippingly, pretty fair maid,
> With your face rosy white and your soft yellow hair?
> Sweet sir, to the well in the summer-wood shade,
> For strawberry leaves make the young maiden fair.

Another song, taken down from a very old Constantine man
in 1930, extols the pleasures of working close to nature and is
very similar to ' The Woodcutter ', a Sussex harvest-home song:

> Here's to the jolly furze-cutter
> Who does his work with ease,
> He goes to work when he minds to
> And leaves off just when he please.

It was unlucky, though, to cut elder-blossom without seeking
permission from the tree itself and to grow an elder in one's own
garden brought doom to the family. Even today the elder is not
a popular tree, possibly because it was once esteemed by witches.
Elms, too, have a peculiar reputation. Near the lychgate at Mylor
Church are three, and not many years ago the local children would
walk around them nine times with the sun; they would then press
their ears against the tree nearest to Mylor Bridge and hear the
Devil himself, roaring in Hell. Elms on the road between St
Austell and Pentewan were said to march around their field each
time the clock struck twelve, until they were felled in 1910.

Ash trees were noted for their curative powers, particularly
against childhood ailments. Robert Hunt actually saw a child passed
naked through a cleft ash; if the two parts of the tree reunited,
the child would recover, but only if he were washed in dew
collected from the branches on three successive mornings. If a

child was beaten with an ash stick, he would stop growing. Hernia could allegedly be cured by crawling through an ash sapling before sunrise and fasting: modern doctors may hold quite different views. A rhyme summed up the power of the ash:

> Even ash, I thee do pluck,
> Hoping thus to meet good luck;
> If no luck I get from thee,
> I shall wish thee on the tree.

In Looe and other east Cornwall villages, oak leaves were worn on 29 May to celebrate Royal Oak Day. Anyone who failed to display a leaf was spat upon. One tree that must have been detested by women was the walnut, for beneath it wives were traditionally beaten:

> A spannel, a wife and a walnut-tree,
> The more you beat 'em the better they be.

In 1902 a visitor to Looe asked a local woman to walk with her through the woods to visit a friend. The woman declined, saying, ' It is the twenty-first of the month and I daren't go through the woods.' When asked why not, she replied, ' Things is said, I should hear all my future and my friends' futures whispered in the trees, indeed I daren't, Miss.' A maidservant in the house also refused to enter the woods on that day. The significance of the date is long since lost, but the whispering forest possibly recalls an ancient reverence for the trees.

It is said that ' Cornwall will stand a shower every day and two for Sundays ', and many unfortunate holidaymakers will probably agree. Cornwall's weatherlore is much concerned with its environment, its animals and birds. A rhyme says, with some justification:

> If the Lizard's clear,
> Rain is near.

while another warns of the treacherous coastline:

> From Padstow Point to Lundy Light
> Is a watery grave by day or night.

The scarlet pimpernel is known as ' the poor man's weather-glass ', for it opens before a dry spell and closes when rain is due. A cock crowing near a house is a sign of good weather, as is a braying donkey; and when a cat washes its face ' over ear ', the skies will be ' fair and clear '. When the cat is running wildly about he has ' a storm in his tail ' and if he sits back to the fire, a frost should be expected. When rooks fly low, watch for rain clouds but if they dart down and fly excitedly, a wind is brewing. Until quite recently beetles were never killed in the St Neot district, because killing them would bring rain. The children, however, liked to torment one red-bellied species with the cry; ' Show your blood, or else I'll kill you! ' The insect would sprawl clumsily in its efforts to escape and usually satisfied its persecutors' demands by rolling onto its back and displaying its red abdomen.

The fishermen of Mevagissey would describe drying clothes waving in the heat of a cottage fire as ' John Liddicoat's cobwebs ' and always expected a gale. Liddicoat is one of the oldest surnames in the Mevagissey area and still survives in nearby Gorran. During a thunderstorm, Ludgvan folk opened all the doors of their houses to let the lightning in and so bring them prosperity. The harvest would not ripen until lightning had flashed, but it was considered dangerous to stand under a whitethorn tree during a storm.

Rainbows were prophetic for farmers, as :

> A Rainbow in the morn, put your hook in the corn;
> A rainbow in the eve, put your hook in the sheave,

and for fishermen :

> Rainbow to windward, foul fall the day;
> Rainbow to leeward, damp runs away.

The unsettled weather in May was summed up neatly in the rhyme :

> Let May come early or late,
> 'Twill make the old cow's tail to shake.

The moon was recognized in old Cornwall as a weather prophet :

> A fog and a small moon
> Bring an easterly wind soon.

It was also advisable to cut one's hair by the growing moon; if it was on the wane, baldness would soon follow. The Gorran men once attempted to trap the moon's reflection in a bucket and throw it over a cliff, having decided that it was responsible for the bad weather. Here is confirmation of the Cornish saying that ' those that are weather-wise are rarely otherwise '.

The Cornish landscape, with its backbone of high granite, is punctuated by strange rock formations and prehistoric constructions. The circles and cromlechs are thought to be mainly the work of early pre-Celtic settlers in Cornwall, probably their temples and burial places. But local legends will always ignore the expert and the fantastic stories attached to the stones are more attractive than the guesswork of historians. The commonest tales concern the county's numerous standing stones. Where these form a circle – at Boscawen-Un in Penwith, for example – the name Nine Maidens is often given to them. One school of thought regards this as a translation of the Cornish *Naw Men* [nine stones], but as the number is rarely nine, a more likely origin is *Maidn Nun* [moorland stones]. Legends, however, suggest otherwise.

The Nine Maidens are the remains of young ladies who broke the Sabbath law against dancing and were turned to stone for their trouble. At Boleigh, near Land's End, the stone circle consisting of 19 stones is called the Merry Maidens and two other stones, standing apart, the Pipers. Originally, only the Pipers stood there and, on certain nights when the moon was full, they came alive and played a fascinating tune on their pipes. A curse fell upon anyone who heard them, so the field in which they stood was avoided as often as possible. One night though, 19 maidens from the local village dared each other to enter the field. Soon, they were all inside, the pipes began their melody and, as the girls danced, they changed into the stone pillars we can see today. A party from the village found them on the following morning, but still, under a full moon, they all revive to dance once again. The Hurlers, a group of stones near Liskeard, were also once human. They chose to play at the Cornish sport of hurling on the Sabbath and met the same fate as the female sinners of Boscawen-Un. The idea of petrification as a form of damnation is not, of course, confined to Cornwall and, for example, similar stories relate to the Somerset stone circle of Stanton Drew.

The maidens, hurlers and their pipers are not the only living stones in Cornwall. The Twelve O'Clock Stone, on Trink Hill in

Nancledra, takes its name from the sun striking on its side at midday, forming a rough sundial; but when the stone ' hears ' a cock crowing it turns itself around. A boulder at Looe, now under water, was called the Cock Crow Stone, for whenever a cock crowed on nearby Hay Farm it turned three times. The same tale was told of the top stone of the Cheesewring, that odd, but apparently natural, formation near Liskeard. In appearance, the Cheesewring is so curious, the smaller stones at the bottom, spreading into a bulbous middle, then lessening in size at the top, that a local quarryman in the last century was convinced that it must be a direct result of the Deluge. In Padstow, Marazion, St Ives and Polperro, roof tiles wake up and roam about at midnight, as do stone eagles from a Launceston house. The stone balls on the gate posts at Trereife knock together when the clock strikes twelve and of similar stones at Heligan House, near Mevagissey, the seat of the Tremayne family, it was said :

> When they stone balls see Squire Tremayne
> They jump on the ground and then back again.

Even the red lion outside an inn in St Columb Major walks at midnight, although this could be strictly in the minds of the clientele!

Above Porthcurno Beach, at Treryn on the Land's End peninsula, stands the most famous Logan Stone in Cornwall. Logan stones are boulders placed so precariously that they rock gently when touched, yet are notoriously difficult to actually dislodge. An old story at Treryn suggested that the stone was once used as a form of court, for no criminal could make it rock. In 1824 a naval lieutenant and 12 of his comrades disproved the notion of the Logan Stone's immovability by pushing it onto the beach below, but the local outcry was so fierce that he was forced to restore it at his own expense. Nevertheless, it has not rocked so freely since. When another Logan stone, at Temple on Bodmin Moor, is touched at midnight the ghost of a black bull appears.

The name Men-an-Tol, given to a stone in Madron parish, means ' the holed stone ' and aptly describes this ring of granite set between two upright pillars. The stone acted as a universal panacaea and, even today, it is believed to be used occasionally. Robert Hunt tells of naked children being passed through it three times, then rubbed on the grass thrice against the sun, as a cure for scrofula; rickets, too, vanished under its influence. Possibly its original purpose was astronomical, as it could have been used to sight the sun, but in later years it was strictly medicinal or prophetic. Adults would squeeze through it to rid themselves of spinal disorders and rheumatism – a ' kill-or-cure ' method, perhaps. If two brass pins were laid across each other on the top edge of the stone, any question was supposed to be answered by the pins' movements under a hidden force. Another boulder, the Crick Stone in Morvah, was used in a similar way to the Men-an-Tol and cured back pains, while the Tolven Stone, near Helford, may have been seen as a birth symbol: to squeeze through it naked ensured fertility.

Cromlechs, or quoits, like those at Lanyon and Trethevy, are the bare remains of prehistoric burial chambers. In popular opinion though, they are quoits once used by playful giants and any recesses in them were caused by the giants' fingers. Two cavities near Boscawen-Un are their footprints and nearby pillars mark their graves. Lanyon Quoit, presumably after the giants had tired of it, was used as a dining-table by Arthur, as well as a group of Saxon kings. Merlin prophesied that a similar gathering would occur there immediately prior to the end of the world, a tale similar to that told of Table Mên, on Land's End. In east Cornwall an extensive earthwork is known as the Giant's Hedge, but a rhyme suggests an alternative builder:

> One day the Devil, having nothing to do,
> Built a great hedge from Lerryn to Looe.

On another occasion the Devil challenged a St Mabyn smith to a trial of strength and skill. The smith suggested that they should see who would be the faster to plough a two-acre field adjoining the smithy. A master of gamesmanship, the smith littered his opponent's path with obstacles and the Devil needed a whetstone time and again. Eventually, he wearied of the unequal struggle and threw his whetstone at the smith. It missed, but landed upright in the soil. As long as it remained there the Devil stayed away from St Mabyn, but one day a Trebetherick farmer knocked it down and the arch-fiend returned to haunt the district. To prove the story, the whetstone was made of granite, while the local stone is friable slate; allegedly, four granite gate-posts still remain in the vicinity.

Witches are also recalled by some of Cornwall's old monu-

K

ments. The Crowz-an-Wra, near St Buryan, means, simply, 'the witch's cross' and at Lewannick is 'Joan's Pitcher', a wishing well perhaps perpetuating the name of a sorceress. The ghost of old Bessy Benarth, a Roseland hag, haunts the crossroads named after her. Near Zennor, a rock formation called the Witch's Rock once marked the Midsummer Eve meeting-place of Cornish covens, and touching the stone nine times at midnight was regarded as an insurance against misfortune. One Land's End witch who may have known the stone was old Madgy Figgy. She would sit in the chair-shaped rock bearing her name, near Tol-Pedn-Penwith, whenever a shipwreck was imminent, gloating and rubbing her hands. When the doomed ship struck she would fly from her chair on a stalk of ragwort and hover over the sea, watching the wreckers awaiting their prize. Once, though, when an Indiaman was wrecked, Madgy Figgy met her match. The body of a woman was washed ashore, adorned with jewels of every type. Madgy claimed the body as her share of the pickings; she took the jewellery and buried the corpse on the cliff. That night a light appeared in the cove, settled on the grave, then moved along to the witch's chair. Each night the light reappeared until a foreigner came to Tol-Pedn-Penwith. Using sign-language, he demanded to be shown the graves from the recent wreck and he sat by them through the day. When night came the weird light shone even brighter than before and it led the stranger to Madgy's hut, where it settled on the chest containing the dead woman's jewels. Madgy Figgy opened the chest and handed the valuables to her unwelcome guest, saying: 'One witch always knows another, dead or living.'

A strange story told of Ludgvan describes how the local stream ran with wine on a certain day of the year. One old woman desperately wanted to see this miracle for herself but peeping from her window she broke the spell forever. We have already noted Roche Rock in the story of Tregeagle, but this huge mound, spiralling from a flat heath, is truly one of the wonders of mid-Cornwall. One could imagine it as a place of religious significance but the only story attached to it is a sad one. The tiny hermitage on the peak of the rock is said to have been the final refuge of a leper, the last member of the Tregarrick family, supported in his hideous existence by a devoted daughter, who each day brought him water from a now-vanished well beneath the Rock.

Along the coastline, more stories exist. The Irish Lady, a rock near Land's End, takes its name from the sole survivor of a shipwreck whose ghost appears on the rock with a rose held in her teeth. Bodrugan's Leap, near Mevagissey, marks the spot where Sir Henry Bodrugan, a supporter of the House of York during the Wars of the Roses, jumped into a boat bound for France when pursued by his Lancastrian enemies. When the boat was far enough from shore, Bodrugan cursed the descendants of his tormentors, Trevanion and Edgecumbe. Perhaps the curse worked, for where are the families now? An old saying suggested that the impossible would be resolved when ' the Rame Head and Dodman meet ' and people like to say that it happened when Sir Piers Edgecumbe purchased both promontories.

As we have seen, the Land's End peninsula contains many ancient earthworks and stones. Carn Kenidzhek [the hooting cairn], on the road between St Just and Penzance, is such a place, so-called because the wind whistles among its rocky crags. When two miners were returning from work late one night, they passed it and found another reason for its name. As they came under the shadow of the hill they heard a low moaning which increased to a shriek when a mysterious light shone through the darkness. In the glow, the terrified miners saw a horse and rider ascending Carn Kenidzhek towards a party of what appeared to be demons. When he reached them, the rider threw off his black cape to reveal himself as the Devil. He and his companions began to stage a wrestling match, and during the first bout a demon was flung against a rock. As he seemed to be seriously hurt, the compassionate miners ran to him and whispered a prayer in his ear. At once the earth shook and the fiendish party disappeared into a black cloud, leaving the two miners to wait for the dawn. Fear of Carn Kenidzhek as the haunt of Satan still existed at least until the middle of the last century.

Throughout the county, there are legends of secret gold hidden beneath old monuments. The Men Scryfa, an inscribed stone in Madron parish, carried such a story and something over a hundred years ago a local man determined to test it. He kept dreaming of a crock of gold under the stone and eventually dug a pit around its base, but the stone collapsed into the pit face downwards and only in recent years has it been restored to its rightful position. The unfortunate searcher discovered no gold, but a legend at Rillaton, near the Cheesewring, may have had a basis in fact. In ancient times a Druid priest is supposed to have lived at Rillaton and would sit on the rocks, in a place still known as the Druid's Chair, offering wine from a golden goblet to passing travellers and huntsmen. However often he offered the cup, it never emptied, until a party of hunters came by from chasing a wild boar over Trewartha Marsh. One man, in a fit of bravado, declared he would empty the cup. He drank and drank to no avail. At last he threw the remains of the wine into the Druid's face and rode off. His horse slipped and plunged over a precipice, killing itself and rider. The man was buried where he fell, still holding the cup. In 1818 excavations near Rillaton unearthed a skeleton, some Bronze Age pottery, a bronze dagger and a golden goblet. The Rillaton Cup is now kept in the British Museum.

8 The Balladeers

CORNWALL ONCE POSSESSED MANY WANDERING BALLADEERS, or 'droll-tellers', who composed songs and poems in traditional style and usually earned their livings as tinkers. They had largely disappeared by the middle of the nineteenth century, although one of their obvious descendants survived until 1974. Bill Chubb of Liskeard obtained a pedlar's licence in 1907, and worked through his life as an umbrella-man and knife-grinder, alternating his tasks with songs and stories. He was also a well-known seer, with a run of successful racing predictions to his credit, but his assertion that the world would end in 1968 lost him some support.

Bill Chubb was a popular man, and his predecessors among the old balladeers also enjoyed the warmth and friendship of their fellow Cornishmen. They wandered around the villages, where they were welcomed at each house, and a meal and a bed could always be found for them. Their rent was seldom more than a song or a story, perhaps with an odd-job completed as an extra token of gratitude. Cornish tradition suggested that the tinker was obliged to wander for his living because he had made nails for the Crucifixion, but whatever the reasons, the travels of the old droll-tellers gave them a wide knowledge of the people and places on their routes. Jim Thomas tells of the Wren family from a village near Camborne, whose sons all married young and happily. The daughters, though, were less fortunate, and finding them husbands proved a difficult task, so a local rhymester produced this verse:

> There is a maid in our town, her name is Jinny Wran;
> She flies about from twig to twig, and looks so very grand.
> Her crinoline is five yards round, her frock and cape to match,
> And on her darling little head she's got a lovely thatch.

One of Cornwall's most famous balladeers was Richard Nan-collas of St Austell, known as 'Rhyming Dick'. He roamed through all the western counties, singing at alehouses and festivals, composing verses to celebrate local events. A pamphlet printed towards the end of the eighteenth century described him as a 'marvellously fruitful genius'; just before his death in 1802, he grew tired of travelling and turned to the church.

'Uncle' and 'Aunt' were terms used commonly by the younger people of old Cornwall to describe their respected elders. 'Uncle' Anthony James of Cury was a blind ex-soldier who travelled in west Cornwall, accompanied by a boy fiddler and a dog, singing traditional ballads, and songs of his own composition. When he boarded at a house, he usually slept until supper time, and then, after a small meal, began singing, mostly long ballads such as 'Chevy Chase' or 'The Unquiet Grave'. Robert Hunt notes that he had 'a knack of turning Scotch and Irish songs into Cornish ditties', and few realized that they were often listening to his own works. A particularly clever transcription was his reworking of 'Barbara Allen':

> In Cornwall I was born and bred,
> In Cornwall was my dwelling;
> And there I courted a pretty maid,
> Her name was Ann Tremellan.

We have heard more than one Cornish traditional singer include

'Ann Tremellan' in their repertoires, so the efforts of Uncle Anthony have not been forgotten.

Anthony sang religious songs, too, but avoided the Methodists, who disliked his art. His own beliefs included a keen awareness of witchcraft, and his tales often contained supernatural elements. Many of his stories described witches' spells and the power of the narratives owed much to his own belief in them.

Possible the most versatile of west Cornwall's rhymesters in the early nineteenth century was Billy Foss, or Frost, of Sancreed, variously described as a blacksmith, clock-cleaner and stone-cutter. His rhymes were spare, sometimes insulting, but they resembled traditional verse and upset the more genteel of his contemporaries. Some of them survived for many years, passed from hand-to-hand on scraps of paper. One, given by Bottrell in a slightly different version, was headed ' A Little Poetry by " Billy Frost ", formerly a St Just Blacksmith ', and libelled an inhospitable Penwith farm:

> As I traversed Boslow I saw an old cow,
> A hog and a flock of starved sheep;
> Besides an old mare, whose bones were so bare
> As to make its poor master to weep.

> A few acres of ground as bare as a pound,
> An old house ready to fall;
> Therein was no meat, for the people to eat,
> And that was the worst of them all.

> No crock, pan or kittle, no goods much or little,
> Was there in the old house;
> No table or chairs, nor bedding upstairs,
> Not as much as to cover a louse.

> No grass for the flocks, but a carn of dry rocks
> Which afforded an horrible sight.
> If you pass that way, you must do so by day,
> For you'd scat [knock] out your brains in the night!

Billy Foss also composed epitaphs, but they were often as unkind as his secular poems; of an old St Just woman, for instance, he wrote:

> Beneath this stone lies a rotten body,
> The mortal remains of Betty Toddy.

His best-known talent, though, was as an impromptu poet, making instant rhymes to suit any occasion and to deflate any antagonist. In 1880, a Newlyn carpenter recalled an occasion many years before when Billy was asked by John Burt, then landlord of a beer shop, or 'kiddlywink', at Nancothan, to write an inn sign for him. Later, as Billy was passing the house, he noticed that some lesser man's work hung above the door. Turning to a companion, he said:

> I'll take no drink in your stinking old wink,
> Your heps and your door I decline;
> I'd had a pint of beer when I came along here,
> If thees' 'lowed me to paint thy sign.

Sometimes, Billy's verse prompted his colleagues to write lines in self-defence, and a travelling tailor called Lewis Grenfell once said of him:

> You go up and down from country to town,
> Cutting letters in wood and in stone;
> By your trade, though, you lose, for it won't find you shoes,
> And as for best clothes, you have none!

Billy Foss would not be defeated at his own game, and retorted:

> I'm honest, at least, for I still pay my debt,
> That's more than a tailor or miller's done yet.

In the 1930s, a very old lady from Treryn, in Penwith, remembered Billy helping a local farmer at harvest-time. Some boys made a rhyme about him:

> As I was walking on the road,
> I saw a mow fell all abroad;
> I'm sorry for the farmer's loss –
> The mow was made by Billy Foss.

Again, though, Billy would not be outdone:

The mow was made, and all complete;
It was a splendid row of wheat.
The rogues and thieves in Buryan Town,
They stole the sheaves, and the mow fell down.

On the one occasion when Billy failed to reply to a scathing rhyme, his wit saw him through. Another rhymester known as ' Blind Dick ' mocked Billy's fondness for dogs with a verse beginning:

I understand both night and day
Two dogs doth in thy bosom lay.

The piece went on to describe Billy as a drunken sot – a charge not confirmed elsewhere – and his friends were amazed Foss did not reply. Finally though, he produced his reason: ' Nobody of note ', said Billy, ' would think anything of a man who wrote such bad grammar – the word *lay* being in the past time when it intended to mean the present!'

There may still be people around Tregonebris, where he lived, who remember the name of Billy Foss, and a milestone which he cut still stands at nearby Crowz-an-Wra, but Billy's memory exists mainly in his verses. Perhaps the majority of them were ill-formed doggerel, but the best-known, about the Balleswidden Mine at St Just, displays a real talent:

And then they had an inyin [engine] good,
That draa'd the water like a flood,
And sucked right up the very mud
Of the Mine of Balleswidden.

Billy Foss's main rival as Cornwall's outstanding rhymester was Henry, or ' Henna ', Quick. Born in Zennor in 1792, he died in his home village at the age of 65, poverty-stricken and forgotten by those who had enjoyed his writings. In west Cornwall's farmhouses, it is still possible to discover Henna Quick's broadsheets, yellow with age, and perhaps including one of his riddles in verse. This example, written in 1852 to describe the death of a cat, shows a greater technique and vocabulary than Billy Foss possessed, but it has a similar native wit:

It happened at Towednack
Upon a certain day,
A white domestic animal
By death was turned to clay.

This animal four-footed were
And was of female kind;
She brought forth young ones every year,
Yet no fruit left behind.

With her sharp crooked teeth and nails
She oft would eat and slay,
And many Thieves or Robbers slew
When they came in her way.

She ever from her youthful days
Did seek to live on prey;
When people kissed her she turned wild
And from them ran away.

She from Goldsithney being brought
When nearly twelve months old,
Four years, five months and thirteen days
Death on her then laid hold.

The third part of her hindmost flesh
Death took nine months before,
But now she's buried in the dust
And feels the smart no more.

People now ignorant of the same
Unto me lend an ear,
Since you would wish to know her name –
See, it doth plain appear!

The last verse forms the acrostic ' PUSS '.

Henna Quick wrote of his parents:

My father laboured underground,
Mother the spinning-wheel put round.

He was, in fact, a man of his people, and yet he must have seemed strange to them. In bearing, voice and stature, he was effeminate, and only his mother was really close to him. When she died in 1843, he struggled on alone, in his own words ' as a water-wheel that had no stream and could not work '. Three years later, he married an elderly woman and enjoyed some comfort until her death four years before his own.

There are still poets and singers in Cornwall, although Liskeard's Bill Chubb was one of the last of the old-style storytellers. Here is Henna Quick's epitaph on his own way of life:

> The Cornish drolls are dead, each one;
> The fairies from their haunts have gone.
> There's scarce a witch in all the land,
> The world has grown so learn'd and grand.

9 Saints and Holy Wells

MANY YEARS AGO THE DEVIL DECIDED to avoid Cornwall as he had no wish to be made into either a squab pie or a saint, and that was the fate of anyone who ventured west of the Tamar. Many Cornish churches were founded between the fifth and eighth centuries, by missionaries from Ireland, Wales and Brittany, although only two of the original buildings now remain, the tiny oratories, or 'praying-places', in the sands at Gwithian and Perranzabuloe. Very few of the holy men were natives of Cornwall, though St Cuby, whose churches stand at Duloe and Tregony, was Cornish by birth. Most were 'voyagers from other parts of the Celtic world'.

Here, of course, we are less concerned with the saints' history than with the folklore that became attached to them, but their desire to christianize virtually everything in sight is of some importance in both fields. Springs, for instance, were regarded by the pagan Celts as objects of worship, so the saints built baptistries over them and they were changed into holy wells. Some of the saints themselves have very dubious backgrounds. St Merryn is a village in north Cornwall, but the church there is dedicated to St Marina, not to the seventh-century Celtic saint, known in north Wales as a disciple of St Comgall. St Dennis, too, a churchtown north of St Austell, has a patron of very obscure origins: far from being a saint, this Dennis could perhaps be a corruption of *dinas*, the Cornish for ' hill-fortress '.

Cornwall's patron saint is St Michael, a common name in the county hagiography and it is interesting that churches dedicated to the Archangel are quite often built in lofty places. In Cornwall this rule is strictly followed, St Michael's Mount being the obvious example among the older churches. In the thirteenth century pilgrims visited the Mount to be cured of blindness. St Michael also had a chapel on Looe Island and Charles Henderson points out that this must have resembled ' a miniature St Michael's Mount '. His name appears again in the tiny hermitage on Roche Rock and in the church at St Michael Caerhays, set on the peak of a steep hill. The old name for Caerhays was Lanvyghal [the church of St Michael]. There is a ruined chapel on Carn Brea, near Redruth, and, while it bears no known dedication, a field below the hill was noted in 1698 as Troose-Mehall, St Michael's Foot.

The saints often arrived in Cornwall by miraculous transportation. St Ia came to St Ives floating on a leaf which she had increased to enormous size by touching it with her staff. The tinners' saint, St Piran – possibly the Irish Kieran – sailed to his new home on a millstone. Some say that a huge skeleton found near Perranzabuloe could be his. When St Petroc landed at Trebetherick, after a more conventional journey, the local people were hostile and distrustful of his powers. He asked some harvesters for a drink, but they told him to get one for himself. At once he rapped his staff upon the ground and a fresh spring appeared; he quenched his thirst and the sceptics became his disciples. Petroc gave his name to Petroc-stow, since corrupted to Padstow, and to other villages in the same vicinity, like Little Petherick. His relics were taken to Bodmin, where the ancient reliquary is still preserved in the vault of a bank. Canon Doble considered the ivory casket, decorated with brass and gold, to be one of the most valuable religious antiquities in Britain.

Two holy men whose names appear regularly in Cornwall are St Mewan and St Issey. In Mevagissey they come together, the double dedication being a rarity in Cornwall. That part of the town where the church stands was formerly called Porthilly and a rhyme was made about the towerless church :

> Ye men of Porthilly, why were you so silly
> In having so little a power?
> You sold every bell, as Gorran men tell,
> For money to pull down your tower.

St Keverne, who lived on the Lizard peninsula, felt that the people showed him too little respect and declared that ' no metal will run within the sound of St Keverne's bells.' In fact, tin has never been discovered in the district. The most famous story of St Keverne concerns his quarrel with St Just, a very unholy gentleman. Just had visited his neighbour and, after a large meal, took his leave. But that was not all he took, for, immediately his guest had gone, Keverne noticed that a valuable chalice was missing from his cupboard. He ran after him, picking up stones from Crousa Downs as he went, and when he came near enough to the fleeing thief began to throw them at him. ' St Just ', says a writer, ' was too deeply absorbed in religious meditation to notice ' and simply kept on running. But eventually the shower of rocks came too close and Just dropped the chalice. Keverne retrieved it and returned to the Lizard. The stones remained where they had fallen and are said to have lain in a field near Germoe until the last century; the field was called Tremen-keverne [the three stones of Keverne]. They were finally broken up for road metal, suggesting that they were a type of gritstone common on Crousa Downs, but quite unknown around Germoe.

St Keyne was a very lovely maiden and retained her chastity by ' the strength of her purity '. She was also able to turn snakes into coils of stone. St Gundred was another virtuous lady. We have seen how a leper languished for years in Roche hermitage. Gundred was his daughter and she had a cell nearby and from it she tended her sick father.

One of the many saints whose name appears in both Cornwall and Brittany is St Mawes, known in Brittany as St Maudez, although there is a Cornish suggestion that he also appears there as St Malo. Mawes was the tenth son of an Irish king. His stone chair is still preserved in the wall of a St Mawes house. One day he was sitting there preaching when a noisy seal came out of the sea and interrupted his sermon. He was an irritable man and after a while he picked up a large rock and threw it at the animal. He missed, but the rock remains, lodged on top of the Black Rocks, half-way across Falmouth Harbour.

St Levan's church lies in a hollow of the granite uplands on Land's End, not far from the sea its patron saint loved. Levan was a keen angler and a rock on the south side of the church, to the left of the porch, once served as his seat when he returned from tiring fishing trips. Before he died Levan decided to leave a reminder of himself in his favourite resting-place, so he struck the rock with his fist and split it open, as it remains today. He prayed over it and prophesied:

> When with panniers astride,
> A pack-horse one can ride
> Through St Levan's Stone,
> The world will be done.

Robert Hunt, writing in 1881, considered that the stone must have been honoured for Levan's sake when the church was built, as it would otherwise have been used in the construction. He adds:

It is more than fifty years since I first made the acquaintance, as a child, with the St Levan Stone and it may be a satisfaction to many to know that the progress of separation is an exceedingly slow one. I cannot detect the slightest difference in the width of the fissure now and then. At the present slow rate of opening, the pack-horse and panniers will not be able to pass through the rock for many thousands of years to come. We need not, therefore, place much reliance on those prophecies which give a limited duration to this planet.

Levan existed on one fresh fish each day and refused to fast even on the Sabbath. One Sunday a local woman, Joanna, was in her garden, gathering herbs for her vegetarian diet when she saw the saint pass on his way to the beach. She hailed him, and rebuked him for breaking the Sabbath, but he retorted that fishing was no worse than gardening. Joanna insisted that Levan was doing wrong, so eventually he called her a fool, and said that any babies born in the parish and christened ' Joanna ' would grow up equally stupid. Since then there have been no Joannas in St Levan, but a patch of ground near the church is still known as Joanna's Garden. Another tale of Levan's fishing told how on one occasion he caught two bream on one hook. Only wanting his usual one, he threw them back, but the fish were determined to be caught and at last he decided to keep both. On arriving home he found his sister, Breage, waiting for him, with two hungry children. The saint cooked the two fish and the children began to eat them, but they were so ravenous that they omitted to remove the bones and choked. Until at least the 1930s bream were known as ' choke-children ' in west Cornwall.

Breage, or Breaca, thought by many Cornishmen to be St Levan's sister, is recalled in the village named after her on Mount's Bay. She, and the patron of a neighbouring village, occur in this saying translated from Cornish :

> Germoe a king,
> Breage a midwife.

In Germoe churchyard stands a three-roofed sedilia, known as St Germoe's chair and believed to be the saint's shrine. Whether Germoe was actually a king or a saint will never be known. There is a rhyme which goes :

> Germoe, little Germoe, lies under a hill,
> When I'm in Germoe I count myself well;
> True love's in Germoe, in Breage I've got none,
> When I'm in Germoe I count myself at home.

Many of the Cornish saints lived close to nature. St Piran's first disciples were said to be a badger, a bear and a fox. Two birds built their nest in St Keverne's hands while he was praying, and he refused to change his position until the chicks had hatched. St Endelenta lived entirely on a diet of cow's milk and died of grief when her faithful cow was killed by a local farmer. On her death-bed she asked that her body be drawn to the grave by six young bullocks. They pulled her over a miry hillside which be-became firm as she passed and there her church of St Endellion was established. Endelenta's sister, Menefreda, met the Devil. He appeared when she was combing her hair, but she flung the comb at him and he slipped down a hole in the cliffs, which can still be seen near the saint's home at St Minver.

When King Constantine of Cornwall was hunting deer, one of his prey took refuge in St Petroc's cell. Constantine was so impressed by the saints' power that he was converted to Christianity. His name survived near Padstow and on the Lizard peninsula.

St Ruan was a popular saint in west Cornwall, but in Brittany, where he was known as Ronan, he was once accused of being a werewolf: a woman said he had eaten her child. The local ruler suggested that he should be exposed to the royal wolfhounds, who would tear a werewolf to pieces. Ronan was exonerated and the child discovered unharmed.

In east Cornwall, the church of St Neot contains the finest stained-glass windows in the county. Some of the pictures show the saint's famous miracles, mostly involving animals and birds. Neot, so legend relates, was a dwarf scarcely 15ins tall, who spent his devotions immersed to the neck in a holy well. When a farmer was plagued by crows attacking his corn, Neot trapped the birds in an open-topped enclosure; they were unable to leave until the corn was reaped. An angel appeared to the little saint one day and showed him three fish in his well. He promised that so long as Neot ate only one fish each day their number would never decrease. Once, however, when the saint was ill, he sent a servant to the well, who brought back two of the fish and cooked them. When he discovered the error Neot prayed for forgiveness and ordered the dead fish to be thrown back into the well. As they touched the water they revived and swam with their fellow. When a fox ate a pair of his shoes, they were pulled intact from its mouth. Wild oxen loved the little saint and drew his plough when his own team was stolen.

The holy wells of the Cornish saints were probably originally wishing-wells venerated in pagan times. Some of the old beliefs lingered on until recent years and many of the wells were believed to hold waters of curative value. To St Cleer, for instance, came the lame and the blind for relief and on Ascension Day crippled children flocked to St Cubert, leaving their crutches by the well when they could walk again; the historian, Hals, wrote that ' the virtues of this water are very great '. Lady's Well, near Mevagissey, and Menacuddle, at St Austell, offered cures throughout the year, but the waters of Chapel Uny Well, in Sancreed, could heal wounds only on the first three Wednesdays of May. Richard Carew describes the powers of St Non's Well at Altarnun, where the insane were taken for their wits to be restored. These unfortunate people were placed with their backs to the

L

well, forced into the water by the village strong men and ' ducked ' until almost unconscious. They were then taken to the church where masses were sung over them.

Possibly the most renowned well in Cornwall was at Madron. In 1640 Bishop Hall of Exeter visited it and witnessed a man named John Trelille, who had been crippled for 16 years, ' suddenly so restored to his limbs, that [he was] able both to walk and to get his own maintenance '; the bishop added that he could find ' neither art nor collusion – the thing done, the Author invisible '. Trelille was paralysed after a game of football when he was 12 years old. At the age of 28 he dreamed of bathing in Madron Well and decided to test his dream. After dipping himself three times he slept on the marshy ground near the well, known as St Madern's Bed, and awoke restored. It did him only temporary good, unfortunately, since he was killed in action four years later, while fighting for the Royalists at Lyme in Dorset. In later years Wesleyans held Sunday morning services at Madron Well, and after the sermon pins or pebbles were thrown into the water while single men and women watched, looking for signs of an early wedding. Until recently rags were hung about the well and spat upon to protect the site from supernatural events.

In Colan, people visited St Nant's Well on Palm Sunday with money for the priest, and were given palm crosses which were thrown in to ensure long life. The waters of Bodmin Well could foretell the future. The field housing the chapel and well at Blisland is called Chapel Park and there is an old superstition that the land should never be cultivated for fear of some disaster befalling the local farmer. In 1878 corn was grown there, but during the harvest the farmer's son fell on a scythe, cutting his leg so severely that it had to be amputated. Another farmer, of Pelynt, decided to move the bowl of St Nun's Well to the foot of a hillside, for use as a cattle-trough. The morning after the basin had returned to its proper place. This happened three times and finally the oxen that had been used dropped dead and the farmer went mad. A similar tale is told of St Cuby's Well at Duloe. Near Helston a flock of crows removed all the stones from Wendron Church, leaving only the porch standing, to be used as a holy well.

Children took their dolls to be baptized at Figgy Dowdy's Well on Carn Marth Hill, near Redruth, and at a well in Morvah parish, but the waters of Ludgvan Well had a more sinister significance. Baptism there was a sure protection against being hanged.

When a local woman suffered this fate, there was great distress in the district, until it was proved that she had been christened in a neighbouring parish.

St Anne was known to 'intercede for the childless', and an oratory was built for her on the old bridge at Looe; a nearby well was believed to ensure fertility, a possible connection with the saint. Not far from Looe stands the well of St Keyne, found earlier this century to be a roughly arched basin full of stagnant water. This is Cornwall's most famous well, for its waters provided mastery in marriage. If a husband drank from it before his wife he would rule the household, but if the wife drank first she took the upper hand. Robert Hunt found a newly-wed couple there in 1881, but the well had earlier been immortalized in a ballad by Robert Southey, who concluded:

> I hastened as soon as the wedding was o'er
> And left my good wife in the porch,
> But i' faith she had been wiser than I
> For she took a bottle to church.

Young people still visit St Keyne's Well, but probably more from curiosity than belief.

10 The Year's Round

STRATTON'S OWN 'Carol of the Months' sets the scene for a year filled with traditional activity:

> January's when cold winds do blow,
> February brings us frost and snow,
> March is when young lambs do play,
> April brings us flowers so gay,
> May is when the fields are green,
> June is when new hay is seen,
> July's days are very warm,
> August brings the thunderstorm,
> September's harvest-fields are clear,
> October's when we brew fine beer,
> November's dreariest days in the year,
> December ends the fleeting year.

The Cornish year is marked out by fairs, or feast days, held in nearly every town and village, and usually falling on the local saints' days. Nowadays they are generally little more than minor funfairs, but until recent times they provided convenient occasions both for local craftsmen and itinerant pedlars to ply their trades. To signal the opening of a fair, gloves were suspended from high poles and, as holding a fair was regarded as a great honour, they were closely guarded by the villagers. However, if the gloves were taken away, the new owner had earned the right to hold his own fair and this apparently occurred in west Cornwall, where the fair transferred from Sithney, near Helston, to Gold-sithney, on Mount's Bay.

The fairs have deteriorated and in some cases vanished altogether, but the great May festivals of Padstow and Helston survive; in St Columb and St Ives, the hurlers play at the Silver Ball; Wassailers and ' Guizers ' continue their songs. All these events and many others form part of the year's round in Cornwall.

JANUARY

An old Cornish toast wished for a :

> Happy New Year
> And a young woman
> And plenty of money with your wife!

Wishes for good luck and prosperity are still a feature of New Year's Day and in Cornwall paying debts at that time is considered foolish, for to do so ensures a trail of payments throughout the year. Also, nothing must be taken from a house, but as much as possible brought in : even dust should be swept inwards and a nineteenth-century writer knew of money left on a windowsill over New Year's Eve and taken indoors on the following morning. A female must never be the first over the threshold on New Year's Day and sometimes young boys were paid nominal sums to cross the step before a lady. In some parts of Cornwall, boys were paid to sand the steps as early as possible, probably as an excuse to continue an old belief in women as New Year bearers of ill-luck: the boys would call at houses, asking to ' sand your step for good luck '.

Guizing, or ' geese-dancing', continued around Twelfth Night until very recently. The term ' guizing ', from which ' geese-dancing ' derives, describes the ancient practice of disguising traditional performers by blackening their faces or clothing them in a grotesque headgear, thus elevating them above ordinary mortals onto a supernatural plane. The Cornish letter s is commonly pronounced as z so ' geese-dancing ' reflects the same source. Until the last century the guizers were regular players all over Cornwall, performing a death-and-resurrection drama, usually involving St George and various adversaries, similar to mumming plays throughout England. Animal hides were sometimes worn and men clad in bullocks' skins took part in festivities on Land's End, while on the Isle of Scilly young men and women exchanged clothes and danced on the Monday after Twelfth Night, which was known as Plough Monday. This is interesting, as the tradition of women's exclusion for mumming is most persistent and active female participation in any ceremony of this nature is unusual. The last New Year guizing in Cornwall was in St Ives, where men with darkened faces danced a type of processional Morris around the town until quite recently, although the original significance of rebirth and fertility had long since vanished.

On 7 January, St Distaff's Day, the islanders of St Agnes in the Scillies held a feast day to celebrate their benefactress, St Warna, whose well stands on the island. The well was thoroughly cleaned and guns were discharged above it to honour the saint, who was said to cause shipwrecks nearby, thus providing the people's only luxuries.

January was one of the months when Loe Bar, a sandbank near Helston separating Loe Pool from the sea, was ' cut '. Loe Pool, Cornwall's largest lake, lies at the confluence of the river Cober and other lesser streams and during winter, when floods were imminent, groups of local men would proceed to Penrose Manor and there present the lord with a leather purse containing three-halfpence in exchange for permission to cut the bar. They then dug a wide trench to allow the escape of the lake's excess water, which discoloured the sea for miles around. One writer of the last century claimed that sometimes this discolouration reached as far as the Scillies. Cornwall's last January festival fell on the 24th, Paul's Pitcher Day, described in an earlier chapter.

FEBRUARY

The Candlemas Fair at Looe inaugurated a very important month in the Cornish calendar and St Blaise's Day follows on the 3rd. This saint, the patron of St Blazey, was believed to cure toothache, sore throats and cattle diseases and candles are still lit to honour him in his village church. In St Ives, on Feast Monday in Candlemas Week, a modified version of the ancient Cornish game of hurling is still played. The game, as we shall see, is better preserved at St Columb Major, but the young people of St Ives still wait for the silver-coated wooden ball to be thrown, or 'dealt', from the parish-church wall by the mayor. It is then passed from hand to hand along the beach and through the streets, each player trying to score a 'goal' in one of two basketball nets. If there is no score at noon the holder of the ball takes the prize – a small sum of money.

In east Cornwall, Shrove Monday was known as 'Paisen Monday', from the habit of eating pea soup on that day. Elsewhere, it was known as 'Hall Monday' and there was a strange early evening custom, not unlike the schoolboy game of 'Knock Down Ginger'. Boys carrying short wooden clubs would roam the village streets knocking loudly at every door and running off quickly if any sounds came from within the houses. If none were heard, they took any objects lying near the houses and displayed them prominently in the village as evidence of their owners' carelessness. The time was known as 'Nicky-nan-night'. Similar customs existed in the Isles of Scilly and in Brittany, where the night was termed *Ninc-kyn-nan-neuf*.

On the following day, Shrove Tuesday, the 'nicky-nan' boys used their clubs again, but this time accompanied their knocking with a rhyme:

> Nick, nicky, nan,
> Give me some pancake and then I'll be gone.
> But if you give me none,
> I'll throw a great stone
> And down your door shall come.

In St Ives and elsewhere, boys walked the streets on Shrove Tuesday with stones tied to lengths of string, crying:

> Give me a pancake now, now, now,
> Or I'll bang in your doors with a row-tow-tow!

In Penzance, until the late nineteenth century, black-faced lads waited at street corners with sooty or greasy hands and tried to rub the faces of passers-by. In Landewednack, young children used to go from house to house begging for 'colperra' and expecting to receive either food – eggs, buns or apples – or money. The term is obscure, but might derive from the Cornish *collan-bara*, meaning a slice of bread, although an invocation from west Cornwall suggests something more sinister: ' Hen-cock, hen-cock, give me a tabban [morsel], or else Colperra shall come to your door!'

Cock-fighting once took place on Shrove Tuesday, and children would often shower the unsuspecting with water, or remove the gates from their neighbours' walls. The old custom of ' shackle-eggs', which still survives at Stoke St Gregory in Somerset, was also popular among Cornish schoolchildren. Each child carried an egg, with his or her name marked on it, to school and placed it with the others in a sieve; this was then shaken until one or more of the eggs cracked. The procedure was repeated until only one egg remained unbroken, when its owner was declared the winner and was crowned with a special cap. Obviously the teacher had to check that none of the eggs was hard-boiled! Eggs were also used for ' battles ', similar to ' conkers ', at St Columb. At noon on Shrove Tuesday the school children ' fought' by rapping their eggs one against another: again, the last to hold an intact egg was declared victor. To save a nasty mess, the schoolmistress held a bowl beneath the eggs while the battles were in progress and later used the contents to make pancakes. This careless use of eggs reflected their price at the time: three for one penny.

Egg battles seem insignificant in comparison with St Columb's other great Shrovetide game, the annual Hurling of the Silver Ball. In contrast to the Irish game in which a stick is used, it is more a type of traditional football, not unlike other games in Derbyshire, Northumberland, Durham and Dorset. Documented for over 400 years, St Columb preserves its heritage with two hurling matches each year, on Shrove Tuesday itself and on the following Saturday week.

Hurling was once played in virtually every town and village in Cornwall, usually in inter-town matches, and Carew, writing in 1602 describes it: ' The ball in this game may be compared to an infernal spirit; for whosoever catcheth it fareth straightways like a mad man, struggling and fighting with those that go about to hold him; and no sooner is the ball gone from him, but he resign-eth this fury to the next receiver and himself becometh peace-able as before.' However, it appears that few players were badly injured and a motto used on several hurling balls was taken seriously: the Cornish *Guare wheag yn guare teag* means ' Fair play is good play.' Carew describes two types of hurling, ' Hurling to Goal' and ' Hurling to Country '. In the former, the players won by scoring a goal, while Hurling to Country meant carrying the ball outside the parish boundary. Twice, exhibitions of hurling were held in London, in 1654 with Cromwell among the spectators and later during the reign of Charles II. The game declined in the last century because of the influence of Wesleyan Methodism, but in St Columb it maintained its traditional hold, largely, according to a contemporary source, through the interest taken in it by *The West Briton*, an influential local newspaper.

Today's games combine the two styles described by Carew with Hurling to Country regarded as an acceptable manner of winning if scoring a goal is impossible, and the teams are made up of men – and, in the last few years, women – living in the town itself and those from the surrounding parish. The ' goals ' – shallow troughs, probably the remains of cross-bases – stand approximately two miles apart: the ' Town ' goal is situated at Cross Putty to the south and the ' Country ' goal at Tregamere to the north. Each game begins at 4.15 pm with the ball ' dealt ', or ' thrown up ', from a step-ladder in the Market Square by either a local dignitary or a specially invited visiting celebrity. More than 1,000 people take part and St Columb on hurling days resembles a town under siege, with all the shop-windows barricaded. The ball is about the size of a cricket ball, consisting apple wood coated with silver gilt; the motto around the centre reads :

> Town and Country do your best,
> For in this Parish I must rest.

The rhyme took a sad twist a few years ago when the ball was stolen by a ' foreigner '. When a hurling match is completed, either by a goal scored or by the ball being carried outside the parish, the players return to the Market Square for ' Town Ball ' or ' Country Ball ' to be declared, and the individual winner is carried off in triumph. The town inns, one of which was recently renamed The Silver Ball, then either celebrate or condole and ' The Hurling Song ' is sung :

> For we roll, we roll the Town [or Country] Ball along,
> And we roll, we roll the Town Ball along,
> And we roll, we roll the Town Ball along,
> And we all come marching home.

Hurling is a test of strength and skill and passing the ball between the players was said to bring good luck to whoever touches it. Once the coating was of gold, only replaced by silver as the latter was cheaper and occasionally mined in Cornwall itself.

Shrovetide precedes Lent and in east Cornwall, at the beginning of the Lenten period, a straw figure clad in rags and known as 'Jack o' Lent' was, until about the middle of the last century, dragged through the streets of each village and afterwards burnt, shot at, or hanged. A slovenly person was often called a 'Jack o' Lent', but the Cornish image was said locally to represent Judas Iscariot.

MARCH

March and April lack much traditional activity in Cornwall. On 1 March people were up before sunrise to sweep fleas from the front-door steps. A similar custom was observed in Carmarthenshire, where it was thought to mark St David's Day. The beginning of March saw the two tinners' festivals described earlier – St Piran's Day and the First Friday in Lide. St Piran's Day was especially important to the miners as a time for celebration and the date is still remembered by traditional feasts in parts of the United States. On 9 March a fair used to be held in Constantine, near Padstow, distinguished by banquets of limpet pies; a hurling match was also part of the entertainment, with a ball presented by the owner of Harlyn, a nearby manor house.

APRIL

As elsewhere, April Fool's Day was celebrated in Cornwall, especially by schoolchildren. Often they would send their fellows to bring them 'a penn'orth of pigeon's milk' or 'memory powder', or ask them to deliver notes telling the recipients to 'send the fools farther'. A boy who succeeded in fooling another would shout: 'Fool! Fool! The cuckoo!'

The Easter period began with numerous customs, starting at Polperro on Palm Sunday when local apprentices were given a day's holiday to visit their parents. At Little Colan, near Newquay, on the same day, the villagers went to St Nant's Holy Well and dropped palm crosses in the water; if a cross sank, its owner could expect an early death. On Holy Thursday, the young people of Roche visited their holy well, where the throwing of pins determined the identity of their future lovers. Good, or 'Goody',

Friday was a day for relaxation and parties of picknickers visited their favourite haunts. It was also a day when shellfish were traditionally collected and oysters from the Helford River were a particular delicacy. Gardeners always sowed their seeds on Good Friday and, strangely, it was believed to be the only day of the year when young ravens were hatched. Hot-cross buns were the children's favourites, with saffron as a special Cornish ingredient. There was a large Good Friday fair at Perranporth.

In Polperro, on Easter Day, it was once the custom to rise very early to 'see the sun dance'. A strange custom was once observed in Lostwithiel, although it disappeared long ago. A 'mock prince' chosen from among the town's freeholders was paraded through the streets dressed in full regalia. He was led to the parish church to hear the service read with great ceremony, then taken to a previously selected house for a banquet. After the meal the 'prince' reverted to his normal standing in the town. It is said that the ritual was a throwback to the times when a real prince ruled at nearby Restormel Castle and Lostwithiel was an important town in Cornwall.

On Easter Monday St Day Fair was held and the working folk of Penzance played at 'lilly-bangers', a dice game held out of doors, usually for prizes of gingerbread cakes and crockery. The second Monday and Tuesday after Easter, Hocktide, was a time for traditional sports and 'binding', or the payment of rents and other debts. Wrestling is a favourite Cornish sport and Hocktide was one occasion when the wrestlers showed their skill. The poet, Chatterton, wrote in the eighteenth century:

> The Saxonne warryer that did so entwyne,
> Like the nesh bryon and the eglantine,
> Or Cornish wrastlers at a hocktyde game.

Towednack Fair is held at the end of the month on the nearest Sunday to 28 April; it formerly included a procession through the streets headed by a fiddler, or 'crowder'.

Throughout Cornwall, on 30 April, the towns and the villages danced to the music of fiddle and drum, while the taverns enjoyed a good trade. The houses were decorated with whitethorn ('May') and other greenery in readiness for the morning's festivities. In Padstow, the townspeople begin preparing for their May Day several days in advance. They practise their dance and song on the quayside and decorate the streets with flags and flowers;

they erect a Maypole in Broad Street, not far from the traditional siting at a cross-roads, and, just before Midnight on 30 April, they assemble outside the Golden Lion Inn. There, as May Day strikes, the night singing begins and Padstow's Obby Oss ceremony is under way.

MAY

The night-singing at Padstow is an experience that can only be appreciated by those who have taken part in it. No-one could fail to be impressed by the haunting air sung in the pitch-dark by massed, unaccompanied voices and the sheer pleasure in the performance. The people – many of them emigrant Padstonians returned especially for May Day – begin their song as May morning opens. They sing first to the landlord of the Golden Lion Inn :

> Rise up, Mr Hawken, and joy to you betide,
>   For summer is acome unto day.
> And bright is your bride that lies down by your side,
>   In the merry morning of May.

Then they set off on their long trek through the town, stopping at certain houses to sing verses appropriate to the occupants. A young girl is greeted :

> Rise up, Miss —— , all in your smock of silk,
> And all your body under as white as any milk.

While a rich man is exhorted thus :

> Rise up, Mr —— , I know you well afine,
> You have a shilling in your purse and I wish it was in mine.

As each verse is sung the person summoned by the words comes to his or her window to wave at the night singers, until, at about 2 am, the choir disbands and its members trudge wearily – and, often, unsteadily – home, for a short sleep in preparation for May Day proper.

The central figure in Padstow's May ceremony is, of course, the hobby horse, or Obby Oss, a grotesque and frightening creature portrayed by a man in a bulbous black cape, topped by a ferocious mask. There are, in fact, two hobby horses, as well as the ' Boys' Osses ', or ' Colts '. Today the Blue Ribbon Oss appears first, on the Institute Steps at 10 am, but it is not until an hour later, when the Old (Red Ribbon) Oss dances from its traditional 'stable' at the rear of the Golden Lion, that the atmosphere in Padstow becomes truly electric. Each horse is accompanied by its team of Mayers, all dressed in white shirts and trousers, sailors' caps and either red or blue sashes denoting their allegiance to a particular horse, and each team is led by a master of ceremonies, wearing a morning suit and top hat. A 'teaser' prances before each horse, brandishing a decorated club: once he, too, was masked, but now goes bare-faced.

Some of the Mayers form bands of accordions, melodeons and drums, and the crowds sing:

> Unite and unite and let us all unite,
>> For Summer is acome unto day,
> And whither we are going we will all unite,
>> In the merry morning of May.
> Where are the young men that here now should dance,
> Some they are in England and some they are in France.
> Where are the maidens that here now should sing,
> They are in the meadows the flowers gathering.

While the song is proceeding the Obby Oss dances and leaps through the streets, sometimes darting toward a pretty girl, as the crowd shouts: 'Oss, Oss, wee Oss!' After a few verses the mood changes and the music slows to a dirge-like rhythm. The horse sinks to the ground in symbolic death and the singers alter their song:

> O where is St George, O where is he-O?
> He's out in his long boat all on the salt sea-O.
> Up flies the kite, down falls the lark-O,
> Aunt Ursula Birdhood she had an old yow [ewe],
> And she died in her own Park-O.

Then, to a frenzied drum beat, the horse revives and dances again:

> With the merry ring, adieu the merry Spring,
>> For Summer is acome unto day,
> How happy is the little bird that merrily does sing,
>> In the merry morning of May.

This continues throughout May Day. In the evening the two main horses meet at the decorated Maypole in Broad Street and dance together for the only time. At about 8 pm the dancing ends and the horses are stabled for another year.

The farewell song, a sentimental ballad not introduced until the 1920s, goes:

> One parting kiss I give thee,
> May nevermore behold thee,
> I go where duty calls me,
> I go whate'er befalls me,
> Farewell, farewell, my own true love.

Documentary evidence of Padstow's Obby Oss reaches back only as far as the beginning of the nineteenth century, but there is a widespread impression that its history is much longer. One story suggests that the horse dances in memory of the women of Padstow who, when their menfolk were away at sea, donned red cloaks to convince a marauding French battlefleet that the British army was waiting on shore: certainly, one stanza from an earlier version of the song substantiates this theory, and a similar tale was told at Fishguard during the Napoleonic Wars.

Hobby-horses are not, of course, unique to Padstow even in Britain and a close, if less spectacular, relative of the Oss still appears at Minehead, in Somerset, also on May Day. Kent's ' Hooden Horses ' once danced at Christmas – one has been revived at Folkestone – and the ' Mari Lwyd ' of South Wales is a mid-winter horse bringing good luck and prosperity to those who see it. Much has been made in the past of the strange resemblance between the Oss's mask and ritual headgear from New Guinea. A sketch dating from about 1835, however, suggests that the mask was originally far less fearsome and possibly the current design could have been introduced into the ceremony by a Padstow sailor returning from distant lands. The letters ' O.B.' inscribed on the teaser's club have also aroused great curiosity: in fact, there is little doubt that they are the initials of a long-dead member of the local Brenton family.

Until fairly recently the horse always visited Treator Pool, outside Padstow town. There, the creature ' drank ' and sprayed the onlookers with water; anyone sprinkled was assured of good luck. Another recent habit of the horse, now discontinued, was to dab a chosen person with soot. The horse itself is black, a traditional colour of fertility, and the propagatory power of soot is exemplified by the custom of inviting chimney-sweeps to weddings. Today any girl touched by the horse believes that she will have a baby within 12 months. The cry ' Oss, Oss, wee Oss!' has been explained in several ways. To some it is a simple ' To we ', or ' Come to us ', urging the beast to favour the caller; to others it is ' wean ', or newly born, a symbol of spring. Most likely, though, it is derived from the horse's whinny. John Fletcher, the dramatist, for example, once wrote of a hobby-horse with its ' lewd Wi-hees '.

All Padstonians believe their song to be unique. In fact, many of the words have parallels in other May songs, notably the ' Old May Song ' of Lancashire, and the air is a variant of a widespread May Day melody. One section of the song does have a particular local interest, however. A verse states that:

> The young men of Padstow they might if they would,
> They might have built a ship and gilded her with gold.

Decorated ships often formed a part of May Day processions, including one in Cornwall, at Millbrook on the banks of the Tamar. Until its harbour became clogged with silt Padstow was a thriving seaport and the gilded ship might be a long-lost part of the festival.

Cornish May Day festivities were not, of course, confined to Padstow. In St Ives the children greeted May with the blowing of rough whistles, known as ' feepers ' or ' pee-weeps ', while in Penzance, the May music was played on fiddles and drums. Some villages kept up the old tradition of lighting bonfires on May evening, and fireballs made of oil-soaked rags were rolled dangerously through the streets. In Hayle, until the late nineteenth century, children walked in procession about the town, singing and clad in gaudy paper clothes decorated with flowers. This is the song they sang:

> O crown the Queen of May,
> O crown the Queen of May,
> Around the ring we'll dance and sing,
> O crown the Queen of May!

In mid-Cornwall, horseshoes nailed to doors as protection against witches were taken down on May morning and turned round without touching the ground. This act was thought to renew the spell. May dew was recognized throughout Cornwall as a valuable cosmetic, but in Launceston had unappealing connections. There, until fairly recent times, the dew was used as a salve to cure neck ailments, but it was only effective if collected from the grave of a newly buried corpse. The importance of dew may have had some link with the May Day practice of ' dipping ', or sprinkling with water, to bring good luck. We have already noted that the Padstow Oss once visited Treator Pool for this purpose and throughout Cornwall dipping was a common custom. In Polperro and Pelynt, anyone seen not wearing a lucky ' may ' blossom was dipped, while in Looe the boys went around carrying bullocks' horns filled with water. They walked through the town singing :

> The first of May is Dipping Day,
> The sixth of May is Looe Fair Day,

and collecting pennies to spend at the fair.

Maypoles were once in common evidence throughout England and no less so in Cornwall, but the Cornish poles involved strange traditions and they were guarded day and night during the first week of the month. It was the custom for neighbouring villages to try to steal one another's Maypoles and fierce battles were often the result. The poles were traditionally decorated with May garlands – streamers being a comparatively recent introduction – and at Looe, May Day was sometimes known as Garland Day. Once, at Merrymeet, near Liskeard, the villagers protected their gaily decorated pole from invading neighbours by cementing it into the ground, but the resourceful men of St Cleer brought a saw with them and carried off the trophy. Guarded Maypoles also stood at Menheniot, Altarnun and Trewen, amongst other places. If they were stolen, they had to be returned to their parent villages by the following morning, or bad luck would follow.

The little village of Lanreath, a few miles inland from Polperro, is mainly famous for its Punch Bowl Inn, with a sign painted by Augustus John, but there, during May, the Maypole-guarding tradition still survives. In 1973 the authors were told, by the mother-in-law of one of the pole's guards, of the intrigue and cunning involved. Spies from Pelynt and other nearby villages try to make the guards drink too much so that they fall asleep on duty; Lanreath's agents spend their time letting down the tyres of their enemies' vehicles. One sees some black eyes in Lanreath during May, but no one is deterred by them and the tradition seems in no risk of dying out. When their long vigil is over, the men chop up their Maypole and make skittles for a game played in the Punch Bowl Inn.

On the first Sunday after May Day it was once customary for Penzance families to visit Rosehill, Poltier and other outlying hamlets for feasts of ' heavy-cake ', described elsewhere. They carried with them flour, currants and the other necessary ingredients and made the cakes in farm dairies, which were always left open for the purpose. They also took tea, sugar and rum and, after paying the farmers for the baking facilities, settled down to enjoy their food. Unlike Lanreath's Maypole, this old practice has long since vanished.

Helston, a small market town at the head of the Lizard peninsula, is probably the most famous place in Cornwall, because of its Furry, or Floral, Dance. Traditionally held on 8 May, Furry Day has now transferred to the nearest Saturday, presumably for the benefit of visitors, when the streets of Helston are decked with May flowers. Throughout the day the people dance around the town, dressed in their best clothes and accompanied by the local brass band. The dancers weave patterns as they move along and occasionally enter houses and shops.

Local legend suggests that Helston was once the resort of fiery dragons and of the Devil himself. Indeed, a large block of granite built into the west wall of the Angel Hotel in the main street is said to have blocked the entrance to Hell. The stone was thrown by Satan at Helston's patron saint, St Michael, but missed him and landed in the courtyard of the old inn. Thus, according to tradition, the town earned its name – Hell's Stone – and the people danced the Furry in honour of their saint's survival. Another story concerned an old lady gathering wild flowers by the shores of Loe Pool, nearby. She was terrified to see a dragon flying above her, heading for the town, but the creature missed its mark and fell into the lake. She made quite sure that it had drowned, then ran into Helston, shouting the good news and waving her flowers – the first-ever Floral Dance.

While the mass media insist on describing the festival as ' Floral Day ', to the local people it remains ' The Furry ' perhaps derived from the Cornish *fer*, meaning ' fair ' or ' feast day '. This indicates that the dance was originally held to celebrate the feast day of St Michael, 8 May, an argument strengthened by the common

M

custom of holding fairs on saints' days. Apart from Furry, another word associated with the Helston dance is ' faddy ', perhaps from the Old English *fadé*, to go: at one time the dance was actually known as ' The Faddy ' and the sycamore as ' the faddy tree ', for local boys would make whistles from its branches for the festival. The Faddy is possibly related to an ancient English dance, ' The Fading ', and to the Irish *Rincce Fada*, or Long Dance, performed before King James on his landing at Kinsale in 1681.

The antiquity of the Furry Dance is hardly in doubt, for Carew describes it as flourishing in his *Survey* of 1602, but the Hal-an-Tow, which traditionally accompanied the dance and has recently been revived, could be far older. Baring-Gould suggests that the Hal-an-Tow formed part of the old English May Games, which included the election and procession of the King and Queen of May, or the Summer King and Queen; the Morris Dance, performed by disguised, sword-bearing men; the Hobby Horse; and the Robin Hood, a form of mumming play. This last section could well encompass the Hal-an-Tow, for the main participants were dressed according to the roles mentioned in the Hal-an-Tow song and presented stock mumming characters. The song itself is perhaps the most interesting survival of the entire festival and, despite Baring-Gould's contrary assertion, its tune bears no relation to the Furry Dance melody. The words, though, are strikingly similar to obsolete versions of Padstow's May Song:

> Robin Hood and Little John, they both are gone to fair-O,
> And we will to the merry greenwood to see what they do
>   there-O,
> And for to chase-O, to chase the buck and doe.
>   Hal-an-Tow, jolly rumble-O
> And for to fetch the Summer home, the Summer and the May-O,
> For summer is acome-O and Winter is agone-O.

> Where are the Spaniards that made so great a boast-O,
> For they shall eat the grey goose feathers and we will eat the
>   roast-O,
> In every land-O, the land where'er we go.

> As for St George-O, St George he was a knight-O,
> Of all the knights in Christendom, St George he was the right-O,
> In every land-O, the land where'er we go.

God bless Aunt Mary Moses, with all her power and might-O,
And send us peace in merry England, both by day and night-O,
And send us peace in merry England, both now and evermore-O.

The first two verses are fairly typical of ' Robin Hood ' mumming songs, although the reference to Spaniards is, like the
French in the old Padstow song, local. The Spaniards made many
attacks around the Cornish coast in Elizabethan times and Mousehole, for instance, was burnt almost entirely to the ground. To
be ' as cruel as a Spanjard ' was a popular simile in the far west
and one historian cites an incident in which a group of marauding
Spaniards forced some local women to ignite bundles of furze in
Paul Church; he also mentions a farmer's wife who cut a Spanish
sailor's throat with a sickle when she found him sleeping beneath
her tree. The goose feathers of the second verse could, therefore,
possibly refer to the flights of the longbow arrows used to fight the
enemy and for a Spaniard to ' eat ' them would be fatal. Verse
three brings in St George, the mumming-play hero, and here the
dragon legend of Helston, mentioned earlier, may be of interest.
An additional verse was added at this point by a Cornish Grand
Bard, the late Robert Morton Nance, but it does little for the
song and, indeed, probably overlooks its original meaning:

But to a greater than St George our Helston has a right-O,
St Michael with his wings outspread, the Archangel so bright-O.
Who fought the fiend-O, of all mankind the foe.

The final verse is, perhaps, the most interesting of all, with Aunt
Mary Moses Helston's counterpart to Padstow's Ursula Birdhood.
At first sight she appears to be a vulgarization of the Virgin
Mary, for the Cornish word for ' maid ' or ' virgin ' was *mowse*;
thus, Mary the Mowse is ' Mary the Virgin '. However, she would
be far nearer the mumming tradition as Robin Hood's Maid
Marian.

The chorus of the Hal-an-Tow song has been described as a
corruption of ' Heel-and-toe ', but this seems dubious. A Cornish
writer in the mid-seventeenth century refers to the ' Haile-an-
Taw ': *Hal*, or *hayl*, is a Cornish word meaning ' moorland ',
while *tyow* means ' houses '. Surely, then, *hal-an-tow* could represent ' in the moorland [the country] and the town '. ' Rumbelow '
is a word denoting jollity and movement, so the full line would
translate as ' in the country and the town, there will be merry-

making '. This explanation seems more logical than a simple heel-and-toe and adequately describes the atmosphere of May Day celebrations. A recent commercial recording of the song includes a verse which has no place in it, since it is a quotation from *As You Like It*, Act IV, Scene II.

On the great day the decorated streets are lined with crowds, all waving at the dancers. The old connections with a processional Morris seem very remote, but the town band still plays the tune in fine style, without the assistance of musical scores. The pomp and gaiety of the past are gone, and happily the days of separate processions for poor and gentry are over. One charming survival of Old Helston is the children's doggerel, sung to the Furry tune and heard recently in a form almost identical to that collected by Miss Courtney in 1890. ' Trawra ', oddly, is Truro, while ' John the Bon ' was, perhaps a local rake, John the Beau, or Bone; Morton Nance, though, noted a John Bon, MP, who was Reeve of Helston in the fourteenth century. No trace has been found of Sally Dover, but she remains, with her lover, immortalized:

John said to me one day; Can you dance the Flora?
Yes, I can, with a nice young man, round the streets of Trawra.
John the Bon was marching on, when he met with Sally Dover,
He kissed her once and he kissed her twice and he kissed her
    three times over.

Helston has more to offer folklorists than the Furry Dance. The Blue Anchor Inn, in Coinagehall Street, has a history dating back to its days as a Monk's Rest in 1400. It stands today as one of only five public houses in Britain licensed to brew their own beer.

After 8 May there are no festivals in Cornwall until the 29th of the month. Then, in Looe and other parts of east Cornwall, it was the custom to wear an oak leaf, for Oak Apple Day. Anyone not doing so was likely to be subjected to spitting, or ' cobbing ', a common protection against ill-fortune. Generally speaking, the customs of May underline an old Cornish saying that one should ' never make mock at a maygum [May game]'.

JUNE
Whitsun in old Cornwall was a time for amusement and relaxation. The children of Polperro would band together and walk into the surrounding countryside, begging for milk and cream from the

scattered farmsteads: to refuse them was to invite bad luck. It was also considered unlucky to venture out of doors on Whit Sunday without wearing some new items of clothing. Children believed that the birds watched for anyone wearing old clothes and fouled them as they walked along. Carew mentions an old Whit Monday custom of collecting for the ' Whitsun Ales ', an outdoor feast no longer celebrated. Whitsun fairs occur at Helston, Lanreath and Truro, with another on 11 June at Menheniot dating from the reign of Henry VI.

During the second week of June the village of Roche once witnessed the Snail's Creep, a curious dance described earlier, while in west Cornwall, a similar dance called ' Roll-Tobacco ' was popular with children on Sunday-School treats. They joined hands, forming a long line with the tallest at the head. Then, while the first child stood still, the others danced round, singing, in decreasing circles, until they joined untidily together. They then wheeled out and retraced their steps, eventually reverting to a straight line.

Midsummer is an important date in most folklore calendars and in Cornwall as elsewhere it was a time for love divination, when girls and boys tried various charms to determine their future partners. It was also the time for lighting Midsummer Bonfires, an ancient custom rescued from extinction by the Old Cornwall Movement in 1929 and still flourishing. Some people like to suppose that bonfires were originally kindled by the Druids in honour of their sun god, whom they identify with Baal. In any case, as elsewhere, the custom was christianized and Midsummer Eve, 23 June, being the Eve of the Feast of St John the church dedicated the bonfires to him. This produced the Cornish name *Goljowan* [John's Feast], though some of the festival's pre-Christian elements survived.

The first fire used to be lit on the Garrack Sans (Holy Rock), near Sennen, from which a chain of fires spread through the length of Cornwall: every Beacon Hill was ablaze – Carn Brea, Castlean-Dinas, Bartinney, Sancreed, St Agnes, Carn Galva, Tregonning, Godolphin, Carn Marth, and many others. In Penzance, youths paraded through the town with burning torches, which they swung around their heads in a circular motion. All Mount's Bay was a mass of fire on Midsummer Eve and the youngsters danced through the streets, ' threading the needle ' : two boys formed an arch with their arms and the others ran beneath it. Cattle were carefully folded at some distance from the fires, but the farmers carried bunches of burning furze to them, allowing the smoke to pass over their stalls; the walk was always made in the direction of the sun. On Midsummer Day itself the people took a holiday and enjoyed fireworks and other amusements. Five days after Midsummer, on St Peter's Eve, the bonfires were lit again and there were more festivities.

Today the bonfires began on Carn Brea, between Camborne and Redruth, continuing in a fiery chain to Kit Hill, on the eastern border of Cornwall. Sometimes young couples leap through the flames to bring themselves good luck and the modern bards of the Cornish *Gorsedd* are usually present. At St Cleer the fire is crowned with a witch's broom and hat, a sickle with a handle of newly cut oak is thrown into the flames and wreaths of St John's wort are hung about the village – all this was traditionally said to banish witches. Herbs are burnt in most of the fires: vervain, clover, tormentil, cinquefoil and restharrow. The ribbons used to tie the bunches of herbs are coloured white, green, blue, red, and yellow. Cornwall's Midsummer Bonfires, in their revived state, are an interesting modern phenomenon which deserve further investigation.

An interesting aspect of Cornish folklore was the election of ' Mock Mayors ' in many of the county's towns and villages. Each election usually took place during the village's feast week and culminated when the ' mayor ', in a drunken stupor, was thrown into a stream or onto a rubbish-tip. A writer in the 1920s stated that, while the proceedings were ' mere burlesques ', the participants ' were firmly convinced that they were as fully authorized by law as they were by custom '. Pelynt's fair day actually falls at Midsummer and its Mock Mayor was treated with great pomp. After a lengthy tour of the village's two inns he was taken at the gallop to the Old Shute Pond, where he was drenched with mud and water.

Two other Cornish Mock Mayor elections were both held on 29 June, St Peter's Day. Peter is the patron saint of Polperro and there the ' mayor ' was wheeled through the narrow streets in a fish-jouster's cart, dressed in tinsel and accompanied by a staff of ' constables '. They stopped at each inn, where the mayor made a speech full of promises to reduce working hours, increase wages and introduce a beer allowance for each man; he then drank a quart of ale. By the end of the circuit he must have been in a sorry state, but his dip in the sea probably revived him. At Four Lanes, near Wendron, the Mock Mayor held a court, called

'Cuckle's Court', perhaps from cuckold. Visitors to the village were usually chosen as victims, sentenced to have their faces blackened until the local authorities stopped the custom. Still quite recently, though, a well-known saying in the district ran:

> Wendron Feast and Cuckle's Court,
> Come every man and stand his quart.

JULY

A traditional remembrance of St Thomas à Becket was once widespread on 7 July, though its celebration was proscribed under severe penalties in 1538. However on the Sunday and Monday following, an important ceremony used to be held in Bodmin – the Bodmin Riding. The proceedings began with the election of two or more young men of the town to represent the 'wardens', who officiated over the ceremony. These wardens, together with the town crier and a fife-and-drum band, went round the town carrying buckets of beer especially brewed for the occasion during the previous October. The crier greeted each household with a toast: 'To the people of this house, a prosperous morning, long life, health and a merry Riding!' Then, after the musicians had played the 'Riding Tune', the householder tasted the Riding Ale and, if satisfied, bought a bottle. The money collected was used later in the day to provide further entertainment for the people.

Next morning a horseback procession, with the riders cracking long-lashed whips, went first to the local priory, St Benet's Abbey, to receive two large garlands of flowers supported on poles, then to the end of the town, where the Riding Games were formally opened. Wrestling was included, with foot- and sack-racing, cudgel-playing for a silver cup and grinning through horse-collars ('gurning') as supporting items. The prizes for wrestling were fairly high by the standards of the day: the *Royal Cornwall Gazette* for 24 July 1824 reported a first prize of £10, £5 for second and £2 for third. The same journal mentions a bell-ringing contest at the sports, carried off by the famous Egloshayle team. The day ended with a ball, held for the town's servant-girls and their escorts, often continuing until 8 or 9 am.

The origins of the Bodmin Riding are obscure, although traditionally it celebrated the return to Bodmin of St Petroc's relics, which had been stolen by a Breton priest in 1177 and taken to St Méen Abbey in Brittany. These relics still remain in a bank vault in the town, but this explanation is dubious since the date of the

Riding has no connection with either St Petroc's Day or the date on which the relics were restored. Certainly, it was well-established by the fifteenth century, when the stewards of the Riding Guild contributed towards a restoration of the church. In 1583 the masters of the Guild of Shoemakers in Bodmin ordered that every member of their organization should participate in the Riding: fines for disobedience reached 12d for masters and 6d for journeymen. The Riding died out in the early nineteenth century, but a few attempts have been made to revive it, the latest being in 1974. A similar custom, held at Liskeard on a smaller scale, died out earlier than at Bodmin.

The Bodmin Riding Games have often been confused with those held on nearby Halgavor Moor at about the same time of the year. Although similar, the Halgavor Games were distinguished by a mock trial, held before a lord of misrule: a young servingman was usually the accused, arrested, in Carew's words, for ' wearing one spur or going untrussed, or wanting a girdle '. He was tried, found guilty and humiliated in some way which was embarrassing rather than painful; for instance, a gullible youngster might be persuaded to fight with an imaginary dragon in Halgavor Moor and usually only succeeded in falling into one of the local bogs. The trial gave the district a saying that long outlasted the actual custom: until quite recently badly dressed individuals were bound to be ' presented in Halgavor Court '.

In 1782 a pyramid-shaped obelisk was erected on Worvas Hill, near St Ives, by instructions of John Knill, once a mayor of the town. Knill intended the monument to be his own mausoleum and his name and family mottoes are inscribed around the three sides. John Knill was greatly respected in St Ives, despite – or, perhaps, because of – his alleged smuggling connections. He, in turn, respected the townspeople and left a deed of trust bestowing an annuity of £10 to be distributed among the poor. He also decreed that every fifth year, on St James's Day, 25 July, a ceremony should be held in his honour: ten young girls of the town, dressed in white, were to dance through the streets to the music of a fiddle. On reaching the mausoleum, where they would be greeted by the mayor and two St Ives widows, they were all to dance around it, while the spectators sang the Hundredth Psalm. The ceremony was first performed ten years before Knill's death, in 1801, and still takes place every fifth year, although the sports and fun that follow it do not play so big a part as they used to; the next ' Knillian Games ' will be in 1976. Ironically, Knill's mausoleum never served its intended purpose, for, just before he died, he willed his body to a group of London anatomists.

AUGUST

Despite the modest size of the village, Morvah held one of Cornwall's largest fairs and an old proverb described a crowd of people as ' three on one horse, like going to Morvah fair '. Gold-sithney Fair falls on 5 August and, as noted before, it once belonged to Sithney; at one time, a proprietor of the fair paid an annual tribute of a shilling to Sithney.

A ' revel ' still takes place at Marhamchurch, near Bude; the patron saint is St Marwenne, daughter of the Christian King Brychan of Brecknock, whose feast day falls on 12 August. ' Revel Sunday ' is a church festival held on the Sunday after this date, but the secular revel, current since at least the Middle Ages, occurs on the following Monday. The central figure in the Mar-hamchurch Revels is the Queen of the Revel, who must be a native of the village and an ex-pupil of the local school. She is elected by the village children, six of whom become her attend-ants, and wears by tradition a white dress and over it a blue cloak, which is handed on from queen to queen. After the new Queen's robing she and her handmaidens walk in procession to the reputed site of St Marwenne's cell, near the war memorial. There, the Queen is officially crowned by ' Father Time '. Dressed in a flowing robe and carrying a scythe and hour-glass, he declares :

> Now look! That this by all be seen,
> I here do crown thee, of this year, the Queen!

The new monarch then rides through the village mounted on a white horse and led by a local farmer dressed for the occasion in a smock and top-hat. The party is headed by the village band, while children in fancy dress bring up the rear. They all proceed through the village, until, near the church, they reach the Revel Field where the Queen declares the Revel formally open. There is wrestling, country dancing, a Maypole, fancy dress, gymnastics and odd events like pram racing. Donations to the Revel fund are passed on to charities.

Mead, metheglin and other drinks based on honey were drunk in early times and today Cornish mead is popular again, mainly due to the efforts of the monks of Gulval, on Mount's Bay. There, in the Mead House, they are again making the drink which is

sweet but surprisingly strong. On St Bartholomew's Day, 24
August, the Blessing of the Mead is carried out at Gulval by the
Almoner of the Fraternity of St Bartholomew of the Craft or
Mystery of Free Meadmakers of Great Britain and Ireland. Bar-
tholomew is the patron saint of beekeepers and honeymakers.

SEPTEMBER

In September 1928 the *Gorsedd* of the Bards of Cornwall was
inaugurated at the old earthwork of Boscawen-Un. The Gorsedd
exists to 'maintain the National Celtic spirit of Cornwall' and,
while there is scant evidence to suggest any historical precedent
for the event, the annual meeting is a spectacular affair. Each
Gorsedd site is chosen for its antiquity and representatives from
Wales, Brittany and other Celtic lands are usually present.
Speeches are in the old Cornish language and it is difficult to
remain unmoved by the occasion.

Cornish wrestling, or 'wrastling', is still a popular sport in
the county and the annual championships are held in September
at specially selected sites. The wrestling style, allowing no kicking,
is peculiar to Cornwall. There is an interesting old British legend
of a wrestling match held on Plymouth Hoe in 1100 BC between
the Cornish champion of the time and a Trojan hero, and Michael
Drayton writes in *Poly-olbion* that Cornish soldiers fought at
Agincourt beneath the banner depicting two wrestlers. The tradition of wrestling in Cornwall is, therefore, very old and in more
recent times local interest in the sport has been maintained.

St Wenn, in the kaolin district of mid-Cornwall, is the natural
centre for Cornish wrestling, since the Chapman family live there:
the Chapmans are the most famous contemporary wrestlers and
two members of the family are also involved in the professional
'all-in' game. Enthusiasts in Cornwall still argue over the great
battle of 1826 between the Cornishman, James Polkinghorne, and
Abraham Cann, champion of Devon, before 17,000 spectators.
Cann finally won, but had to resort to the Devonian style, including kicking, to do so. Local feeling for a village's own wrestlers
runs high and, while this type of rhyme –

> Chacewater boobies up in the tree,
> Looking as wisht [sad] as ever could be;
> Truro men, strong as oak,
> Knock 'em down at every stroke,

– has now died, the excitement at a wrestling match is still intense. Today's competitors, dressed in loose-sleeved sailcloth jackets, shorts and socks, swear the Wrestler's Oath:

I swear that I will wrestle fairly,
Without any treachery or false move,
For my honour and that of my country,
In testimony of sincerity and following the way of my forebears,
I shake my opponent by the hand.

Harvest-time in Cornwall was an occasion of great importance, when master and men worked for a good crop and a general celebration followed. Today, the work is still hard, but the ceremonies have diminished. In recent years the Old Cornwall Society has helped revive the old custom of Crying the Neck, mostly in the area around Helston, although it disappeared as a spontaneous event at about the turn of the century. Crying the Neck took place as the last handsful of corn were cut by the reapers. The men stood in the middle of the last field to be harvested and split into three groups. As the reaper cut the last 'neck' of corn the first group cried: 'We have it! We have it! We have it!' 'What have 'ee? What have 'ee? What have 'ee?' asked the second party, and the third responded triumphantly. 'A neck! A neck! A neck!' Then there were cheers for the farmer, while cider and cake were passed out to the men.

After the ceremony the neck was plaited into a corn-dolly, decorated with cornflowers and hung over the chimney-place in the farmhouse kitchen. Sometimes the plait was long and straight, but an old woman from North Hill saw one neck twisted into four loops with the ears of corn in the middle.

When the cornfields were clear it was the custom for the farmer to hold Harvest Suppers for his workers. In the far west, around Penzance, they were known as 'gooldize', from the Cornish *gôl deis*, [a feast of ricks], and the entertainments included much eating and drinking. There were songs, too, and old favourites like 'The Barley Mow' were popular. It was customary to have at least one song thanking the farmer and his wife for their support throughout the harvest:

Our day's work is done, to the farmhouse we steer,
To eat of our supper and drink some brown beer.
We'll eat and we'll drink health to him and his wife,
Here's prosperity be with them all the days of their life.

Cornwall's largest fair is held at Summercourt, a straggling village on the main London-to-Penzance road, on 25 September. Summercourt, or 'Old' Fair was once known throughout the west as a centre for trading, as well as a place of entertainment, with a travelling theatre and waxwork and puppet shows. The fair is still of considerable size, but its former importance is underlined in this rhyme from the childhood of A. L. Rowse:

> 'Ere we'm off to Summercourt Fair;
> Me mother said ' Ess ',
> Me Faather said ' No ';
> An' dash me buttons if I dun't go.

There was plenty to drink at Summercourt and Billy Treglase, a local balladeer, had this advice for the ladies:

> All the women of Summercourt Fair,
> I'll give 'ee advice, then you can beware.
> If your men do drink too much beer or gin,
> You must scat [knock] 'em down with a rolling pin.
> So, women, I hope you'll follow this plan,
> If you should be plagued with a drunken man.

A ' Mock Mayor ' ceremony was formerly held in Penryn towards the end of September, organized by journeymen tailors from the area. Bonfires blazed and the drunks enjoyed themselves until one year, when the real mayor of Penryn took exception to this caricature of his office. He and his constables met the impostors outside the town, but there were too many for the law to handle; the constables were themselves ' arrested ', and spent the night in their own cells.

OCTOBER

The village of Paul, near Penzance, holds its feast day on the nearest Sunday to 10 October and, if the weather is bad, local people look forward to a difficult year, for there is an old proverb: ' Rain for Paul, rain for all '. On the following day, Feasten Monday, there used to be a bowling match between Paul and Mousehole. Roast Goose Fair, held in Redruth on 12 October, was a time when working people enjoyed a rare meal of meat.

In west Cornwall, the nearest Sunday to All Hallows' Eve, 31 October, is known as Allantide, or Allan's Eve. St Just-in-Penwith Feast is held at this time:

> St Just bugs, leathern jugs,
> Curdy milk and whey;
> Boil the maggots in the crock,
> On Allan feasten-day.

It was the custom in St Just, St Ives and other villages in the district for children to take apples to bed with them at Allantide and eat them on the following morning. This was thought to bring good luck. Some adults also practised the ritual, especially women who wished to dream of their lovers.

NOVEMBER

Many Cornish villages celebrated 4 November as ' Ringing Night ', when the church-bells rang out to announce the Gunpowder Plot ceremonies on the following night. In Bude, the local fife-and-drum band led a procession similar to the famous anti-Popery carnival held each year in Lewes, Sussex; the festival ended with a bonfire and firework display on nearby Stamford Hill. Margaret Courtney recalls this children's rhyme attached to Bonfire Night:

> Please to remember the fifth of November!
> A stick or a stake, for King George's sake,
> A faggot or rope, to hang the Pope,
> For Gunpowder Plot shall never be forgot,
> Whilst Castle Ryan stands upon a rock.

Camborne feast day falls on the nearest Sunday to Martinmas, 11 November, and on the previous Saturday a group of local people, known as ' The Homage Committee', carried hampers around the market place to collect marrow-bones from the butchers: they afterwards visited the inns of the town as ' tasters '. This custom was briefly revived in 1884.

The St Ives Pig Fair, or *Fair Mo*, fell on the Saturday before Advent Sunday. As the pilchard-fishing season generally ended in November, there was plenty of money available and the fair was regarded as a great event. The main street was filled with stalls, or ' stannens ', many of them with little gingerbread figures, perhaps in imitation of the saints' images sold when the fair was a religious event. Packets of ' fairings ' contained sugar almonds or macaroons. One writer recalls a pieman selling pigs made of pastry with currant eyes. He walked through the town, shouting:

> Who'll buy, who'll buy?
> A long-tailed pig or a short-tailed pig,
> A straight-tailed pig or a curly-tailed pig,
> A pig without a tail or a tail without a pig?

Another popular figure was the ice-cream salesman :

> Hokey-pokey, penny a lump,
> You all know what I mean,
> That's the stuff to make you jump.
> God save our Gracious Queen!

The fair's attractions included wrestlers and acrobats, and on one occasion a booth stood on Skidden Hill containing Daniel in the Lion's Den. Daniel's proprietor announced to the potential customers that his star could be distinguished from the lions ' by his wearing a green umbrella under his arm '.

DECEMBER

St Nicholas is the patron of children and on his day the choir-boys of Par choose themselves a leader. Known as the Boy Bishop, he dresses in fine robes and directs the hymn singing. The second Thursday before Christmas marked two tinners' festivals: White Thursday and Picrous Day, when the workers were given a holiday.

In Mousehole, on 23 December, the fisherfolk celebrate Tom Bawcock's Eve. The day is said to commemorate a period of local famine eased by the efforts of one fisherman, Tom Bawcock, who put to sea and returned with seven different varieties of fish to feed the villagers. A song, restored by Robert Morton Nance, commemorates the event:

> A merry place, you may believe,
> Was Mousehole 'pon Tom Bawcock's Eve;
> To be there then who wouldn't wish
> To sup of seven sorts of fish?

On Christmas Eve, the mummers performed their ' St George ' plays. In Cornwall they were all of the ' hero-combat ' type, with the central character overcoming a villain, who was then resuscitated by a comic doctor. The Mullion play, which continued until

the late nineteenth century, was a mime, while in Stithians, up to
the outbreak of World War I, the play's hero was not the usual St
George, but simple Jack. Most of the lines were crude and ill-
shaped, but the Cadgwith play gave this verse to Father Christmas:

> As I lay on my silent bed,
> I dreamt my only son was dead.
> Thou cruel monster, what hast thou done?
> Thou'st ruined and killed my only son!

In Polperro, to be ' as good as a Christmas play ' was a certain
delight.

The Cornish Yule log was called a ' mock ' or ' block ' and
was usually ignited with a piece of the previous year's log, sometimes with the figure of a man engraved upon it; it was thought
to deter witchcraft. Until quite recently Cornish children were
allowed to sit up until midnight on Christmas Eve, to drink to
the mock and sing carols around the flames. Carols have long
been a part of Cornish life and most pub singers in the county
include a number of them in their repertoires:

> Welcome, Christmas, which brings us all good cheer,
> Pies and puddings, roast pork and strong beer.

Sets of carols were used in certain Cornish towns: St Ives, Redruth, Morwenstow and St Keverne had their own versions, but
Padstow has the only remaining set. There, each Christmas time,
the townspeople gather on the quay and walk through the streets,
singing their own carols.

Carhampton, in Somerset, probably has the most complete
survival of wassailing in Britain today, but Cornwall keeps up
the tradition, too. In Bodmin, on Christmas Eve, the wassail bowl
is carried around the town by four men clad in full evening dress;
they walk from door to door, collecting for charity and singing:

> Our Wassail Bowl is full with apples and good spice,
> Grant to taste it once or twice,
> And joy come to our jolly Wassail.

The bowl once contained moveable wooden pegs to mark the
amount of liquor – cider or beer – that had been consumed on

its travels. The word ' wassail ' appears to derive from the Old English *waes hael*, meaning ' be whole ', or ' be of good health ', and is comparable with the modern ' Cheers '.

Festivities continued in old Cornwall throughout the Christmas period, until New Year's Eve, when the Wassailers again took to the streets. In Truro, today, they still do so. The Truro Wassailers, with their gaily decorated apple-wood bowl form a tightly knit community, each family preserving the right to carry on the Wassail until the last member has died, then passing on the honour to another family. They sing outside houses and inns, beginning with this verse :

> Now Christmas is over, our Wassail begin,
> Pray, open your door and let us come in.

and ' beg ' for money or drink without embarrassment :

> Now we poor Wassail Boys are growing weary and cold,
> Drop a small piece of silver into our Bowl,

then deliver their blessing :

> I hope that your apple-trees will prosper and bear,
> And bring forth good cider when we come next year.

Notes

INTRODUCTION, pages 9–45
Most of the folklore elements in the Introduction are expanded in the relevant chapters of the book, with sources detailed in the complementary notes. The story of the pair of boots was related orally by Mrs Morel Duboil of Plymouth, formerly of Warleggan on Bodmin Moor.

ABBREVIATIONS
O.C.   *Old Cornwall*
J.F.S.   *Journal of the Folk Song Society*
J.R.I.C. *Journal of the Royal Institute of Cornwall*
E.D.S.   *English Dance and Song*
F.L.   *Folklore*

The Life Cycle, pages 47–61

BIRTH AND CHRISTENING: Margaret Courtney, *Cornish Feasts and Folk-lore*, 1890, 156–62; *O.C.*, II, 5, 1933, 41; A. K. Hamilton-Jenkin, *Cornwall and its People*, 1945, 250; letters from Mrs M. Saunders of Bradoc, near Lostwithiel, 1973.
CHILDHOOD: M. Courtney, *op. cit.*, 156–62; G. F. Northall, *English Folk Rhymes*, 1892, 497; Lucy E. Broadwood and J. E. Fuller Maitland, *English County Songs*, 1893, 176; William Hone, *The Every Day Book*, 1826, 363–4; A. L. Rowse, *A Cornish Childhood*, 1942, 11–32; Iona and Peter Opie, *The Lore and Language of Schoolchildren*, 1959, 77; notes collected by Tony Deane from Gorran schoolchildren, *c.* 1965; information supplied by Mrs A. M. Honey, Boscastle, 1969; J. Thomas, *Randigal Rhymes and a Glossary of Cornish Words*, 1895, 63; *O.C.*, April 1926, III: 5.
COURTSHIP: *O.C.*, Summer 1933, 41; M. Courtney, *op. cit.*, 164–6; modern St Valentine's Day rhyme supplied by Mrs Morel Duboil of Plymouth, 1969.
MARRIAGE: *O.C.*, April 1926, 36; A. K. Hamilton-Jenkin, *Cornwall and Its People*, 1945, 247–50; *O.C.*, Winter 1930, 22; M. Courtney, *op. cit.*, 166–71; wife-selling is mentioned in various reports in *The West Briton* newspaper, e.g. 13 November 1818 and as late as 1853.

RABBIT TRAPPER STORIES : Two letters from elderly man in Camborne in 1967

FOOD AND DRINK : A. K. Hamilton-Jenkin, *Cornwall and Its People*, 1945, 367–77; Stanley J. Coleman, *Cornish Lore and Legend*, no date, 3; Louis T. Stanley, *A Journey Through Cornwall*, 1958, 109–12; personal recollections : the authors have seen starry-gazy pie cooked in different parts of south Cornwall; recipes supplied by various informants.

MIRACLE PLAYS : Sabine Baring-Gould, *A Book of Cornwall*, 1899, 302–3; A. K. Hamilton-Jenkin, *Cornwall and Its People*, 1945, 128–30; F. E. Halliday, *The Legend of the Rood*, 1955, 11-51.

FAIRS AND SONGS : For fairs, see notes for *The Year's Round*; songs from Sabine Baring-Gould, *Songs of the West*, 1913 edition, 168; Inglis Gundry, *Canow Kernow*, 1966, 48.

BELL RINGING : Sabine Baring-Gould, *Cornish Characters and Strange Events*, 1925, 222–7; I. Gundry, *op. cit.*, 22; John Keest, *The Story of Fowey*, 1950, 136.

DEATH : Information supplied by Mrs M. Saunders of Bradoc, 1973; Mrs Odessa Tomlin of Lostwithiel, 1973; Mrs G. Knight of Nottingham formerly of Withiel near Bodmin, 1972; S. J. Coleman, *op. cit.*, 13; M. Courtney, *op. cit.*, 166, 171; A. K. Hamilton-Jenkin, *Cornwall and Its People*, 1945, 283–6.

EPITAPHS : G. A. Cooke, *A Topographical and Statistical Description of the County of Cornwall*, 1830, 289; letter from Mrs E. H. Pengilly of Higher Sticker, near St Austell, 1965.

The Tinners and their Legends, pages 62–76

ATTAL SARSON : A. K. Hamilton-Jenkin, *The Cornish Miner*, 1927, 29.

BIBLICAL LEGENDS : Rev. H. A. Lewis, *Christ in Cornwall*, no date, 1–14; Robert Hunt, *Popular Romances of the West of England*, 1881, 261.

ST PIRAN : W. C. Borlase, *The Age of the Saints*, 1893, 22–5; R. Hunt, *op. cit.*, 272.

WHISTLING UNDERGROUND : Oral information from an ex-miner in Redruth 1971; same belief held by miners in Wales and Northumberland.

MINERS AND FISHERMEN : A. K. Hamilton-Jenkin, *The Cornish Miner*, 1927, 29; quotes from William Pryce, *Archaeologis Cornubiensis*, 1790.

ANIMAL SUPERSTITIONS : Joseph Hammond, *A Cornish Parish*, 1897, 350–67; information also given by Rev. T. W. M. Darlington, formerly of Gwennap parish, December 1972; Arthur Caddick, *Curiosities of Cornwall*, 1957, 6.

HAT BURNING : *O.C.*, II : 11, 1936, 17; P. H. Ditchfield, *Old English Customs*, 1896, 200.

POLDICE : Rev. T. Darlington, 1972; *O.C.*, Summer 1931, II : 1, 10.

SONGS : S. Baring-Gould, *Songs of the West*, 5th edition 1913, 190; Ralph Dunstan, *Cornish Dialect and Folk Songs*, 1932, 13; Inglis Gundry, *op. cit.*, 23, 53–5.

KNOCKERS : *Choice Notes from Notes and Queries*, 1849, 68; William Bottrell, *Traditions and Hearthside Stories*, 1880, III : 193; R. Hunt, *op. cit.*, 346; information received from Robert Husband of Penare, near Gorran, 1973.

TOM TREVORROW : W. Bottrell, *op. cit.*, II : 186.

BARKER'S KNEE : Informant in Redruth, *c.*, 1971; R. Hunt, *op. cit.*, 88.

ST AGNES : Noted from an old miner living in St Agnes by David Watts of Edenbridge, Kent, *c.* 1970.

DORCAS : R. Hunt, *op. cit.*, 354–5.

GHOSTLY WARNING : J. Hammond, *op. cit.*, 360; similar tales are still to be heard in mining districts; other warning stories appear in Hunt, *op. cit.*, 350.

MINERS' CHARACTER : Richard Carew, *Survey of Cornwall*, 1602, reprint 1953, 88–93.

PAUL'S PITCHER DAY : W. Carew Hazlitt, *Popular Antiquities of Great Britain*, 1870, I : 23; P. H. Ditchfield, *op. cit.*, 53.

ST PIRAN'S DAY : Hitchins and Drew, *History of Cornwall*, 1824, I : 725; Hamilton-Jenkin, *The Cornish Miner*, 300; American survival from Theodora Fitz-Gibbon, *A Taste of England, the West Country*, 1972, 58.

FRIDAY IN LIDE : T. F. Thistleton-Dyer, *British Popular Customs*, 1891, 120; M. Courtney, *op. cit.*, 24

MIDSUMMER CUSTOM : See notes on Midsummer bonfires in *The Year's Round*.

WHITE THURSDAY : P. H. Ditchfield, *op. cit.*, 29; Hitchins and Drew, *op. cit.*, I : 725.

METHODISM : T. R. Harris, *Methodism and the Cornish Miner*, 1960.

The Sea, pages 79–89

PILCHARD FISHING : S. W. Paynter, *Old St. Ives*, 1927, 37–42; A. K. Hamilton-Jenkin, *Cornwall and Its People*, 1945, 81–116; S. P. B. Mais, *The Cornish Riviera*, 1928, 28, 106

SONGS : R. Morton Nance, *Folklore Recorded in the Cornish Language*, 1928, 7 records at Cecil Sharp House, Vaughan Williams Memorial Library; Louis Hind, *Days in Cornwall*, 1907, 226; Ralph Dunstan, *Cornish Song Book*, 1929, 69; I. Gundry, *op. cit.*, 39–41, 52, 60.

PORTHGWARRA LOVERS : Song from Ken Stubbs's collection; R. Hunt, *op. cit.*, 247.

ANIMALS : Oral information from John Affleck of Fowey, 1973, and Sheila de Burlet of Polperro, 1972.

GHOSTS : L. T. Stanley, *A Journey Through Cornwall*, 1958, 117; *O.C.*, *Winter* 1935, 38; R. Hunt, *op. cit.*, 357–70.

LYONESSE : Alasdair Alpine MacGregor, *The Ghost Book*, 1957; oral information obtained in the Land's End area, 1969.

MONSTERS AND MERMAIDS : *O.C.*, October 1928, 42; R. Hunt, *op. cit.*, 148–55.

MERMAID OF ZENNOR : A. L. Salmon, *The Cornwall Coast*, 1910, 226–9; L. T. Stanley, *op. cit.*, 129–31.

CRUEL COPPINGER : S. Baring-Gould, *A Book of Cornwall*, 1899, 272–4; A. K. Hamilton-Jenkin, *Cornwall and Its People*, 1945, 16; M. Courtney, *op. cit.*, 89.

THE WRECKERS : J. Vivian, *Tales of the Cornish Wreckers*, 1969, 5–47; L. E. Elliott-Binns, *Medieval Cornwall*, 1955, 141; M. Courtney, *op. cit.*, 89; A. K. Hamilton-Jenkin, *Cornwall and Its People*, 1945, 45–8.

SMUGGLERS : R. Pearse, *The Ports and Harbours of Cornwall*, 1963, 26, 78, 114, 133–4; Henry Carter, *The Autobiography of a Cornish Smuggler,* 1894 (complete book); Jonathan Couch, *The History of Polperro*, 1871, reprinted 1965, 29–44.

Fairies and Giants, pages 90–100

PISKEY-LED : *O.C.*, 3, 1926, 8; M. Courtney, *op. cit.*, 1890, 123; information given orally in Bodmin, 1965.

JACK O'LANTERN : T. Q. Couch, *Choice Notes from Notes and Queries*, 1859, 73.

PISKEY FEET : M. Courtney, *op. cit.*, 126.

PISKEY RING : Oral information from Miss S. P. Jennings of Penryn, 1972, *J.R.I.C.* 1915, xx : 62, part one, 170.

MURYANS : M. Courtney, *op. cit.*, 125.

FAIRY OINTMENT : R. Hunt, *op. cit.*, 109.

BABY'S NIGHTGOWN : Oral information from a lady in Fowey, 1972.

CHANGLINGS : *West Briton*, 14 July 1843; R. Hunt, *op. cit.*, 85; W. Bottrell, *op. cit.*, II : 200–2.

BETTY STOGS : R. Hunt, *op. cit.*, 103; W. Bottrell, *op. cit.*, II : 205.

LOST CHILD OF ST ALLEN : R. Hunt, *op. cit.*, 86.

ANNE JEFFRIES : S. Baring-Gould, *Cornish Characters and Strange Events*, 1925, 531; William Turner, *Remarkable Providences*, 1697, 82; R. Hunt, *op. cit.*, 127.

SPRIGGANS : R. Hunt, *op. cit.*, 90; W. Bottrell, *op. cit.*, III : 193; M. Courtney, *op. cit.*, 120–6.

GOGMAGOG : Geoffrey of Monmouth, *History of the Kings of England*, (c. 1136), Folio Society, 1969, 53.

TRERYN GIANT : R. Hunt, *op. cit.*, 47; personal notes made in Land's End area in 1969.

CARN BREA: *O.C.*, no. 11, 1930, 44.

BOB-BUTTONS: B. Spooner, in *F.L.*, Spring 1965, LXXVI: 17; R. Hunt, *op. cit.*, 51.

CORMORAN: R. Hunt, *op. cit.*, 46.

MORVAH FAIR AND FEAST: *F.L.*, Spring 1965, LXXVI: 16; R. Dunstan, *The Cornish Song Book*, 1929, 13.

GIANT BOLSTER: R. Hunt, *op. cit.*, 73.

TREBEGEAN: Richard Carew, *op. cit.*, 237.

TREBIGGAN: R. Hunt, *op. cit.*, 53.

RALPH'S CUPBOARD: B. Spooner, in *F.L.*, Spring 1965, LXXVI: 20.

JACK THE GIANT KILLER: J. O. Halliwell, *Rambles in Western Cornwall*, 1861, 197; *The Story of Jack and the Giants*, 1851 (Chap Book).

TOM OF BOWJEYHEER: R. Hunt, *op. cit.*, 55–60; W. Bottrell, *op. cit.*, 1870, I: 5–11.

REAL LIFE GIANTS: *O.C.*, 1931, II: 2, 40; S. Baring-Gould, *Cornish Characters and Strange Events*, 181.

Ghosts and Demons, pages 101–113

FARMHOUSE BOSSINNEY: Oral information from Miss S. P. Jennings and Mrs G. Jennings of Penryn, 1972.

COLD PATCH: *O.C.*, Winter 1933, 14.

DOCKACRE HOUSE: Information given by R. Buckeridge, the owner of Dockacre, January 1973.

ST AUSTELL: Local informants, 1969, 1970.

LADY OF THE LANTERN: Cyril Noall, *The Story of St. Ives*, 1970, 26.

JAMAICA INN: J. Hallam, *Haunted Inns of England*, 1972, 39; L. T. Stanley, *op. cit.*, 1958, 201.

DOLPHIN INN: J. Hallam, *op. cit.*, 41; personal recollections, 1972.

LOOE ISLAND: *O.C.*, October 1928, 16–25.

TREWOOFE: W. Bottrell, *op. cit.*, II: 1; *O.C.*, Summer 1932, 38.

FOGOU: W. Bottrell, *op. cit.*, I: 245–86.

PENGERSICK: R. Hunt, *op. cit.*, 322; W. Bottrell, *op. cit.*, II: 251.

PARSON GHOST LAYERS: *O.C.*, April 1926, 7, Summer 1931, 37, Winter 1931, 1, Summer 1933, 14, Summer 1934, 40; R. Hunt, *op. cit.*, 219–24, 254; W. Bottrell, *op. cit.*, III: 26; research in Talland area by Tony Shaw, 1970–2.

DOROTHY DINGLEY: S. Baring-Gould, *Cornish Characters and Strange Events*, 1925, 72; Christina Hole, *Haunted England*, 1940, 35; R. Hunt, *op. cit.*, 255.

PORTHCURNO: R. L. Hadfield, *The Phantom Ship*, 1937, 46; R. Hunt, *op. cit.*, 362.

JACK HARRY'S LIGHTS: R. L. Hadfield, *op. cit.*, 63.

SUBMARINE: C. Hole, *op. cit.*, 96; information supplied orally in Looe, 1972.

NANCY TRENOWETH AND FRANK LENINE: R. Hunt, *op. cit.*, 233.

WHITE HARE: S. P. B. Mais, *op. cit.*, 125; C. Hole, *op. cit.*, 157; information supplied orally in Looe, 1972.

BLACK COCKEREL: Related by Mrs M. Saunders of Bradoc, 1973. (A fictionalized version appears in A. L. Rowse, *West Country Stories*, 1945, 1–10, under the title *The Wicked Vicar of Lansillien.*)

WHITE HORSE: Cyril Noall, *op. cit.*, 26.

BLACK DOG: *O.C.*, April 1929, 23.

DEVIL AND HIS DANDY DOGS: R. Hunt, *op. cit.*, 233; T. Q. Couch, *op. cit.*, 78.

TREGEAGLE: B. Spooner, *Jan Tregeagle, Man and Ghost*, no date; S. P. B. Mais, *op. cit.*, 68, 129; R. Hunt, *op. cit.*, 132–42.

Witchcraft and Herbal Lore, pages 114–126

WITCH TRIALS: W. Notestein, *History of Witchcraft in England*, 1911, 276–9; G. L. Kitteridge, *Witchcraft in Old and New England*, 1929, 219; C. L'Estrange Ewen, *Witchcraft and Demonianism*, 1933, 374; *Calendar of State Papers*, domestic series 1671, 105, 171 – two letters from Thomas Holden to Williamson, the second of which states 'The witches I wrote to you about the assizes being over are freed, although their familiarity with cats and rats are plainly proved against them.'

WITCH IN HARE'S FORM: Oral information from a lady in Bodmin area, 1970; J. Couch, *op. cit.*, 68.

WITCH'S INITIATION: *West Briton*, 3 December 1841.

ILL-WISHING: *West Briton*, 25 July 1845; A. K. Hamilton-Jenkin, *Cornwall and Its People*, 1945, 286–99.

BLOOD-LETTING: *O.C.* I: 10, 1929, 40; A. K. Hamilton-Jenkin, *Cornwall and Its People*, 1945, 292–5.

WITCH BOTTLE: *F.L.*, LXVI, 1955, 196.

ANIMAL HEART: *F.L.*, XLIV, 1933, 114; *Western Morning News*, 5 December 1931; M. Courtney, *op. cit.*, 147.

MILLPREVE: *O.C.*, no. 9, 1929, 45; A. K. Hamilton-Jenkin, *Cornwall and its People*, 1945, 305–6.

TAMSON BLIGHT: *O.C.*, no. 9, 1929, 31, II: 11, 1936, 37; R. Hunt, *op. cit.*, 316; A. K. Hamilton-Jenkin, *Cornwall and Its People*, 1945, 291–305; *Western Morning News*, 4 June 1928.

SATOR CHARM: Thomas R. Forbes, *The Midwife and the Witch*, 1966, 84–93; M. Courtney, *op. cit.*, 143.

HANGMAN'S ROPE: *West Briton*, 10 October 1845.

MOUSE: J. Hammond, *op. cit.*, 353.

RINGWORM: Information from Mrs G. M. Knight of Nottingham, formerly of Withiel, nr Bodmin, 1973; *O.C.*, XII: 9, 1935, 43.

WART CHARMING: Information from Mr C. C. Stidwell of Milton Damerel, Devon, 1973.

SNAKE CHARM: *O.C.*, II: 10, 1935, 29; *F.L.*, LXIV: 1953, 304 (also contains information on rat charmer and blood charmer); M. Courtney, *op. cit.*, 156.

BLOOD CHARMER: *J.R.I.C.*, XX: 62, part 1, 1915, 52.

HERBAL CURES: Billy Bray story supplied by Rev. T. W. M. Darlington, formerly of Gwennap, 1972; Rev. Polwhele, *History of Cornwall*, 1806, VII: 26; A. K. Hamilton-Jenkin, *Cornwall and Its People*, 1945, 348; the majority of cures were supplied by Mrs M. E. Saunders of Bradoc, 1973, with additional notes from N. Culpeper, *English Physician and Complete Herbal*, 1961 (reprint of the 1789 edition); and R. C. Wren, *Potter's New Cyclopaedia of Botanical Drugs and Preparations*, 1970 edition.

HUGH ATWELL: T. Brian, *The Pisse Pot Prophet*, 1637, 95.

CURSED FIELD: *Sunday Express*, 25 March 1973; personal notes made on the Lizard, 1972.

Animal, Vegetable and Mineral, pages 127–144

BEAUTIFUL AND UGLY SIGHTS: Personal correspondence from Mrs M. E. Saunders of Bradoc, 1973.

CRUELTY: L. T. Stanley, *op. cit.*, 27, 90; A. K. Hamilton-Jenkin, *Cornwall and its People*, 1945, 288–91.

BENCH ENDS: S. Baring-Gould, *A Book of Cornwall*, 1899, 225; *O.C.*, Summer 1932, II: 3, 19.

BLACK BULL: *O.C.*, April 1928, no. 7, 12.

KITTENS AND DOGS: *O.C.*, Winter 1930, no. 12, 4.

PILCHARDS: J. Harris Stone, *England's Riviera*, 1912, 43–53.

BATS: M. Courtney, *op. cit.*, 163.

RIDDLES: *O.C.*, Winter 1933, II: 6, 33.

OLD DADDY FOX: Ralph Dunstan, *Cornish Dialect and Folksongs*, 1932, 46.

BIRDS: *O.C.*, Winter 1930, no. 12, 1–6; Jonathan Couch, *op. cit.*, 83; Edward E. Armstrong, *The Folklore of Birds*, 1958, 213.

CUCKOO: M. Courtney, *op. cit.*, 163; E. E. Armstrong, *op. cit.*, 202–4; oral information obtained in Gorran, 1972.

ROBIN AND WREN: *O.C.*, Summer 1930, no. 11, 4; E. E. Armstrong, *op. cit.*, 141–66, 176, 177.

INSECTS AND SPIDERS: *O.C.*, Summer 1932, II: 3, 44, Winter 1933, II: 6, 23; M. Courtney, *op. cit.*, 60; Venetia Newall, *Discovering the Folklore of Birds and Beasts*, 1971, 5.

SNAILS: *O.C.*, Winter 1930, no. 12, 1–6, Winter 1933, no. 6, 23; M. Courtney, *op. cit*, 39, 131, 138.

INCANTATIONS: *O.C.*, Winter 1932, II: 4, 12–16.

PLANTS: *O.C.*, Winter 1930, no. 12, 1–6; Jonathan Couch, *op. cit.*, 82.

MAY FERN: *O.C.*, Summer 1936, II: 11, 40; M. Courtney, *op. cit.*, 28.

STRAWBERRY LEAVES: Cyrus Redding, *Illustrated Itinerary of the County of Cornwall*, 1842, 123.

FURZE CUTTER: *O.C.*, Winter 1930, no. 12, 1–6

TREES: *O.C.*, Winter 1930, no. 12, 1–6.

WHISPERING FOREST: *F.L.*, August 1902, XIII, article by M. E. Hall.

WEATHER: *O.C.*, Winter 1930, no. 12, 1–6; Summer 1931, II: 1, 38–40; G. F. Northall, *English Folk Rhymes*, 1892, 460–6, L. T. Stanley, *op. cit.*, 178.

DANCING STONES: *O.C.*, Summer 1934, II: 7, 23–4; H. O'Neill Hencken, *The Archaeology of Cornwall and Scilly*, 1932, 52–5, 293; B. Spooner, *Stone Circles of Cornwall*, in *F.L.*, LXIII/LXIV, 1952/53, 484–7.

TURNING STONES: B. Spooner, *op. cit.*, 484–7; *The Liskeard Gazette and East Cornwall Advertiser*, 5 January 1856.

LOGAN STONE: *O.C.*, Summer 1936, II: 11, 31; J. T. Blight, *A Week at the Land's End*, 1861, 129.

CURATIVE STONES: S. P. B. Mais, *op. cit.*, 98; J. T. Blight, *op. cit*, 17.

QUOITS AND THE DEVIL: J. T. Blight, *op. cit.*, 16, 74–5; L. T. Stanley, *op. cit.*, 193–4; S. P. B. Mais, *op. cit.*, 32.

WITCHES: R. Hunt, *op. cit.*, 330–2; L. T. Stanley, *op. cit.*, 115–6.

LUDGVAN WATER: *O.C.*, April 1926, no. 3, 8.

ROCHE ROCK: H. M. Cresswell Payne, *The Story of the Parish of Roche*, 1946, 74–8.

COASTLINE: Arthur L. Salmon, *op. cit.*, 25; J. T. Blight, *op. cit.*, 108.

CARN KENIDZHEK: R. Hunt, *op. cit.*, 216; J. T. Blight, *op. cit.*, 166.

HIDDEN GOLD: S. Baring-Gould, *A Book of Cornwall*, 1899, 107–8; J. T. Blight, *op. cit.*, 20

The Balladeers, pages 145–151

BILL CHUBB: *Cornish Life*, I: 9, July 1974, 2–3; personal recollection from Padstow, May Day 1969.

TINKERS: *O.C.*, no. 8, October 1928, 40.

THE WREN FAMILY: *O.C.*, no. 8, October 1928, 40.

RHYMING DICK: *O.C.*, no. 5, October 1927, 37–8.

UNCLE ANTHONY: R. Hunt, *op. cit.*, 26–7; Ralph Dunstan, *The Cornish Song Book*, 1929, 55.

BILLY FOSS: W. Bottrell, *op. cit.*, III: 112; *O.C.*, no. 10, October 1929, 6–15; R. Hunt, *op. cit.*, 27.

HENNA QUICK: *O.C.*, II: 5, 36–40; A. K. Hamilton-Jenkin, *Cornwall and Its People*, 1945, 314, 329.

Saints and Holy Wells, pages 152–159

ORIGINS: S. Baring-Gould, *A Book of Cornwall*, 1899, 1; William J. Ferrar, *The Saints of Cornwall*, 1920, 7–8; L. E. Elliott-Binns, *op. cit.*, 4-6, 280.
ST MERRYN AND ST DENNIS: Nicholas Pevsner, *Cornwall*, 1951, 148; S. J. Coleman, *op. cit.*, 4.
ST MICHAEL: Gilbert H. Doble, *Miracles at St. Michael's Mount in 1262*, no date, 3; Charles Henderson, *Essays in Cornish History*, 1935, reprint 1963, 197–201.
TRANSPORT: Peggy Pollard, *Cornwall*, 1947, 41–3; Arthur L. Salmon, *op. cit.*, 265–6.
ST PETROC: F. I. Cowles, *The Magic of Cornwall*, 1934, 60; L. T. Stanley, *op. cit.*, 178–9; W. J. Ferrar, *op. cit.*, 35–9.
MEVAGISSEY: L. T. Stanley, *op. cit.*, 27.
ST KEVERNE AND ST JUST: R. Hunt, *op. cit.*, 262–4; Arthur L. Salmon, *op. cit.*, 115–7; L. T. Stanley, *op. cit.*, 43–4.
ST KEYNE, ST GUNDRED AND ST MAWES: H. M. Cresswell Payne, *op. cit.*, 79–85; R. Hunt, *op. cit.*, 268–9; S. J. Coleman, *op. cit.*, 4–11.
ST LEVAN: R. Hunt, *op. cit.*, 265–8; F. I. Cowles, *op. cit.*, 107–8; A. L. Salmon, *op. cit.*, 188–9.
BREAGE AND GERMOE: W. J. Ferrar, *op. cit.*, 13–14; A. L. Salmon, *op. cit.*, 154.
ANIMALS: Peggy Pollard, *op. cit.*, 41–3; A. L. Salmon, *op. cit.*, 319.
ST. NEOT: R. Hunt, *op. cit.*, 275–7; S. J. Coleman, *op. cit.*, 4; W. Ferrar, *op. cit.*, 53–5.
CURATIVE WELLS: M. & L. Quiller-Couch, *Ancient and Holy Wells of Cornwall*, 1894, 36–41, 113.
MADRON WELL: J. O. Halliwell, *op. cit.*, 79–81; M. & L. Quiller-Couch, *op. cit.*, 125–38; R. Hunt, *op. cit.*, 293–6.
WISHING WELLS: *O.C.* April 1928, 7, 41; M. & L. Quiller-Couch, *op. cit.*, 11–13, 52–3, 122–4, 165–6; A. K. Hamilton Jenkin, *Cornwall and Its People*, 1945, 308–11.
ST ANNE AND ST KEYNE WELLS: *O.C.*, April 1928, no. 7, 41; R. Hunt, *op. cit.*, 292–3; F. Cowles, *op. cit.*, 203–4; W. Ferrar, *op. cit.*, 26–7.

The Year's Round, pages 160–188

STRATTON CAROL: *O.C.*, Winter, 1936, 20.
FAIRS: S. Daniell, *Old Cornwall*, 1970, 42; F. E. Halliday, *History of*

Cornwall, 1959, 127, 153; Elliott-Binns, *op. cit.,* 183, 203–5; A. K. Hamilton-Jenkin, *Cornwall and Its People,* 1945, 395–7.

JANUARY

TOAST: Theodora Fitz-Gibbon, *A Taste of England, the West Country,* 1972, 118.
NEW YEAR'S DAY: A. R. Wright, ed. T. E. Lones, *British Calendar Customs: England,* 1938, II: 3; R. Hunt, *op. cit.,* 382; J. Couch, *op. cit.,* 73
GUIZING: Christina Hole, *English Custom and Usage,* 1941, 28–9; R. Hunt, *op. cit.,* 392; A Salmon, *op. cit.,* 247; W. Paynter, *op. cit.,* 1927, 46.
ST DISTAFF'S DAY: A. R. Wright, *op. cit.,* II: 92.
LOE BAR: C. A. Johns, *A Week at the Lizard,* 1848, 215–9; H. Spencer Toy, *History of Helston,* 1936, 385–6, 392–5.

FEBRUARY

CANDLEMAS: A. R. Wright, *op. cit.,* II: 120.
ST BLAZEY: M. Courtney, *op. cit.,* 19.
ST IVES HURLING: W. Paynter, *op. cit.,* 45–6; A. Ivan Rabey, *Hurling at St. Columb,* 1972, 5–19; local sources and personal recollections, 1969.
PAISEN MONDAY: M. Courtney, *op. cit.,* 21.
NICKY-NAN-NIGHT: Thistleton-Dyer, *op. cit.,* 58; J. Couch, *op. cit.,* 73.
ST IVES RHYMES: W. Paynter, *op. cit.,* 47; M. Courtney, *op. cit.,* 51; R. Hunt, *op. cit.,* 383.
PENZANCE SHROVETIDE: A. K. Hamilton-Jenkin, *Cornwall and Its People,* 1945, 428.
COLPERRA: M. Courtney, *op. cit.,* 22.
COCK-FIGHTING: A. K. Hamilton-Jenkin, *Cornwall and Its People,* 1945, 150–6; M. Courtney, *op. cit.,* 23.
SHACKLE-EGGS: *Word Lore,* I: 1, 27; oral information in Looe, 1971.
EGG-BATTLES: M. Courtney, *op. cit.,* 24.
ST COLUMB HURLING: Claud Berry, *The Portrait of Cornwall,* 1949, 42–145; *The West Briton,* 2 March 1972; J. C. Trewin, *Down to the Lion,* 1952, 181–4; A. Ivan Rabey, *op. cit.,* 5–19; personal recollections, 1968–70.

MARCH

FLEAS : M. Courtney, *op. cit.*, 24.
CONSTANTINE FAIR : M. Courtney, *op. cit.*, 25.

APRIL

APRIL FOOL'S DAY : M. Courtney, *op. cit.*, 27.
PALM SUNDAY : J. Couch, *op. cit.*, 74.
HOLY THURSDAY : M. Courtney, *op. cit.*, 25.
GOOD FRIDAY : M. Courtney, *op. cit.*, 25, 150, 159.
EASTER DAY : J. Couch, *op. cit.*, 74; Thistleton-Dyer, *op. cit.*, 162.
EASTER MONDAY : M. Courtney, *op. cit.*, 26.
HOCKTIDE : Thistleton-Dyer, *op. cit.*, 188.
MAY EVE : Thistleton-Dyer, *op. cit.*, 216; A. K. Hamilton-Jenkin, *Cornwall and Its People*, 1945, 430–42; personal recollections, 1966–69.

MAY

PADSTOW : Donald R. Rawe, *Padstow's Obby Oss*, 1971, 2–27; *J.F.S.*, v, 1916, 273–6, 328–39; P. Maylem, *The Hooden Horse*, 1909, 65, 85, 104; *Ethnic*, I : 3, 4–19; M. Oldfield Howey, *The Horse in Magic and Myth*, 1923, 84; I. Gundry, *op. cit.*, 14–17; Richard Polwhele, *History of Cornwall*, 1803, III : 54; S. Baring-Gould, *Book of Cornwall*, 1899, 168–70; local information supplied by Charlie Bate, Mervyn Vincent, John Buckingham, Dick Goddard, Richard Larque and personal recollections 1965–71.
ST IVES : A. K. Hamilton-Jenkin, *Cornwall and Its People*, 1945, 433.
PENZANCE : Thistleton-Dyer, *op. cit.*, 236.
HAYLE : A. K. Hamilton-Jenkin, *Cornwall and Its People*, 1945, 433; M. Courtney, *op. cit.*, 29.
LAUNCESTON : A. R. Wright, *op. cit.*, II : 206.
POLPERRO, PELYNT AND LOOE : G. F. Northall, *op. cit.*, 1892, 239; M. Courtney, *op. cit.*, 29; J. Couch, *op. cit.*, 74–5; Thistleton-Dyer, *op. cit.*, 235–6.
MAYPOLES : A. K. Hamilton-Jenkin, *Cornwall and Its People*, 1945, 431–2; research in the Looe area by Tony Shaw, 1970–72.
LANREATH : Oral information from Mrs Libby of Polperro, whose son helped to guard Maypole, 1973, and Tony Foxworthy, formerly of Lanreath, 1973.

SUNDAY AFTER MAY DAY: Thistleton-Dyer, *op. cit.*, 236.
FURRY DAY: E. M. Cunnack, *The Helston Furry Dance*, 1963, 2–19;
R. Nettle, *Sing a Song of England*, 1954, 43–5, 55–6; S. Baring-Gould,
Songs of the West, 1913, 48, 50; L. T. Stanley, *op. cit.*, 66–70; I.
Gundry, *op. cit.*, 10–13; Spencer Toy, *op. cit.*, 368–79.
OAK-APPLE DAY: Thistleton-Dyer, *op. cit.*, 302.
MAYGUM: *O.C.*, Summer 1930, 11, 3.

JUNE

WHITSON: J. Couch, *op. cit.*, 75; Thistleton-Dyer, *op. cit.*, 279.
ROLL-TOBACCO: M. Courtney, *op. cit.*, 39.
MIDSUMMER CHARMS: J. Couch, *op. cit.*, 76.
MIDSUMMER BONFIRES: M. Courtney, *op. cit.*, 40–4; A. Howard,
English Cavalcade, 1964, 139–40; *O.C.*, (pamphlet) 1963; W. Carew
Hazlitt, *Popular Antiquities of Great Britain*, I: 178; A. K. Hamilton-
Jenkin, *Cornwall and Its People*, 1945, 420-34.
MOCK MAYORS: *O.C.*, April 1926, no. 3, 15–24; A. K. Hamilton-
Jenkin, *Cornwall and Its People*, 1945, 453–69.

JULY

BODMIN RIDING: *The Western Morning News*, 26 June 1973; Thistleton-Dyer, *op. cit.*, 338; L. T. Stanley, *op. cit.*, 198–9, A. K. Hamilton-
Jenkin, *Cornwall and Its People*, 1945, 466.
HALGAVOR GAMES: Thistleton-Dyer, *op. cit.*, 339; M. Courtney, *op. cit.*,
47; R. Hunt, *op. cit.*, 402–3.
JOHN KNILL: M. Courtney, *op. cit.*, 48; L. T. Stanley, *op. cit.*, 141-3;
A. K. Hamilton-Jenkin, *Cornwall and Its People*, 1945, 272; no
author, *John Knill*, 1936, 3-14; J.J.R., *John Knill, 1734–1811*, 1936,
1–12.

AUGUST

MORVAH FAIR: M. Courtney, *op. cit.*, 51.
MARHAMCHURCH: Personal recollections by Sally Shaw, 1970.
GULVAL: *E.D.S.*, Spring 1971, article by Tony Foxworthy, 16.

SEPTEMBER

GORSEDD: Programme of the Gorsedd 1969; personal recollections 1968–9.

WRESTLING: *O.C.*, Summer 1951, v: 1, 13–14; *The Cornish Magazine*, October 1965, VIII: 6, 132–4; Sir Thomas Parkyns, *The Inn-Play*, 1713, complete book; *The Cornish Magazine*, July 1960, III: 3, 70–1; personal notes made in 1969–70.

CRYING THE NECK: *Western Morning News*, 1 September 1954; *O.C.*, Summer, 1951, v: I, 20; A. K. Hamilton-Jenkin, *Cornwall and Its People*, 1945, 408–10; M. Courtney, *op. cit.*, 52.

HARVEST SUPPERS: *O.C.*, Winter 1932, 12–13; A. K. Hamilton-Jenkin, *Cornwall and Its People*, 1945, 412–5; I. Grundy, *op. cit*, 25; Carew, *op. cit.*, 141.

SUMMERCOURT FAIR: A. L. Rowse, *A Cornish Childhood*, 1942, 11–32; correspondence from Mrs E. Knowles of Grampound, 1969.

PENRYN MOCK MAYOR: *O.C.*, April 1926, no. 3, 17.

OCTOBER

FAIRS: M. Courtney, *op. cit.*, 2
ALLANTIDE: Thistleton-Dyer, *op. cit.*, 395; M. Courtney, *op. cit.*, 2, 3.

NOVEMBER

RINGING NIGHT: M. Courtney, *op. cit.*, 4.
MARTINMAS: M. Courtney, *op. cit.*, 5.
FAIR MO: M. Courtney, *op. cit.*, 5; W. Paynter, *op. cit.*, 48–9.

DECEMBER

ST NICHOLAS' DAY: Thistleton-Dyer, *op. cit.*, 432–7.
TOM BAWCOCK'S EVE: *O.C.*, April 1927, no. 5, 20; R. Dunstan, *Cornish Dialect and Folk Songs*, 1932, 7; oral information from Michael Kessell of Carnkie, near Redruth.
MUMMERS: Cawte, Helm and Peacock, *English Ritual Drama*, 1967, 11–36, 42; *O.C.*, October 1928, no. 8, 4; R. J. E. Tiddy, *The Mummer's Play*, 1923, 144–8; R. Hunt, *op. cit.*, 389; Thistleton-Dyer, *op. cit.*, 468.

THE MOCK: A. K. Hamilton-Jenkin, *Cornwall and Its People*, 1945, 419-20; J. Couch, *op cit.*, 79.

CAROLS: *E.D.S.* Spring 1971, 26; A. K. Hamilton-Jenkin, *Cornwall and Its People*, 1945, 416; oral information from Richard Larque, 1973.

BODMIN WASSAIL: *O.C.*, Winter 1932, 14; *E.D.S.*, Spring, 1971, 16; A. K. Hamilton-Jenkin, *Cornwall and Its People*, 1945, 420; M. Courtney, *op. cit.*, 14; R. Hunt, *op. cit.*, 386–8; A. R. Wright, *op. cit.*, II: 54; oral information supplied by Peter Wood, 1973.

TRURO WASSAIL. *E.D.S.*, Winter 1971, 132–3; Topic Records, *Folk Songs of Britain*, IX.

Select Bibliography

The following books are the main sources for Cornish folklore and history. Magazines and periodicals dealing with specific aspects of the subjects are mentioned in the Chapter Notes where relevant.

S. BARING-GOULD, *Book of Cornwall*, 1899
  Cornish Characters and Strange Events, 1908
  Songs of the West, 1913
R. M. BARTON, *Life in Cornwall in the Early Nineteeth Century*, 1970
  Life in Cornwall in the mid-nineteenth century, 1971
C. BERRY, *Portrait of Cornwall*, 1949
J. T. BLIGHT, *A. Week at the Land's End*, 1861.
W. BORLASE, *Observations on the Antiquities of Cornwall*, 1754
  The Age of the Saints, 1893 edition
W. BOTTRELL, *Traditions and Hearthside Stories*, 3 vols, 1870–80
A. CADDICK, *Curiosities of Cornwall*, 1957
R. CAREW, *Survey of Cornwall*, 1602
S. JACKSON COLEMAN, *Cornish Lore and Legend,* no date
W. COLLINS, *Rambles Beyond Railways*, 1851
I. COLQUHOUN, *The Living Stones*, 1957
J. COUCH, *The History of Polperro*, 1871
M. COURTNEY, *Cornish Feasts and Folklore*, 1890
W. P. COURTNEY & G. C. BOASE, *Bibliotheca Cornubiensis*, 3 vols, 1874
F. I. COWLES, *The Magic of Cornwall*, 1934
G. H. DOBLE, *The Saints of Cornwall*, 1965
D. DU MAURIER, *Vanishing Cornwall*, 1966
R. DUNSTAN, *Cornish Song Book*, 1929
  Cornish Dialect and Folk Songs, 1932
L. E. ELLIOTT-BINNS, *Medieval Cornwall*, 1955
P. DERRESFORD ELLIS, *The Cornish Language and its Literature*, 1974
W. J. FERRAR, *The Saints of Cornwall*, 1920
DAVIES GILBERT, *Christmas Carols*, 1822
  The Parochial History of Cornwall, 4 vols, 1838
I. GUNDRY, *Canow Kernow*, 1966
J. O. HALLIWELL, *Rambles in Western Cornwall*, 1861
W. HALS, *History of Cornwall*, 1750
J. HAMMOND, *A Cornish Parish*, 1897
J. HATCHER, *English Tin Production and Trade before 1550*, 1973.
H. O'NEILL HENCKEN, *The Archaeology of Cornwall and Scilly*, 1932
C. HENDERSON, *Essays in Cornish History*, 1935

L. HIND, *Days in Cornwall*, 1907

F. HITCHINS & S. DREW, *History of Cornwall*, 2 vols, 1824

R. HUNT, *Popular Romances of the West of England*, 1865

A. K. HAMILTON JENKIN, *The Cornish Miner*, 1927
The Story of Cornwall, 1934
Cornwall and Its People, 1945.

C. A. JOHNS, *A Week at the Lizard*, 1876

J. KINSMAN (editor), *The Cornish Handbook*, 1931

S. P. B. MAIS, *The Cornish Riviera*, 1928

E. W. MARTIN, *A Wanderer in the West Country*, 1951

A. MEE, *Cornwall*, 1931

J. MURRAY, *Handbook for Travellers in Cornwall*, 1882

C. NOALL, *Smuggling in Cornwall*, 1971

P. POLLARD, *Cornwall*, 1947

R. POLWHELE, *History of Cornwall*, 5 vols, 1803–6

M. & L. QUILLER-COUCH, *Ancient and Holy Wells of Cornwall*, 1894

A. IVAN RABEY, *Hurling at St. Columb*, 1972

D. R. RAWE, *Padstow's Obby Oss*, 1971

C. REDDING, *An Illustrated Itinerary of the County of Cornwall*, 1852

A. L. SALMON, *The Cornwall Coast*, 1910

L. T. STANLEY, *A Journey Through Cornwall*, 1958

J. HARRIS STONE, *England's Riviera*, 1912

J. C. TREGARTHEN, *Wildlife at the Land's End*, 1904

B. WALKE, *Twenty Years at St. Hilary*, 1935

Note: folklore and country-craft museums may be found at Looe (The Cornish Museum), Polperro (The Smugglers Museum), Boscastle (The Witchcraft Museum), Tintagel (King Arthur's Hall), Helston (Borough Museum), St Ives (Town Museum), Zennor (Wayside Museum), Harlyn Bay (for Celtic Relics), Fowel (Noah's Ark Museum) and Mevagissey (two museums on the quay). Most Cornish borough museums will also be of interest, especially the County Museum at Truro.

Index of Tale Types

Numbers preceded by AT are from Antti Aarne and Stith Thompson, *The Types of the Folktale*, 1961; those with ML are from R.Th. Christiansen, *The Migratory Legends*, 1958; those with ML and an asterisk are from K. M. Briggs, *A Dictionary of British Folktales*, 1970-1.

Motif Index

These numbers are from Stith Thompson, *Motif-Index of Folk Literature*, 1966.

o

General Index